D0368918

Shatner

Shatner

MICHAEL SETH STARR

APPLAUSE THEATRE & CINEMA BOOKS
Guilford, Connecticut

Applause Theatre & Cinema Books
An imprint of The Rowman & Littlefield Publishing Group, Inc.
4501 Forbes Blvd., Ste. 200
Lanham, MD 20706
www.rowman.com

Distributed by NATIONAL BOOK NETWORK

Library of Congress Cataloging-in-Publication Data available

ISBN 978-1-4950-8268-9 (hardcover)
ISBN 978-1-4930-5065-9 (e-book)

♾™ The paper used in this publication meets the minimum requirements of American National Standard for Information Sciences—Permanence of Paper for Printed Library Materials, ANSI/NISO Z39.48-1992.

Contents

Preface

Any biographer tracing the rollercoaster arc of William Shatner's career faces a formidable challenge in chronicling the life of an American icon who continues to lead an active and very public life as he nears his ninetieth decade.

I undertook this challenge and spent three years researching and writing about William Shatner's life, interviewing friends and colleagues with whom he interacted at one point or another during his long career, reading hundreds of interviews with him and about him, and screening as much of his onscreen work as I could—occasionally venturing down rabbit holes for information that was tough to come by. (Example: *The Butler's Night Off*, Shatner's first onscreen appearance, filmed in 1951 when he was still a student at McGill University and about which little is known.)

Once I felt I had covered all the bases of Shatner's life—from his birth in Montreal in 1931 to his picking fights on Twitter eighty-eight years later—I needed to choose a title for this book. I wanted to avoid any allusions to *Star Trek*, no matter how cleverly they might be cloaked—to me, that was just too obvious. I know, I know—this book would not exist had not Gene Roddenberry's television series jump-started William Shatner's career fifty-odd years ago. And, yes, Captain James T. Kirk is, without a doubt, his defining role. But as I hope you will learn in reading this book, William Shatner's career in show business existed for over a decade before *Star Trek* and certainly encompassed so much more after the series' initial three-season run on NBC. So it felt too easy to peg the book's title to *Star Trek*. Besides, it's been done countless times before in the thousands (millions?) of newspaper and magazine articles written about William Shatner once the series completed its initial run. He himself has used *Star Trek*-ian verbiage in a few of his own book titles (including *Star Trek Memories* and *William Shatner: Live Long and . . .*).

I also wanted to avoid using the word "definitive" *anywhere* in the book's title. It's an adjective that I have always found somewhat pretentious, particularly when used by an author (or by an overenthusiastic publisher) to describe a biographical work. No written account of a person's personal and professional life can ever be "definitive," even when chronicled in memoir form—when one's memories, in recalling their life, tend to be selective (or, worse, self-serving).

But in the end, choosing a title for this book wasn't as difficult as I first imagined it would be. It was, in fact, *right there* from the day I began this project, since whenever someone would ask me about my next book, I usually answered in one word: "Shatner."

The name itself triggers so many images: Shatner as Captain Kirk in *Star Trek*, of course, but also as bug-eyed, sweaty, hysterical Robert Wilson in *The Twilight Zone*, confronting that furry gremlin no one else sees ("There's a man out there!"). Or Shatner as Denny Crane ("Denny Crane." "Denny Crane.") savoring a cigar with Alan Shore on their *Boston Legal* balcony. Or Shatner as the Priceline Negotiator, karate-chopping his way through another witty ad. Or the late-sixties Shatner, crowned with various iterations of hair, slow-talking his way through versions of "Mr. Tambourine Man" and "Lucy in the Sky with Diamonds." Or the swingin'-seventies Shatner guesting on daytime game shows with his second wife, Marcy, and appearing in a string of forgettable movies, summer-stock stage productions, and television shows. (And let us not forget those margarine commercials . . . "Promise.") There's *Barbary Coast* Shatner (OK, so maybe not so memorable) and Shatner as tough LA cop *T. J. Hooker* and Shatner reviving Captain Kirk (and his career) on the big screen in various *Star Trek* iterations, both in front of the camera and in the director's chair (for *Star Trek V: The Final Frontier*). There's Shatner as beauty pageant host Stan Fields in *Miss Congeniality* and its sequel and as grouchy Ed Goodson in the CBS sitcom *$#*! My Dad Says*. There's Shatner as a cable TV interviewer (*Shatner's Raw Nerve*). There's the funky, spoken-word-album Shatner working with Brad Paisley and Iggy Pop and Henry Rollins and covering everything from country music to old standards to Christmas tunes. There's Shatner as the subject of several websites, including the now-defunct Shatner's Toupee (Shatnerstoupee.blogspot.com), the extremely well-researched "Definitive Oracle" that tracked the subtle weaves and styles of his (alleged) hairpieces at various stages of his career—with essays, accompanied by topical photographs, to substantiate theories regarding the hairpieces' handiwork. There's the late-in-life Shatner picking yet another Twitter fight with *Outlander* fans or with "snowflakes" or with someone from *Dancing with the Stars* or with the #MeToo movement or with a half-dozen other targets . . . or, more likely than not, with his go-to *Star Trek* frenemy George "Oh My" Takei in a back-and-forth squabble that's lasted over twenty-five years and continues to this day.

So *Shatner* it is.

In the course of researching and writing this book, I was hoping to speak to The Man himself. I had interviewed William Shatner once, back in 2009, when I wrote about his new celebrity interview show, *Shatner's Raw Nerve*, for the *New York Post*, where I have covered television for the past twenty-four years. Our interview was conducted over the phone and was pleasant enough; it took a slight detour to the off-ramp of awkwardness when I mentioned his, shall we say, *checkered* history with some of his costars. "I really haven't rubbed anyone the wrong way. I think you're referring to some cast members from *Star Trek*," he said, a bit testily. "I've asked them numerous times to see if I can assuage their bitterness. I don't know what their problem is, quite frankly, so I've given up on trying to make it better. I don't like any ill-feeling, and if there was something I could do to correct it I would. But nothing seems to work." That exchange passed quickly enough and we got back on track. I found Shatner to be quick-witted and perceptive, two attributes that were on full display in *Shatner's Raw Nerve*. (If you've never seen it, you can find episodes online. Check it out.)

But getting an interview with William Shatner for this book was not in the cards. In 2016, after signing the contract to write what would morph into *Shatner*, I contacted his representatives to inform them of this project and to request an interview with their client. I had an "in" with one of Shatner's agents (through a friend) and I was cautiously optimistic, though I had heard he could be prickly and I wasn't holding out much hope. I heard nothing for several months and then circled back. Crickets. On my third try, I finally received a reply via e-mail: "Mr. Shatner" could not participate in my project, it said, "due to an overcommitted production schedule." Fair enough. At least they didn't tell me to get lost or threaten the legality of my endeavor. I appreciated the civility of the tone, since that's not always the case in these scenarios. It's a tricky proposition writing a book about someone who is still alive but is not participating in the project—and, in William Shatner's case, is still heavily invested in his career and works at a pace that would exhaust someone half his age.

Later, I considered it a badge of honor when Shatner blocked me on Twitter, although I'm still not sure why he chose to do that. Maybe he was upset that when I wrote to Walter Koenig (Chekov from *Star Trek*) requesting an interview, he sent back this reply: "Unless you will have several photos in your book showing Mr. Shatner having sex with a horse I must politely decline. Walter Koenig." It was the best turndown for an interview I've ever received, bar none. And it *somehow* found its way into the pages of the *New York Post's* renowned Page Six gossip column. I have no idea how that happened.

William Shatner did, though, ask several people I contacted for this book not to speak to me, including a friend of his since their days at McGill University in Montreal. When I initially contacted the friend, he told me he was visiting Los Angeles and would be having dinner with "Bill" (his intimates all call him Bill). He would ask Bill if it was okay to talk to me for this book. As expected, Bill put the kibosh on that one. It's a frustrating scenario for a biographer, but I get it, and it's not an unusual occurrence when writing a book that is, by definition, "unauthorized"—a word that conjures up seamy scandal but, in reality, means only that the book's subject did not cooperate with the author or endorse the project in any fashion. I was fortunate, though, to interview many of William Shatner's friends, colleagues, and associates spanning nearly the entire breadth of his life and career—including a future Canadian diplomat who, as a young, frightened, shell-shocked Jewish refugee in the late 1940s, learned to speak English with help from his summer camp counselor: a guy named Bill Shatner. You'll read more on that later.

*   *   *

No book writes itself, and I was helped throughout the long process of researching and writing *Shatner* by many people who contributed in one way or another, even if it was to share a story that I didn't use in the book or to steer me in another direction vis-à-vis William Shatner's life and career.

So here we go.

I would like to thank John Cerullo, Carol Flannery, and Marybeth Keating at Applause Books; David Klimek (who provided invaluable research assistance and advice from Montreal and kept me apprised of Shatner's activities in Canada); Patty Bergamaschi (transcriptionist par excellence); Roger Corman; Arnold Shapiro; Tom Bleecker; Christopher Plummer; Pierre Epstein; Bruce Raymond; Greg Evigan; Pierre Lafond; Fred Bild; Justin Halpern; Steve Holland; Rick Husky; Richard Donner; Stephen McPherson; Angie Dickinson; Joel Katz; Alan Dean Foster; Nancy Kovack Mehta; William F. Nolan; Howard Ryshpan; Arthur Weinthal; *Breakfast Television* and *Global News* in Montreal; Michelle Lafond; Scott Sternberg; Library and Archives Canada; Nancy Jacoby; Henry Winkler; Lionel Caplan; Lionel Tiger; Joan Collins; Bill D'Elia; Austin Beutel; Vicki Kaywood; William F. Nolan; Ron Goulart; George Foreman; Scott Faris; Steve Carver; Ken Connors and Terry DiMonte at CHOM (97.7 FM) in Montreal; Brenda Carroll at the Canadian Broadcasting Corporation; and the archival photo staffs at the Associated Press, Alamy, Photofest, Getty, and the Canadian Jewish Archives. My apologies in advance for anyone I have inadvertently left off this list. It was not intentional.

Last but certainly not least, a special thank you to my daughter, Rachel, and especially to my wife, Gail, for her unwavering love, support, and encouragement over the past thirty-six years. This book would not have existed without you.

CHAPTER 1

In the Beginning

Producer Joel Katz knew his upcoming television series, *For the People*, was dead on arrival as it sped toward its premiere on CBS in January of 1965.

That was a shame, Katz thought, since the series, a legal drama created by future *Cool Hand Luke* director Stuart Rosenberg, boasted an unusually strong pedigree. Its two stars, William Shatner and Jessica Walter, were young but seasoned.

Shatner, thirty-three years old and a Shakespearian-trained actor, had a decade of live television and series work on his resume and several big-budget Hollywood movies under his belt. He was also a hot Broadway commodity, coming off successful starring roles in *The World of Suzie Wong* and *A Shot in the Dark* and three guest-starring appearances on *The Defenders*, a popular CBS series executive-produced by Herbert Brodkin (who was also the executive producer of *For the People*).

Shatner was confident in his newest television role as earnest assistant district attorney David Koster, fighting the good fight in the labyrinthian New York City legal system. "I've been in a lot of shows headed for Broadway, and there's a smell of success about the hit ones. I sense the same about this TV series, an excitement on the set, a feeling of victory," he said. One week before the premiere of *For the People*, Shatner, looking dapper in a tuxedo, promoted the show, appearing as a guest panelist on the CBS television game show *What's My Line?* alongside Kitty Carlisle (filling in for Arlene Dahl), Bennett Cerf, columnist Dorothy Kilgallen, and host John Daly.

("It's on right after *Ed Sullivan*," Shatner told Daly about *For the People*. That week's "mystery guest" on *What's My Line?* was actor Jack Lemmon, who was there to promote his new movie, *How to Murder Your Wife*. He was correctly identified by a blindfolded Carlisle.)

Jessica Walter, twenty-four, had also appeared on *The Defenders* and on several other high-profile television shows, including *The Alfred Hitchcock Hour*, *Ben Casey*, and *Route 66*. She, too, was a Broadway veteran, most recently starring in the comedy *A Severed Head*. The *For the People* cast also included, most notably, Howard Da Silva and Lonny Chapman, who had over forty years of acting experience between them.

But *For the People* was a midseason entry on the CBS schedule, replacing the Craig Stevens series *Mr. Broadway*, which premiered the previous fall to disappointing viewership numbers and was cancelled after thirteen episodes. The network's executives, showing little faith in *For the People*, slotted the series to air on Sunday nights at nine opposite NBC's *Bonanza*, the top-rated series on television.

Katz still felt the sting over fifty years later.

"CBS just needed a thirteen-week fill-in, and they had something 'big' coming in behind it," he recalled. "They didn't promote [*For the People*]. It was probably predestined to have just that one run. It did well enough for [CBS] to say, 'Okay, moving on.'" The series premiered on January 31, 1965, and in late March, CBS pulled the plug, burning off the remaining episodes, which aired through mid-May. The network ultimately replaced *For the People* with its veteran legal drama, *Perry Mason*—and it, too, was demolished on Sunday nights by *Bonanza*. "*For the People* was opposite *Bonanza*, which was the most popular show at the time," Shatner said. "And *Bonanza* killed us, so we went off the air after thirteen weeks."[1]

But the television gods work in mysterious ways, and the cancellation of *For the People* allowed Shatner to explore other opportunities, including a new science fiction series at NBC. A pilot episode for the series had been shot throughout the fall of 1964 and into early 1965, but network executives found it "too cerebral," and there were problems with its star, Jeffrey Hunter. NBC officials believed in the project and, in an unusual move, gave its creator, Gene Roddenberry, the green light to shoot a second pilot.

Star Trek was looking for a new leading man—and William Shatner was available.

*   *   *

An acting career didn't seem to be in the cards for William Alan Shatner when he entered the world in Côte-Saint-Luc, Montreal, on March 22, 1931, the first son of Joseph, a clothing manufacturer, and his wife, Ann.

Joseph Schattner was born in Austria in 1898 to Wolf and Freyda Schattner. At the age of fourteen, Joseph became the first member of his large extended Jewish family, which included ten brothers and sisters, to emigrate to North America. In 1912, he boarded a steamship in Austria bound for Montreal, which had a thriving Jewish community that comprised roughly 7 percent of the city's population. Joseph changed his surname to the more Anglicized "Shatner" and made a living in his new country by holding down several odd jobs, including selling newspapers, before entering the clothing business. He did well enough, those first few years, to bring the rest of his brothers and sisters to Montreal, where they branched out into various life-styles. Joseph's younger brother, Louis Shatner—William's uncle—was arrested in 1956 for allegedly running a gambling ring in Montreal. He claimed he his lost his life savings in a bad mining investment.[2]

Ann Garmaise, who was seven years younger than Joseph, was born in 1905 into a financially comfortable Jewish family in Montreal. Her parents, Jacob Garmaise and Yetta (née Kahn), were from Eastern Europe; Jacob emigrated to Canada from Lithuania and Yetta from Germany. The fam-ily—which also included Ann's brothers, Max and Bernard, and her sister, Pearl—was "relatively well off," and Ann grew into a brash and boisterous young woman who enjoyed being the center of attention. Years later, when her son became famous, she would tell anyone within earshot that "I'm Wil-liam Shatner's mother," much to his embarrassment. "My mother was a bit of a clown and never really pursued her acting in a professional way, but she had talent," Shatner's sister recalled.

Joseph and Ann were married in 1926 in Montreal and settled in Notre-Dame-de-Grâce, a heavily Catholic, mostly English-speaking middle-class neighborhood in the city's West End. The locals called it "NDG" for short. They moved into a house at 4419 Girouard Avenue with William and his older sister, Farla. There are Internet records showing that a son, David Shat-ner, was born to Joseph and Ann in April 1935. David died that December at seven months old and was buried in Back River Cemetery in Montreal. There is no mention of a David Shatner in any of William Shatner's of-ficial biographies, and Bill has never publicly mentioned or written about a deceased brother, so the veracity of this information is unclear.[3] Farla and William's little sister, Joy, arrived eleven years later.

Joseph worked his way up in the clothing business by tackling different facets of the trade, from packing boxes to eventually becoming a salesman before starting his own company called Admiration Clothing. The factory was located on 8 Briardale Road in Montreal's Hampstead section and manufactured men's suits for French-Canadian stores—or, as William Shatner recalled, "basically suits for working men who owned only one suit."[4] Joseph was, his son recalled, "a stern but loving man"[5] who worked extremely hard, smoked heavily, and relaxed on Saturday, the Sabbath, when he would recline on the family room couch and listen to the Metropolitan Opera crackling over the radio from New York City.

The tools of Joseph's trade were burned into his son's memory; Bill recalled the smell of his father's factory, the "unforgettable aroma of raw serge and tweed in rolled-up bales, mixed with the smell of my father's cigarettes."[6] Joseph imagined that Bill would, one day, take over the business (after going to college, of course). He gave Bill a job in the factory—packing suits. As a teenager, Bill, dressed in his best suit, would sometimes accompany his father on sales calls to clients in and around the Montreal area (and sometimes to far-flung locales).

When Bill was three or four years old, the family moved to a larger house on Marcil Avenue in a neighborhood where both French and English were spoken freely. "Many of my young friends were French so I spoke French on the streets somewhat easily," he said later. "Both of my parents spoke French; my mother, being Canadian, was taught it in school and my father, being a businessman, had learned it as a necessity. I learned it by osmosis on the streets of Montreal."[7]

While Ann raised her children, she found time to give elocution lessons to the neighborhood children as well. Bill thought, in hindsight, that she was a frustrated actress, and that the elocution lessons gave her the chance to emote, sometimes rather theatrically. She would often act out monologues at home, entertaining her family. Ann kept a kosher home, and the Shatner family joined a Conservative Jewish synagogue, Shaare Zion, where Bill attended Hebrew School. The original synagogue held Shabbat and holiday services at Victoria Hall in the city's Westmount district; in 1939, Shaare Zion moved to a new facility on Côte-Saint-Luc Road, where Bill was Bar Mitzvahed in 1945.

Sundays were spent visiting Ann's parents and other relatives who lived nearby. At night, the Shatners listened to their favorites on the radio, including comedians Jack Benny and Fred Allen, ventriloquist Edgar Bergen (with his sidekick, Charlie McCarthy), and Arch Oboler. Bill had a special affinity for Oboler, "a mastery of mystery and suspense" with shows such as *Lights Out*. He was also an avid fan of radio dramatist Norman Corwin.

(Years later he had the chance to work with both of his idols. He costarred in Oboler's *Night of the Auk*, which aired on New York City's public television station in 1960 and, decades later, acted in a Corwin radio play called *The Curse of 589*, broadcast on National Public Radio.)

Sports on the radio was also big; when he was around nine, Bill rushed home to listen to the Joe Louis–Billy Conn fight, only to find the front door locked. He pounded on the door until someone let him into the house. In a similar story, younger sister Joy was listening to a hockey game on the radio. "Billy was ringing the doorbell to come in to listen. I did not hear the doorbell and he kept ringing and ringing and I still did not hear it, and so he broke into a window on the side [of the house] and came in and practically killed me, he was so upset. So, he had a little bit of a temper."[8]

As he got older, Bill's personality began to take shape. He was slight of build, though ready for a fight if necessary, and earned the nickname "Toughie" for never backing down from a challenge. He claimed to be a rather quiet, shy boy who didn't have many friends. When he was around six years old, or so the story goes, he found a five-dollar bill in a field and, wanting to share it with his best friend, tore it in half. In another oft-repeated Valentine's Day scenario, young Bill would send himself a valentine in school, knowing that none of his classmates would include him in this juvenile rite of passage. "There was love at home, but there was still a loneliness," he said. "I've always had to deal with loneliness and how to overcome it."[9]

He was "a bit of a prankster," his sister, Farla, recalled. "I remember when I would have little birthday parties and my brother would come in in the middle [of the party] and start telling ghost stories and close the lights and make everyone scared to death."[10] In another family story, he was walking with his mother and his sister, Joy, in downtown Montreal. "Suddenly Billy disappeared, and we finally found him dancing to the organ grinder," Joy recalled. "Billy got everybody watching him and dancing with him and laughing with him and he loved performing in front of that organ grinder."[11]

He dreamed of being just like the kids who lived in the upper-class Westmount section of Montreal where, he figured, the constant undercurrent of anti-Semitism was not as prevalent as it was in the NDG. When he walked to Hebrew school, Bill would cross to the other side of the street and pretend he didn't know where his synagogue was—looking both ways before bolting inside to make sure no one saw him. "There was a lot of discrimination in those years for being Jewish," he recalled. "I had to fight . . . quite regularly with kids who would take me on. There was a lot of scuffling; nothing horrible beyond children throwing punches but it was nightmarish at the time."[12]

Shatner wasn't exaggerating, according to his boyhood friend, Arthur Weinthal, who grew up near Bill in Montreal's West End. "There was an anti-Semitic environment in Montreal," he said. "The city had a lot of French-speaking people—it was their province—but the aura that emanated out of the politics of the city was anti-Semitic. I always felt separate and alone and segregated, in my mind. One of the great anomalies of Montreal was that on Sherbrooke Street, near Decarie Boulevard, there was a place called the NDG Kosher Meat Market. As an adult I always thought, 'Isn't that interesting, Our Lady of Grace Kosher Meat Market, since that's what 'NDG' means—'Our Lady of Grace.'"[13]

Bill struck up a friendship with his Marcil Avenue neighbor Pierre Lafond, who was slightly older and whose father owned a French-Canadian summer camp for boys. "Bill lived downstairs, and we lived upstairs," Lafond recalled. "He was a year younger than I was, but we became close friends because of the proximity, for one thing, but also in those days, there was a lot of street life and we were all together. We played football on the streets; we played baseball and hockey." Pierre's younger sister, Suzanne, recalled one day when Bill and Pierre, playing baseball in the street, accidentally shattered a neighbor's windshield with a batted baseball; they both fled to the relative safety of a darkened theater nearby and never fessed up.[14]

Bill and Pierre joined the "Marcil Gang," a group of kids who lived on the street and who gave themselves nicknames like "Peanut" and "Sweet Pea." Bill's first pangs of lust were ignited by a local girl named Betty— Pierre remembered her as Betty Beck—who was part of the Marcil Gang. "Betty was my entrée into sexuality, not necessarily sex, but being aware of a voluptuous girl," Shatner said. "We used to play tackle football—and, if you tackled Betty, it could change your life."[15] Despite his claims that he was lonely, Pierre remembered Bill as "being very attractive," claiming that "the girls loved him" and that he was quite talkative when it came to the opposite sex. "He was extroverted. He wasn't afraid to talk."

During the school year, Bill walked to nearby Willingdon Elementary School, where he earned decent grades. He didn't share the walk with Pierre, who attended a different elementary school because his French-Canadian father wanted him to improve his English-speaking skills.

When Bill was around seven or eight years old, Ann, the frustrated actress, began taking her son each Saturday to the Montreal Children's Theatre, which was established in 1933 by Dorothy Davis and Violent Walters and was originally located in a residential basement. The theater's stated mission was "not necessarily to create young actors and actresses"; instead, it claimed that "good speech, self-esteem and confidence were primary goals."[16] Both Davis and Walters would live well into their nineties, and the school, now called the Children's Theatre, has staged over seven hundred plays. Young Bill Shatner's classmates included Richard Easton, a future Tony Award-winning actor, and Beatrice Picard, later to become a star on French-speaking Canadian television (and with whom Shatner had one of his very first onstage love scenes, which ended with a kiss). "He was exposed to the theatre early on and given a sense of ambition, I think, by his mother," Shatner's boyhood friend, Hilliard Jason, recalled years later. "His mother, I think, dreamed that her son would be a star one day."[17]

It was during his time at the Montreal Children's Theatre that Bill caught the acting bug. "I don't remember being taught how to act because I don't believe you can be taught how to act," he said. "But you can learn the discipline of learning words and having to appear and to say them. I don't ever recall thinking, 'I'm too scared to do this, therefore I won't do this.' To me the show had to go on and I understood that concept from a very early age."

Bill and his fellow Children's Theatre actors would stage plays at the local Victorian Theatre, in a nearby park, and on local radio, where Bill appeared on a show called *Saturday Morning Fairy Tales*. He was "madly in love" with Violet Walters, who with her dyed black hair and violet lips he thought "bore a striking resemblance, all of it manufactured, to some of the silent-screen stars." He was one of the few males at the school: "I think she was desperate for any male to say the words."[18] Young Bill would anger Davis and Walters by hiding behind the curtain when it was time to rehearse, but he was an overall likeable kid and the women never took his unruliness too seriously. Ann Shatner never missed a performance; if Bill auditioned for a radio role and didn't get the part, she would be on the phone, screaming at the poor producer on the other end for not hiring her son.

Bill caught the eye of Rupert Caplan, a producer at the Canadian Broadcasting Corporation (CBC), and started to appear regularly in roles both big and small on CBC radio shows, including an adaptation of *Lies My Father Told Me*, Ted Allan's tale about an Orthodox Jewish boy growing up in 1920s Montreal, and *Daddy Long-Legs*, which merited a local newspaper photograph of teenaged stars Bill Shatner and Elizabeth Karabiner. Bill played Jimmie McBride in the Children's Theatre stage production of *Daddy-Long-Legs*, which was based on the 1912 Jean Webster novel. The CBC's reach was expansive; Shatner's voice was heard not only in Montreal but on radios in Toronto, Vancouver, Winnipeg, and even five hundred miles away in Halifax. He participated in the Children's Theatre on weekends all the way through to his high school years.

*   *   *

When he reached the age of six, Bill started spending summers away from home at Jewish sleepaway camps that dotted the picturesque Laurentian Mountains north of Montreal. He had his first summer camp experience at Camp Rabin, owned by one of his aunts. He loved the athletics—playing baseball, swimming, and, especially, boxing—but he felt lonely and homesick. His older sister, Farla, was also at Camp Rabin, so that helped a bit, and his parents would often drive up to visit on a summer Sunday. He recalled a starring role in a camp production of *Winterset*, in which he played a young Jewish boy in Europe forced to leave his home and his beloved dog (played by a fellow camper "costumed in painted newspaper") as the Nazis approached. "The people at the camp, the parents, were very much aware of the situation, and that a massacre was going on [in Europe]," he said. Shatner remember crying onstage, which, in turn, brought the camp audience (mostly parents) to tears.[19] "I remember the warmth of my father holding me as people told him what a wonderful son he had. Just imagine the impact that had on a six-year-old child. I had the ability to move people to tears. And I could get approval."[20]

In the fall of 1944, Bill entered West Hill High School, not too far from the duplex on Marcil Avenue. He tried out for the school's football team and made the cut, becoming, as he said in a self-deprecating manner, "part of a great high school dynasty that won the city championships for several years . . . I was on the second team and, quite clearly, I was, at most, second best."[21] Bill had always enjoyed skiing in the Laurentian Mountains and joined the West Hill High School ski team. He kept a busy social schedule, dating a few girls off and on, but there was no high school sweetheart in the picture.

Bill began to lose touch with his upstairs Marcil Avenue pal, Pierre Lafond, who went to a different high school. Their friendship trailed off, and they eventually lost touch. Pierre, like his boyhood friend, found later success in California. After graduating from McGill University with a degree in architecture, he moved to Santa Barbara in 1957, inherited his father's liquor store there, and expanded the business—eventually starting the Santa Barbara Winery, which continues to operate to this day on one hundred and five acres in the Santa Ynez Valley, and Lafond Winery & Vineyards.

*   *   *

Bill spent many of his boyhood weekends at the movies, often watching two double bills on the same day, starting at noon on Saturday and not leaving the theater until later that evening. Sometimes Bill and his pals would cut class on Friday and head to downtown Montreal to catch a burlesque show at the Gayety Theatre on Sainte-Catherine Street. "Lily St-Cyr was usually there stripping, and they had the comics and I used to cry with laughter at the burlesque," he said.

Bill joined the high school drama department and acted in several plays, and while he devoted more and more time to studying and absorbing the craft of acting, his grades began to suffer. It wasn't that he couldn't do the work—he was bright, intuitive, and curious—but all he cared about, at this stage of the game, was acting and sports. He felt more complete as a person, more at ease when he was on the stage inhabiting someone else's skin, and he enjoyed the adulation of the audience. Perhaps the acting and the warmth of an audience was a panacea to the loneliness he claimed to feel in his everyday life as Bill Shatner. His devotion to acting was frowned upon by his buddies on the football team, who thought it was "weird." It was, he said, "tantamount to carrying your violin case while passing the school."[22] But he persevered, seeking out new avenues for his passion and accepting any acting jobs that came his way, including a production of the Clifford Odets drama *Waiting for Lefty* that was staged at a Communist meeting hall in Montreal.

He was sixteen and didn't understand the play's message, or know the first thing about Communism, but said later he was lifted emotionally by shouting "Strike! Strike!" on the stage.[23]

When Bill was fifteen and "oh so terribly naïve," he got a job as a stage manager at the Orpheum Theatre in Montreal, where he caught the fancy of a French singer who was performing there. The male singer (Shatner never identified him by name) invited Bill out for dinner at a nice restaurant. The eatery's dress code required a jacket, which Bill didn't have. No problem, the singer told him, he had a jacket back at his hotel room that he was sure would fit Bill. They went upstairs to retrieve the alleged jacket, and the situation spiraled into a farcical scene as the romantically aggressive singer chased Bill around the bed before he could make a panicked escape. "I didn't know that men could be attracted to other men," he said. "It was not something spoken about in middle-class Jewish homes."

Bill continued to spend his summer vacations at various (mostly) Jewish summer camps throughout his high school years and eventually graduated from camper to counselor. For several summers, he worked as a counselor at Camp B'nai Brith, located on a lake in the Laurentian Mountains in Sainte-Agathe-des-Monts. One of his co-counselors, Howard Ryshpan, was two years younger and, like Bill, was bitten by the acting bug. Their paths would cross again a decade later when they were both working in Canadian television.

"Saint Agathe at the time was like the Catskills. There were a lot of Jewish hotels and people went there for the summer," Ryshpan recalled. "A lot of the guys who worked the Catskills worked up in Saint Agathe. The camp itself was very pretty; there was no electricity at the time, and, at night, we'd have to spend an evening on duty in case the kids got up during the night. We had kerosene lamps on the porch of each of the bunks. So, you would see these lamps in the darkness, and you would hear the loons out on the lake at night and it was very lovely."

Shatner was a popular personality in the camp and made some lifelong friends, including Hilliard Jason, who later embarked on a distinguished medical career. (He insisted on being called "Hilliard," even back in their camp days, Shatner said.)

Camp B'nai Brith was comprised of thirteen bunks, each with two counselors, and was nonsectarian, though most of its campers were Jewish and attended the Friday-night Sabbath services. World War II had ended just a few years earlier, and many of the kids at Camp B'nai Brith were refugees from Eastern Europe who had witnessed unspoken horrors during the Holocaust, losing family members, including parents and friends. "I was in charge of arts and crafts, Hilliard Jason was in charge of the waterfront and Bill was in charge of drama," Shatner's boyhood friend, Arthur Weinthal, recalled. "I think one year he did a Gilbert and Sullivan something-or-other."

Over sixty years later, Weinthal could still remember the refugees who arrived at Camp B'nai Brith, "kids who had been released from camps in Europe."

> Most of these kids were orphans. The Jewish Community Service in Montreal gave each of them a little suitcase with a T-shirt, soap, a towel, a toothbrush and a pair of shorts. I was also a counselor in addition to being in charge of arts and crafts, and I had a bunk of eight to ten kids—and the sounds you heard at night from those kids were incredible. They were shell-shocked . . . and in the morning we used to take their bedsheets, which were covered in urine, and hang them over the balcony.
>
> Over the course of three weeks the number of bedsheets over the balcony would lessen and the noise at night would lessen and the faces which were haunted and pale when they arrived were now sunburnt.[24]

"It stretched us a great deal," Hilliard Jason said. "You had to grow up very fast . . . taking care of kids who needed you in a parental role—in some cases rather desperately."[25]

One of those frightened young campers was future Canadian diplomat Fred Bild, who arrived at Camp B'nai Brith as a thirteen-year-old Jewish refugee from Belgium. Seven years earlier, Fred's father was grabbed off a street in Brussels and sent to his death at Auschwitz; Fred's mother hid him and his younger brother on a farm in the Belgian town of Lubbeek for two years. The family was reunited after the war, and Fred's mother remarried, moving with her new husband and children to Montreal. Because he was Jewish, Fred was not allowed to attend a French school (one of the rules back then), and he spoke no English that first summer at Camp B'nai Brith in 1948.

One of his counselors was Bill Shatner.

"To me, he was a grown up. He certainly had this sense of authority. But he was a very, very congenial person," Bild said, vividly recalling Shatner seventy years later.

He obviously took his job seriously. I didn't know what a counselor was. I had been in organizations like that for young people,
where they were put together and there were supervisors over
them. I guess that's kind of what he was, but he immediately . .
. I can remember the first words he spoke to me. I didn't speak a
word of English when I arrived. I only spoke French and German.
He immediately spoke French to me. His French wasn't perfect;
it was the kind of French that Montreal boys spoke. But it was
certainly understandable and made me feel at home.

He asked me where I came from and if was this my first time
at camp, and he asked me what sports I liked. And I didn't know
what to say because I hadn't practiced any sports. There were a
couple of other boys like me who were recent arrivals and he was
very solicitous of us. He didn't make a huge fuss over us, but he
did take special care of us.

Bill spent a lot of time with Fred and the other recent arrivals from Europe, taking them on nature hikes, teaching them how to play baseball ("I
didn't understand the usefulness or the entertainment value in it," Fred said),
and trying to help them improve their English skills. Fred spent three weeks
at Camp B'nai Brith that summer and returned the following summer with
one year of Canadian schooling under his belt. His English had improved
to the point where he didn't have much trouble communicating. And, once
again, Bill Shatner took Fred under his wing.

"The second summer, that was '49, he put on a play," Fred recalled. "By
that time, I had improved my English. He congratulated me; he thought
I made tremendous progress. But he continued to correct me, to show me
how to pronounce words and to phrase certain sentences. That's why I say
he 'taught me English.' We didn't have formal sessions of learning English,
but he would say 'This is what you normally say.' He didn't make me feel
I was doing something wrong or that I needed correcting—nothing of the
sort—and that's what I remember most about him. Anything he ever taught
you, he did in the nicest way. It was very natural."

Bill gave Fred a part in the camp play, which was "something with Cowboys and Indians" that included a rousing song. "It wasn't great theater, but
it did give me a role which I was very pleased with," he said. Fred formed a
gang within his bunk, tattooing an anchor on everybody's arm with a ball-
point pen. Shatner helped the boys compose a song in the vein of Gilbert and
Sullivan. "He was an extremely nice guy," Fred said. "He took his counseling

duties seriously. He never lost his temper, never insulted us like some other counselors did that. They would berate their kids and say, 'You'll never amount to anything because you're not as good as the kids next door.' He never did anything like that. He was encouraging, he was full of praise for us and he considered it his job to teach us things."

That was Fred's last summer at Camp B'nai Brith. He eventually graduated from Concordia University in Montreal, earned a diploma from University College in London and a foreign student's diploma from the Ecole nationale d'administration in Paris, and went to work for the Canadian government. He held diplomatic appointments in Japan, Korea, and France; was the Canadian Ambassador to Thailand; and, in 1990, was appointed as Ambassador to the People's Republic of China and Mongolia. But he never saw Bill Shatner again, and never had the chance to thank him. Until now.

There were other, more lighthearted camp adventures. At the end of one summer, when Bill was eighteen or nineteen, he and a group of his Camp B'nai Brith staff members were invited by the camp director to accompany him on a "wooden war canoe" trip from the Laurentians to New York City—a journey of over nine hundred miles. Shatner retold the story many times over the years, recounting how he couldn't pee in the middle of Lake Champlain (too embarrassed in front of his canoe mates) and how this group of guys from Canada were supposed to be feted by local Jewish groups in Kingston or Schenectady (the city often changed in Shatner's retelling) but were forced to bypass the welcoming committees for various reasons. They finally made it to Manhattan, tying up their canoes at the Seventy-Ninth Street marina (sometimes the Seventy-Second Street marina) and walking through the midtown streets. In one version of the story, Shatner said he was asked by a male passerby to accompany him to a show at Radio City Music Hall—where the man attempted to seduce him. In another version, Shatner and his pals were featured on a local newscast recounting their canoeing exploits. Where the group stayed in Manhattan, or for how long they were in the city, is lost to the mists of time.

*   *   *

Bill Shatner graduated from West Hill High School in June of 1948, three months after his seventeenth birthday. Despite his mediocre academic record, he was accepted into McGill University, most likely because the school needed to meet its quota of Jewish students. The McGill campus was only two miles from Marcil Avenue in Montreal, and Bill saved himself considerable expense by living at home during his four years attending the school. He was passionately devoted to acting, but his father still expected him to join his clothing business, so Bill acquiesced by enrolling in McGill's School of Commerce. He attended classes infrequently and relied on the kindness of classmates to lend him their notes, "passing exams by one or two marks, getting fifty or fifty one percent right on answers" while devoting as much time as he could to the school's drama department.

He recalled spending "eighteen hours a day"[26] writing plays and musicals, acting in student productions and doing whatever he could to stay involved in the school's theatrical life. "It didn't occur to me that I could be an actor," he said. "I was in Montreal and was going to do something else, probably be in my father's clothing business, but I continued this routine of not going to school and reading other people's notes."[27] Given his background and experience in radio, he was hired for some local radio productions, which helped him earn some extra cash. He also earned some money doing voice-over work as a part-time announcer at the CBC. He joined McGill's five-member radio workshop and became its vice president, eventually ascending to its presidency; he staged and produced the school's annual *Red and White Revue* (Hilliard Jason was its technical director), joined the Players' Club, and acted in a production of Lillian Hellman's *The Children's Hour* and Agatha Christie's *Ten Little Indians*. "He had good time, a good voice, and was a very accomplished performer," recalled Lionel Caplan, a fellow Camp B'nai Brith counselor who became friendly with Shatner when they reconnected at McGill. They were soon joined by Camp B'nai Brith alum Arthur Weinthal, a future Canadian-television executive, and the trio became fast friends.

"He was the one who encouraged me to join the *Red and White Revue*," Caplan recalled. "In one *Revue* he played a thick, punch-drunk gangster, which was extremely funny. In our third year at McGill he produced and directed the *Revue*. I was the script coordinator. At the end of the run, at the last performance, it was customary for the producer to say a few words and Bill said something like, 'For a rounded University education all you need to do is take Philosophy 101,' which he had done, and participate in the *Red and White Revue*." Shatner also directed one of Caplan's "pretty awful" plays which was meant to be an anti-war anthem, but, according to Caplan: "One of the critics accused of us of being Communists. This was the period of McCarthyism."[28]

Weinthal remembered "going to movies together," saying: "I never knew him as 'William Shatner,' only 'Bill,' that's who he was. The three of us would go to the Monkland Theatre and the Empress Theatre and then we'd go out and have a hot dog and some fries on the Strip. We were very good friends and we were particularly good friends with Lionel Caplan because he was the only one who could get his father's car. Lionel was a hero to us."[29]

Bill's later stage career encompassed the works of Shakespeare, but there's no record of him acting in any Shakespearian productions at McGill—unlike his fellow B'nai Brith camp counselor Howard Ryshpan, who appeared in the school's production of *Twelfth Night*. One of Ryshpan's castmates in *Twelfth Night* was Leonard Cohen, who graduated from McGill in 1955. Born into a Jewish family in Montreal in September 1934, Cohen grew up only blocks away from Shatner; separated by three years, they attended different elementary schools and high schools (Cohen graduated from Westmount High School) and were not friends at the time. (If they were, neither man recalled any interactions between them.) There is some evidence, unearthed by online historians, that Bill Shatner and Leonard Cohen were related to each other as fourth cousins through their shared Garmaise lineage (Shatner's maternal side of the family). After graduating from McGill, Cohen achieved international acclaim as a folk singer-songwriter, poet, and novelist. He was inducted into the Canadian Music Hall of Fame, the Canadian Songwriters Hall of Fame, and the Rock and Roll Hall of Fame, and in 2010, he was awarded a Grammy Lifetime Achievement Award. He died in November 2016 at the age of eighty-two.

*   *   *

In 1951, while at McGill, twenty-year-old Bill Shatner somehow found the time to make his big-screen debut playing "a crook" in a low-budget movie called *The Butler's Night Off*. (He was credited as "Bill Shatner" for the only time in his professional acting career.) The details surrounding his involvement in the movie are murky; directed by trained cinematographer Roger Racine, *The Butler's Night Off* was shot in and around Montreal and had noirish pretensions and a labyrinthian plot. Bill was most likely asked to appear in the movie by Stanley Mann, who wrote the screenplay and who had directed the *Red and White Revue* at McGill the year before Shatner (and who, like Bill, was a veteran of CBC radio). *The Butler's Night Off* cast included Henry Ramer, Paul Colbert, Peter Sturgess, and Maurice Gauvin.

The movie, less than an hour in length, has been lost to history, but thanks to the digital age, a few choice clips can be found on YouTube. Mann would go on to a successful television and Oscar-nominated screenwriting career, including credits on *The Mouse That Roared*—which put Peter Sellers on the map in North America—*The Collector*, *Eye of the Needle*, *Conan the Destroyer*, and *Damien: Omen II*.

That summer of 1951, Bill and Lionel Caplan decided to take a road trip to the United States, winding their way in the direction of California. They (wrongly) assumed they needed to obtain a permit to travel, but when they went to the US Consulate in Montreal, they were told they needed to post a bond—about $400—to ensure they would not disappear in America without returning to their native country. "While I had some savings and could manage, Bill didn't, and had to borrow money from his mother which, being proud and independent, annoyed him intensely," Caplan recalled. The two friends joined a couple who were on their way to Kansas and wanted passengers to share the driving and the expenses. "He was a theology student, so there were many interesting discussions along the way and Bill lost no opportunity to challenge his beliefs, which didn't always endear him or us to our hosts," Caplan said. "Most nights [the couple] spent in motels along the way, but to save money we slept in their car." After reaching Kansas, Bill and Lionel hitchhiked to Colorado, where they visited Arthur Weinthal, who was spending the summer with his sister and her husband in Denver, working at an inner-city day camp for underprivileged children.

From there it was on to Utah, hitchhiking there with a group of Mormons, and then on to Nevada after getting a lift from two drivers from New Jersey. "They dropped us in front of a brothel which they were intending to visit," Caplan said. "Brothels were about to be declared illegal in this part of Nevada." Once they arrived in California (finally!), they spent a few days with an aunt of Bill's, who was married to a professor who taught at the University of California, Berkeley. "We heard all about the rampant McCarthyism affecting many academics," Caplan recalled. "On the West Coast, when we weren't visiting relatives, we spent our nights in cheap hotels—but if we arrived somewhere after dark we would sometimes sleep on beaches. I especially remember Santa Barbara."[30] They hitchhiked up the West Coast to Vancouver—"to earn money we worked for a very short time humping sacks of something or other around the railway yard"—and Bill, selling his acting experience, was able to get a part in a radio play on the CBC, "which helped with the finances," Caplan recalled. "Then through a relative of his we got a lift to Chicago with an elderly couple who wanted us to drive them." After a short stint in Chicago, Bill and Lionel headed to New York City, where they saw several Broadway shows, including *Guys and Dolls*, before returning to Montreal.

The traveling was a fun diversion, but Bill knew that his father expected him to join the business after he graduated from McGill—and that expectation "hung over him like a cloud"[31] (though not enough to stop him from cutting classes). "I knew this is what I loved to do," he said about acting, "but it was . . . beyond *concept* to even think about that. I don't remember even thinking that I could possibly become an actor. I put myself through school . . . although I lived at home, I paid my dues and bought my books and had my spending money by acting on radio in Montreal." He occasionally joined his father at the office, where he "got instantly tired" and realized he could never be happy in the clothing business—in which he had absolutely no interest or acumen.

Bill's grades at McGill plummeted as he devoted more and more of his time to the theater, acting onstage and in productions produced through McGill's radio workshop. Finally, in his junior year, he screwed up the courage to tell his father what he really wanted to do with his life. It was, he said, "one of the most difficult things I have ever done."[32] He was in his bedroom on Marcil Avenue when Joseph asked his son if he'd thought about what he would do after he graduated. He dropped his bombshell, and it hit Joseph like a ton of bricks; Bill remembered his father sitting on the bed, trying to absorb the news that his son wanted to be an actor—an actor!—while Bill paced back and forth, trying to explain his decision. "He was very upset, totally against it," he said. "He argued with me for days. And I had to keep saying, 'I want to try.'"[33]

Eventually, his father came around to the idea. Sort of. "Well, do what you want to do," he told his son. "There's always a place for you here. I don't have the money to support you, but I'll help you the best I can."[34] Bill figured that if he could earn one hundred dollars a week, he could support himself as a working actor. "I could live, and that was my ambition when I was in my twenties."[35]

Bill graduated from McGill in the spring of 1952 with a degree in commerce and chose a quote from the nineteenth-century English Romantic poet John Keats to accompany his graduation photo in the school's year-book: "There is not a fiercer hell than the failure in a great object." He did not attend the graduation convocation; he'd failed a math class and needed to pass that hurdle before getting his college degree.

*   *   *

If Bill was going to pursue an acting career, he needed a job. Shortly after his college graduation, he was thrown a lifeline by Ruth Springford, who had directed him in several plays at McGill. She also ran a summer theater in Northern Ontario called the Mountain Playhouse, which was billed as "the only English-speaking Summer Theatre in the Province of Quebec," and she sent Bill to see its actor/manager, Bruce Raymond. "My one and only fifteen minutes of fame were realized in the summer of 1952 while I was ac-tor/manager of a now long-gone summer theater, the Mountain Playhouse, situated at Beaver Lake on the top of Mount Royal," Raymond remembered nearly sixty years later. "A newly minted BCom graduate approached and asked for a job as an actor. As he wanted the then-princely salary of thirty-five dollars a week, I could only afford to hire him if he also took on the job of the Assistant Box-office Manager. William Shatner agreed."[36]

Bill's main job was to oversee ticket sales for the Mountain Playhouse, and he failed miserably shortly after arriving there. "I didn't know anything about the business," he said. "I flunked accounting two years in a row. And my father tried to dissuade me from taking the job. But we made a deal. He gave me five years to make it as an actor. If I didn't, I'd go into his busi-ness."[37] His career as the theater's assistant manager was short-lived; Ruth Springford fired him shortly thereafter but kept Bill on as a performer, which is when he "began playing all those happy young man roles."[38] He costarred in a 1952 Mountain House production of *Castle in the Air* and, that same year, played Richard Stanley in *The Man Who Came to Dinner* starring Barry Morse, Corinne Conley, and Jack Creley. (Bill was also billed as Assistant Manager.) In 1953, he costarred in *When the Sun Shines* opposite Creley and Suzanne Finley.

He wasn't exactly starving; Joseph had given him a few thousand dollars after he graduated from McGill, and now he used that money to support himself. "I always thought, 'Well, I can go back to Montreal if this doesn't work out,'" he said. "I thought that for years."[39]

Springford's connections in the Canadian theater world ran deep, and when the 1952 summer season ended, she recommended Bill to a friend at the Canadian National Repertory Theatre, housed in the La Salle Academy Playhouse in Ottawa. Bill was hired as an actor-manager for thirty dollars a week and was, initially, relegated to mostly playing roles as juveniles—more "happy young man" parts. "I went there as an assistant manager and couldn't keep track of the money and tickets and I was fired again but hired as an actor." Again.

One Academy Playhouse anecdote landed Bill in the gossip columns nearly a decade later, once he attained a modicum of stardom in Canada. The story, perhaps invented by an imaginative publicity agent, found young Bill Shatner appearing in a production of *The Seventh Veil* and playing a piano, onstage, while waiting for the leading lady to make her entrance. Bill didn't know how to play the piano and was supposed to mime his movements on the keys while accompanied by an actual (unseen) pianist playing offstage. A blanket was placed inside Bill's piano to muffle the sound; on opening night, as he started to "play" his piano on cue, the offstage pianist was silent for around thirty seconds, leaving Bill to mime in silence—until the real pianist finally came crashing in just as Bill lifted his arms off the keys to stretch them. "The unexpected comedy broke up the audience and for the balance of the play they laughed at everything," the item noted. "The heavy drama wound up as a farce."[40]

Still, the theater company was important enough to warrant a mention in the *New York Times*, which ran a brief item in November 1953 about the Noel Coward comedy *Relative Values*, making its North American premiere at the La Salle Playhouse later that month with star Araby Lockhart, the Toronto-born actress known for her work on the Canadian stage and on television. "The supporting players include Lynne Gorman, William Hutt, and William Shatner," the story noted.[41] *Relative Values* costar Amelia Hall had appeared opposite Alec Guinness at the esteemed Stratford Festival in Ontario the previous summer—Shatner's next destination as he climbed the acting ranks.

CHAPTER 2

The Montreal Star

One of the guest directors at the La Salle Playhouse had recommended Bill Shatner to Tyrone Guthrie. In 1953, the legendary British-born director, then fifty-three years old, had cofounded the Stratford Festival in Stratford, Ontario, with Canadian native and journalist Tom Patterson. Patterson's vision for the Stratford Festival was to create a theater featuring only Canadian actors performing the stage classics. He was given a grant of $125 by the Stratford City Council to seek "artistic advice" for his idea from Laurence Olivier in New York City. When he failed to connect with Olivier, Canadian theater pioneer Dora Mavor Moore arranged a transatlantic phone call between Patterson and Guthrie—who, intrigued by the idea, flew to Stratford, surveyed the physical and cultural landscape, and agreed to become the Festival's first Artistic Director.[1]

At the time of Guthrie's arrival, the Festival's outdoor venue was almost literally a pit covered by a giant canvas tent. It could accommodate around two thousand people. The stage facilities, or lack thereof, mattered little to Guthrie's colleagues in the theater; such was his stature and influence that he was able to lure British stars Alec Guinness and Irene Worth to Stratford—Guinness to star in its inaugural production of *Richard III* in 1953, and Worth following as the star of its second production, *All's Well That Ends Well.*

Guthrie was a giant in the theatrical world who inspired mostly fear in those who met him for the first time. He was, Bill Shatner recalled, "a giant, like a god from Olympus"[2] when he met Guthrie for the first time in 1954, after packing his belongings into the car his father bought for him (a British-made Morris Minor) and making the four-and-a-half-hour drive from Ottawa to Toronto in a fierce rainstorm—narrowly avoiding being forced off a bridge into the Ottawa River by a passing truck.[3] He arrived in Stratford in time for the start of the new Festival season.

Bill was in good company; his fellow players included Ottawa native and future *Bonanza* star Lorne Greene—who once convinced a naïve Shatner to invest $500 in uranium commodities (he lost it all)—and Christopher Plummer. "He was the most extraordinary genius, really," Plummer said of Guthrie. "He was funny, and he could absolutely collapse you with laughter. He worked with all the greats; he taught Charles Laughton. He worked with Laurence Olivier and Ralph Richardson. He was just extraordinary in how he let you go absolutely free and then reined you in. One day I remember we were improvising and making bloody fools of ourselves in rehearsal and he said, 'Absolutely terrible taste. But keep it in.'"[4]

Shatner and Plummer were not strangers to each other when they joined the Stratford Festival. They'd worked together before, both in theatrical productions and in radio and on television (mostly in Toronto). "Radio was huge in the late forties and early fifties and television hadn't really made its big mark quite yet," Plummer said. "We were doing theater and radio. Radio to make a living, and the theater because it was the best coach in the world. Bill was in all those productions. We were both used to playing leading roles, even then."[5] They worked in both English- and French-speaking radio shows, including French-language soap operas and a weekly Bible series. Shatner and Plummer costarred in a production of Shakespeare's *Cymbeline* staged by the Russian director-designer Fyodor Komisarjevsky, affectionately known as "Kommie," who Plummer called "the guru of all time." Kommie arrived in Canada having already headed the Imperial and State Theatres of Moscow and the Old Vic in London. Bill Shatner was "Kommie's favorite of all," Plummer said. "We adored him, and I think he liked us. One particular line Kommie said to both Bill and me was, 'When you play king, everyone else stand up and you sit down.' It was a wonderful, simple piece of direction I'll remember all my life."[6]

Money was tight in those early days, and Bill was burning through the funds his father had given him after his graduation from McGill. He was working semi-steadily in radio and television, but those jobs didn't pay much (around thirty-five dollars apiece). Bill rented a room in the top floor of a rooming house just blocks away from the CBC; the bed, he remembered, had a rope mattress. He was "desperately homesick" that first year and lived in fear of just about everything—his new colleagues, his future, and even "of being knifed in the back when I walked down the dark streets."[7] He ate most of his meals, alone, at a nearby restaurant with a cheap buffet and a sketchy bar that opened for business once the cafeteria closed. He became friendly with the prostitutes who hung out there and worked in the upstairs rooms; eventually he began a relationship with one of them that lasted "several months," claiming, "It wasn't a love affair, we weren't in love with each other, but it was warm and soothing and nurturing."[8]

Bill's loneliness was offset, in part, by the local work in Toronto and by the Stratford Festival, which staged three plays each season, from May through September. The company's actors appeared in all three productions, with the new guys, including Shatner, relegated to supporting roles or to the chorus. "Getting a few lines was an accomplishment," he said, but no one complained. "We were all vying for roles and . . . we struggled for roles and opportunities and we wanted bigger roles to play the next year," he said. "There was security in being the member of a [theater] company but we wanted to be better than a member of a company."[9]

They were all in awe of the six-foot-six-inch Guthrie, whose protuberant belly and hawk nose complemented his dominating mien.[10] After a time, Guthrie, recognizing something in Bill Shatner's acting ability, started to take him under his wing—even likening him to "an actor in the tradition of Olivier."[11]

"All of us little actors in Canada saw the horizon advance toward us" with Guthrie's presence, Shatner said. "We trembled in his sight. One time he put his arm around me and said, 'Bill, tell me about method acting.'" Shatner prattled on about a subject he knew nothing about, trying to impress his mentor, when Guthrie stopped him. "He paused and said, 'Why don't they think of a beautiful sunset?' rather than trying to call up some emotion. He was a master at crowds and panoply and grand design; perhaps less successful at 'Here's how to read a line' or the meaning of the words."[12]

Bill found work on the CBC in live television productions that ran the gamut from classical literature to situational comedy. It helped to pay the bills. In 1955 alone, he costarred in an adaptation of Herman Melville's *Billy Budd* opposite big-screen star Basil Rathbone—who was said to have admired Shatner's elocution and his use of "universal English." Bill remembered the stately Rathbone telling him that he wasn't too nervous about their live production of *Billy Budd*; after all, Rathbone said, he acted on live television productions in America before an audience of thirty million viewers. *Billy Budd* would be a piece of cake, seen by maybe five million viewers if the television stars aligned. On opening night, Rathbone proceeded to accidentally step into a bucket on stage, which got stuck on his foot as he frantically tried to shake it off. "He blew his lines and was destroyed from that moment," Shatner said with some satisfaction.[13] There were other television appearances that year: *The Coming Out of Ellie Swann*, alongside Hugh Webster and veteran actress Kathleen Kidd; *Forever Galatea*, in which he costarred opposite Jane Graham; and *On a Streetcar*, costarring Janet Reid.

When Bill Shatner wasn't acting in the festival or in television or radio productions, he was expanding his performing repertoire with singing, dancing, fencing, and voice lessons. And he was also writing, furiously. They were, mostly, television plays, including *Dreams*—"a story of a young couple who meet and fall in love under false pretenses"—which he wrote for the CBC's *On Camera* series.[14] One of the *Dreams* cast members was a young actress named Gloria Rand (née Rosenberg), and Bill fell hard for her. She was, he said, "a lovely, doe-like woman who came and was tremulous and on the edge of the pasture of life and just struck my fancy."[15] They began dating and he was soon calling her every night from Stratford, telling her he loved her and imploring her to join him there. "We were on the phone so often that the operator from the Canadian Exchange felt sorry for me and allowed me to call for free," he said.[16] She eventually acquiesced and followed him to Stratford. They were engaged four months later.

In the meantime, Bill's roles in the Stratford Festival's productions were growing bigger as his first year segued into his second year and then into his third year as a member of the company. He started to be cast in high-visibility roles, including *Julius Caesar* and *Castle in the Air* with Canadian stage veteran Amelia Hall. "William Shatner, a newcomer, is making an excellent impression as individualistic Scots man-of-all work—incidentally the only actor who adopts an accent and sticks to it," noted one critic. [17] The *New York Times* singled him out for praise for his role in *The Merchant of Venice*: "As Gratiano, William Shatner has a boyish swagger that refreshes another commonplace part."[18]

By Bill Shatner's third year in Stratford, Michael Langham had succeeded Guthrie as the festival's Artistic Director. Christopher Plummer, too, was enjoying a lot of success at the festival and, in the summer of 1956, was tapped by Langham to star in *Henry V*, with Shatner as his understudy. In August, Plummer, who was "plagued by kidney stones,"[19] was forced to miss a performance, later attributing his pain to a sexual encounter the night before. "I woke up alone the next morning . . . (pain) all around my groin and lower abdomen . . . I started to whimper like a whipped dog. 'So, this is what syphilis is like?' I thought. 'I suppose I deserve it, but Christ, how the hell was I to know?'"[20] (It was, indeed, a kidney stone.)

Plummer's understudy, Bill Shatner, stepped into his shoes. Would it be the proverbial big break? "I heard that he was totally original in the part," Plummer said diplomatically, over fifty years later. "He sat down where I stood up. He stood up where I laid down. I mean he completely did the opposite to what I did, which was very brave, actually, for an understudy. And I thought, 'That son of a bitch!' He made a big hit and I couldn't wait to get back to dethrone him."[21]

Shatner insisted that he wasn't trying to upstage the show's star, attributing his contradictory stage movements to not knowing what he was doing, since he didn't have enough practice as Plummer's understudy to nail the role note for note.[22] "Without one word of rehearsal . . . I pulled it off because I was understudying one of two plays we were rehearsing to begin with," he said. "I was there all the time and saw the choreography and learned the lines—that was the key thing."

As Plummer's understudy, the thought never crossed his mind that he would be called upon to fill in for the star. "I hadn't even talked to those actors," he said of the play's other leads. "We'd butted heads a couple of times and I'd spoken to the other understudies. But the lead actors in the parts? I'd barely spoken to them and now I was going to have to deliver lines of great verve and force and wear a costume I never wore before and walk in steps I never had gone before and face two thousand two hundred people . . . and none of that daunted me."[23]

He froze once, in a later scene after the Battle of Agincourt when Henry is on the battlefield with his brother, the Duke of Gloucester (the role Shatner was supposed to play). He approached the actor playing the Duke, hoping for help with his next line. He was met by a blank stare. "That guy had memorized everybody's line in the play," he said, still baffled years later at the memory. "Later, someone said, 'What a brilliant piece of choreography—exhausted, brother goes to brother and leans on him for strength and comes back, renewed.' Little did they know."

The reviews of Shatner's performance the following day were, for the most part, excellent (with a few minor quibbles).

"To sum up the performance in a word, Shatner rose magnificently to the occasion," observed a writer for the *Montreal Gazette.* "But he is not yet equipped to play Henry to the hilt . . . He can assume the confident swagger and the knowing leer. Those who saw him in *Julius Caesar* will also remember that he can also move an audience with quiet sincerity."[24]

Sydney Johnson wrote a lengthy critique of Shatner's *Henry V* performance in *The Montreal Star,* praising the actor's ability to emote "not in the great speeches but in the short dialogue passages, though he reached great heights of eloquence in the prayer before the battle in Act IV . . . Shatner had practically everything except a majesty of delivery."[25] He (gently) critiqued Shatner's inability to vocally carry those scenes requiring lengthy speeches, writing that "his characterization lacked nobility of expression . . . he needs more training and experience to play a king . . . Still and all, considering the circumstances this was a truly great performance and Mr. Shatner thoroughly deserved the ovation he received from the audience and his fellow players."

"Understudy Shatner, with only a few afternoon hours' rehearsal, took over Friday night and earned three curtain calls—one solo," noted the Canadian Press wire service, following up with some incorrect information about Gloria. "Today he is scheduled to marry Gloria Rand, a blonde English beauty he met in Toronto last winter. He said a honeymoon will be postponed until after the Stratford company's appearance at the Edinburgh Festival later this month."[26]

It was quite an eventful August for Shatner. Less than two weeks before his one-night starring role in *Henry V,* he was one of four winners of the Stratford Festival's third annual Tyrone Guthrie Award. Shatner and fellow winners David Gardner, Robin Gamell, and Marie Day were given their citations by Canada's governor general, Vincent Massey, in a private ceremony. The award came with a $750 scholarship "for furthering their knowledge and experience in acting."

Shatner also appeared in his second movie, a filmed (color) version of the Stratford Festival's production of *Oedipus Rex* that was directed by Tyrone Guthrie and starred Douglas Campbell as Oedipus. Most of the actors wore masks in the tradition of ancient Greek theater. (The *New York Times,* reviewing the movie in January 1957, called the masks "monstrous and grotesque.") Shatner, a member of the chorus, also wore a mask. However, in the beginning of the film, he appears sans mask (briefly) as he appears onstage and gives the chorus leader (William Hutt) his mask. "For students and all with classical interests, this film is a jewel of great price," noted the *New York Times* in its review. Shatner was not mentioned.[27]

Bill Shatner and Gloria Rand married after a four-month courtship on August 12, 1956, in her parents' home in Toronto. Lionel Caplan was among the guests. "It was held in the garden of her parents' house, a pleasant but by no means extravagant occasion," he said. "And while in many Jewish weddings the bridegroom is accompanied to the *chuppah* by one or both of his parents, Bill, typically, walked down the aisle on his own."

He was twenty-five, riding high on a burgeoning acting career, and setting his sights on more television work. So, too, was Gloria. In February 1955, she flew to New York City to costar in an episode of *Goodyear Playhouse*, NBC's live television anthology series. The episode, "Backfire," revolved around a sociology professor (Larry Gates) who reassesses his principles after witnessing a crime. Her role was visible enough to earn her a bit of newspaper ink. "Young Gloria Rand was the horrified daughter and Mark Richman was the young man who helped show the professor that people must be adjudged as separate individuals, not in scientific groupings. 'Backfire' turned out to be excellent, thought-provoking drama from start to finish."[28] She followed that up a year later with a costarring appearance in an episode of the CBC's *GM Theatre* called "Tolliver's Travels." For both Bill and Gloria, it seemed like the sky was the limit. "As far back as I can remember there were only two things I always wanted to do," Shatner said at the time. "Be an actor and see America."

✳   ✳   ✳

He was able to check off the second box earlier that year, when Tyrone Guthrie cast Shatner in a bit role (as Usumcasane, a name Shatner loved to pronounce) in a short-lived Broadway production of *Tamburlaine the Great*, which ran for twenty performances at the Winter Garden Theatre from mid-January to early February of 1956. It had the unfortunate timing to open among such stellar shows as *Auntie Mame*, starring Rosalind Russell, and *Inherit the Wind*, starring Paul Muni—not to mention *My Fair Lady* and *Cat on a Hot Tin Roof*. Guthrie directed the production, which was originally scheduled to run for twelve weeks with Lloyd Bochner in the lead role and David Gardner and Colleen Dewhurst among the show's large cast. "Maybe

I wasn't the toast of Broadway," Bill said later, "but I certainly was a shot glass of whisky of Broadway."[29]

Later accounts of Bill Shatner's short time on Broadway—in a small role that mostly required that Usumcasane help carry Tamburlaine (Anthony Quayle) on a sedan chair—had him being offered a seven-picture movie deal by an executive at 20th Century Fox, who saw the show and promised Bill the princely sum of $500 a week. (He was making eighty dollars a week at Stratford.) But he declined to sign the deal on the advice of a fellow actor (or of "some weird guy at some party"—he told several versions of the story). Bill's agent "gnashed his teeth" over his decision.[30] In another version of the story, Bill was being represented by his cousin, a recent law school graduate whose mother was a secretary at 20th Century Fox. Cousin Bill was his first case. It's unclear if that's the way it really played out.

After *Tamburlaine* closed and he returned to Canada, Bill was offered a television role in New York and was scheduled to return to Manhattan in March. But he and fellow actor Robert Christie were denied permission to enter the country under the McCarran Act, which stipulated that Canadian actors taking jobs in the United States were required "to be outstanding artists or to play a part no American citizen could fill." The Actors' Equity Association of Toronto filed a grievance on the actors' behalf, but to no avail.[31]

Bill would get his artistic revenge soon enough.

*   *   *

The Shatners were optimistic about their careers as the calendar changed to 1957. They both had eyes on the New York television and theatrical world, and they moved to the city from Toronto early that year, settling into a small apartment in the Jackson Heights neighborhood of Queens, a short subway ride from Manhattan. Live television was experiencing its "Golden Age" and New York City was its hub in a medium that exploded in the past decade and virtually wiped out serial radio dramas. (Los Angeles was still playing catch-up vis-à-vis television production but was quickly gaining steam on its way to supplanting New York.) CBS, NBC, and the fledgling ABC networks were all headquartered in Manhattan. Live dramas including *Studio One*, *Lux Video Theater*, *Kraft Television Theater*, and *The United States Steel Hour* ruled the nightly airwaves along with variety shows (*The Jackie Gleason Show*, *The Ed Sullivan Show*, *The Red Skelton Show*) and sitcoms. A plethora of cheap-to-produce soap operas (*As the World Turns*, *Guiding Light*, *The Edge of Night*), game shows, and fifteen-minute early-evening newscasts rounded out the networks' schedules.

Bill Shatner had attracted notice the previous year during his short run in *Tamburlaine the Great*; now, the television floodgates opened and the work came fast and furiously for the handsome young actor: *Lamp Unto My Feet, Goodyear Playhouse, The Kaiser Aluminum Hour, Playhouse 90, Omnibus* (in which he costarred with his old pal, Christopher Plummer), and *Climax!* He played a young pathologist in a two-part *Studio One* drama, "No Deadly Medicine," written by Arthur Hailey and costarring Lee J. Cobb, James Broderick, and Gloria Vanderbilt. "William Shatner was very good as the younger pathologist," noted Jack Gould in the *New York Times*.[32] What Gould and the viewers at home did not know is that Shatner had a fit of stage fright in the middle of the live telecast, during a scene where he had to walk across the stage. It was a minor blip and went unnoticed (by everyone except Shatner).

He appeared on *The Ed Sullivan Show*, performing a scene from *Henry V*, and he filmed an episode of *Alfred Hitchcock Presents* called "The Glass Eye" with costars Jessica Tandy and Tom Conway. He played an embittered young man opposite crusty Ed Begley in an episode of ABC's *The United States Steel Hour*—his performance was labeled "superior," and *Variety* gushed that he was "unforgettable as the young priest." He seemed to get every role he auditioned for. He couldn't miss. "Very quickly I became one of the busiest actors in the city," he recalled. "It seemed like I was always working."[33] He started to be recognized on the street; he was offered several television commercials, which he turned down. Sure, the money would come in handy, but acting in commercials wasn't "serious" work—and he was working with some of the biggest names in show business. How would that look? "I was one of the most popular actors on live television, getting role after role after role," he said. "But they only paid six hundred dollars and it took about two or three weeks to do a live TV play. The rent was one hundred dollars. So, by the time you got through with all your expenses—you could never get ahead—for years."[34]

He loved the adrenaline of live television, the sport of learning his lines, hitting his mark (usually a piece of masking tape on the stage floor), and getting into the "zen" zone of separating himself from the audience while being aware that millions of eyeballs were watching his performance. There was little room for error. He even loved the whirring noise that emanated from the bulky television cameras as their internal fans cooled down the hot camera tubes. "For all you might know it was breathing," he said. "There was this warm camera, there was someone behind it, but he was kind of hidden behind this massive thing . . . I thought the camera was alive; if you make an entrance, it purred at you."

His acting in those heady New York days didn't go unnoticed by Richard Matheson, a thirty-year-old writer living in Brooklyn. "He so often gets a bad rap for overacting, but I just don't see that," he said later. "I used to go out of my way to watch Bill perform on TV in New York in the early part of his career. And he was fascinating to watch . . . very theatrical." Matheson went on to carve a legendary career as a screenwriter and novelist and, in the 1960s, wrote two classic episodes of *The Twilight Zone* starring Shatner ("Nightmare at 20,000 Feet" and "Nick of Time") and the 1966 *Star Trek* episode "The Enemy Within."[35]

While Bill Shatner's television career became a frenzied existence of hopping from job to job—sometimes flying to Los Angeles, other times shuttling back to Canada for the occasional one-off—Gloria's career was stalling. It wasn't for lack of trying; she auditioned for roles but wasn't getting called back, and that began to wear on her fragile nerves. She won a small role on an episode of *Goodyear Playhouse* but couldn't build on the momentum—and had to watch from the sidelines while her husband became a hot commodity. It was frustrating to her, and Bill tried not to talk too much about his work once he arrived home at night in order to not upset his wife: "So I acted all day and then went back to Queens and played another role."[36]

Many of the industry's biggest movie actors, during that "Golden Age" of television, were wary of the small screen. Most of them considered television below their station, maybe even a passing fad (they knew better, but had a tough time admitting it). It was unusual for big-screen actors to cross the line from movies into series television; Broderick Crawford was an early exception, signing on for the syndicated series *Highway Patrol* in 1955, five years after his Oscar-winning turn in *All the King's Men*. Crawford made millions from *Highway Patrol* and enjoyed fame far beyond his movie work. Those actors working primarily in television, including Bill Shatner, had a different mindset: the steady work was great and provided a decent paycheck.

But the brass ring was a Hollywood movie.

CHAPTER 3

Entering a New Stage

Hollywood came calling in 1957. Early in the year, Bill signed a two-picture deal with MGM that would launch his movie career while giving him room to continue working in television. It seemed to be the best of both worlds, and the Shatners, both tiring of Bill's bicoastal ping-pong commute, decided to relocate to Los Angeles, keeping the apartment in Jackson Heights so Bill had a place to stay when he worked in New York. They rented an apartment, for $125 a month, in the Los Angeles neighborhood of Westwood; the complex had a pool and was a popular short-term landing spot for people in the show-business community. Bill and Gloria made the four-day cross-country drive in Bill's new Austin Healy sports car, but it seemed anything but celebratory; later, he recalled the hours of ominous silence as they drove to California. Gloria got pregnant in early 1958, and that August, their first child, daughter Leslie Carol, was born.

Bill's first movie for MGM would be *The Brothers Karamazov*, starring Yul Brynner, Lee J. Cobb, and Claire Bloom. Legendary Hollywood heavyweight Pandro S. Berman was producing the picture; he'd seen Shatner in an episode of *Studio One* on CBS and thought he would be perfect for the role of Alexey Karamazov, an idealistic monk (with "Mamie Eisenhower bangs," as one pundit wrote) who was the youngest brother of Dmitri Karamazov (Brynner). Shatner met with MGM casting director Mel Balarino and then with Berman, who sent him to meet the movie's director, Richard Brooks (*The Blackboard Jungle, The Catered Affair*). Bill tested for the role, and MGM executives thought his cheekbones resembled Brynner's facial structure. Alexey and Dmitri Karamazov could easily pass for brothers . . . at least on the big screen.

There were rumors that Marilyn Monroe was negotiating to play the role of Grushenka; when that fell through (for various unconfirmed reasons), Carroll Baker was considered, but she was on suspension at Warner Brothers for refusing to appear in *Too Much, Too Soon* and the studio refused to loan her out to MGM. The role went to Austrian actress Maria Schell, the older sister of actor Maximillian Schell, who was making her American screen debut.

Shooting on *The Brothers Karamazov* began on the MGM lot in Los Angeles in June and lasted for several months, including on-location filming in Paris and London. Bill Shatner's introduction to Hollywood studio life began inauspiciously; when he arrived at MGM for the first time, he was barred from passing through the studio gate because the security guard (whose name, Shatner claimed, was Ken Hollywood), didn't know who he was. (Why he wasn't on the studio call sheet remains anyone's guess.) Bill returned to his apartment and got a frantic phone call from the studio, wondering why he wasn't on the set. He rushed back—and, this time, Ken Hollywood let him through the gates. Parts of the movie were also filmed on location in Paris and London.

Shatner's main job in *The Brothers Karamazov* "was to stand in the background looking saintly," and he got along swimmingly with his costars. He was, though, unsure of how to interpret Yul Brynner's habit of literally kicking him in the pants. (Was it a form of initiation? Hostility? A practical joke? He was never quite sure, though years later Brynner had nothing but good things to say about working with Shatner.) Bill had memorized the entire script before shooting began—thanks to his years of stage training—and was surprised to watch as a few of his costars learned their lines, on the set, the day they shot their scenes. Such was the Hollywood way.

The October 26, 1957, issue of *Maclean's*, Canada's popular weekly newsmagazine, turned Bill Shatner's introduction to Hollywood vis-à-vis his role in *The Brothers Karamazov* into a feature-length article. The story was headlined "Bill Shatner's Adventures in Hollywood" and was written by Barbara Moon. It provides a snapshot of Shatner's first foray into big-time moviemaking, both on the set and during his off-hours with Gloria, "a beautiful, shy Toronto-born girl with wheat-colored hair, high cheekbones, wide eyes and a wide soft mouth." (Moon mistakenly claims Gloria met Shatner when he was acting in *Tamburlaine the Great* on Broadway, saying: "[Gloria was] dancing in the Copacabana line. 'The Copacabana,'

Gloria explains in her breathless young-girl's voice, 'is the one where they wear clothes.'")[1]

Shatner was earning around $5,000 every three weeks, Moon reported, and right after signing his MGM deal, he was going to buy a house "with two fireplaces, a pool, a barbecue pit and a glass-enclosed living room" before his agent talked him out of it—warning Bill not to "mortgage yourself to Hollywood!" The article described Shatner's "tiny disquietude" at being ignored by the studio and at not being introduced to his *The Brothers Karamazov* cast members before filming began—and not meeting director Richard Brooks until a few days before shooting his first scene. He ate his lunch, alone, in the studio commissary on day one; his initiation into moviemaking improved as the long days on the set progressed.

The Shatners bought a second car, a used Nash station wagon, for Gloria to drive when her husband was working; on weekends, they sometimes sailed to Catalina Island or drove to Tijuana to watch the bullfights. Director Richard Brooks seemed to be pleased with Bill's performance; Brynner gave his rookie costar one of his "big-bowled" pipes. Gloria, Moon reported, enrolled in a ballet school but wasn't having any luck landing an acting job of her own. "In short, Shatner has found nothing in Hollywood that he can't relate to his familiar routine as an actor or to the film world he's read about," Moon wrote. "He knew it would not be glamorous. He was not really surprised to find that it was nerve-wracking, occasionally lonely, often uncertain. 'This is just the big break, the first plateau,' he says. 'From here I could go forward, or I could go back.'"

Filming on *The Brothers Karamazov* wrapped in August and the movie opened in February 1958 to mixed reviews. Bill was surprised at his star billing—"because I have so little to do in the picture," he told journalist Sidney Fields—but he was pleased with the critiques of his performance opposite heavyweights Brynner, Cobb, Bloom, Schell, and Richard Basehart.

"Shatner is a very good actor—still only at the halfway mark insofar as his potential is concerned," said his *Brothers Karamazov* costar Cobb, whose work in the movie earned him an Oscar nomination as Best Supporting Actor. (Burl Ives won for *The Big Country*.) "The third son, William Shatner, has chosen his way of survival in contest with his father; he has retreated into the church as a monk," *Variety* noted in its review of the movie. "The explosion that these figures ignite comes when Brynner imagines Schell has gone to his father in preference to him . . . William Shatner has the difficult task of portraying youthful male goodness, and he does it with such gentle candor that it is effective."[2] Director Richard Brooks praised the entire cast, including Shatner, as "actors of great talent and sensitivity."[3]

*   *   *

With his first Hollywood movie under his belt, Bill went back to his busy schedule of television work. He played the role of a gentle English priest on an episode of *The U.S. Steel Hour* and won kudos as the villain in Rod Serling's *A Town Has Turned to Dust*, a *Playhouse 90* drama about a lynching. "Mr. Shatner gave one of the best TV performances of his career," noted *New York Times* television critic Jack Gould. "As the town bully and ringleader of the lynching party, he was the embodiment of hate and blind physical passion. Mr. Shatner's attention to detail in putting together the picture of an ignorant and evil social force was remarkable."[4]

He reappeared on *The U.S. Steel Hour*, this time in a Western-themed episode called "Old Marshals Never Die." "This time I'm a good guy," he told the *New York Times*. "As a matter of fact, it's a Western in which we're all good guys. The only type of role I've never had on TV is a young romantic one."[5] There was talk that Bill was being considered for a role on Broadway in a new Budd Schulberg drama called *The Disenchanted*, a fictionalized version of the life of F. Scott Fitzgerald (that never materialized); television directors Sidney Lumet and Robert Mulligan called him "one of the brightest and most sensitive young actors we've ever directed."[6]

In June of 1958, veteran Broadway producer Joshua Logan announced that he'd chosen William Shatner to star in a dramatic version of *The World of Suzie Wong*, based on British author Richard Mason's 1957 novel about Robert Lomax, a British artist living in Hong Kong who falls in love with a local prostitute named Suzie Wong. Bill flew to New York to meet with Logan and co-producer David Merrick at Logan's country house and reportedly left their meeting fifteen minutes later with a signed contract paying him $750 a week. "By the time I got back to the city I had the job," he said.[7] The show was scheduled to open in October at the Broadhurst Theatre on Fifty-Fourth Street. "The male lead in *The World of Suzie Wong* goes to William Shatner, a comparatively unknown performer on Broadway," the *New York Times* reported. "In 1956, the Canadian player made his local debut in *Tamburlaine the Great*. Although he was listed in the program, his chore was a minor one."[8]

Signing the Broadway deal for *The World of Suzie Wong* meant that Bill now had to extricate himself from his MGM contract, which took him longer than he expected and forced him to forfeit $100,000. Bill and Gloria moved into a small house in Hastings-on-Hudson to make his commute into Manhattan bearable. Gloria stayed at home, taking care of six-month-old Leslie. Once they were settled in, Bill spent the following weeks sitting in with Josh Logan and Paul Osborn, who was adapting Mason's book for the stage, while a parade of actors tried out for the other leading roles. "There was much rewriting and here too I was brought into the discussions," he recalled.[9] In a nod to Shatner's Montreal roots, Logan and Osborn decided to make Robert Lomax a Canadian artist. (Which also negated Bill having to adopt a British accent.) For the role of Suzie Wong, Logan and Osborn chose France Nuyen, a nineteen-year-old Vietnamese-French actress who was discovered on the beach in 1955 by *Life* photographer Philippe Halsman while working as a seamstress. Three years later, she graced the cover of *Life* magazine.

France Nuyen's resume was like Bill's in that it included one major Hollywood movie, the musical *South Pacific*—produced by Logan and written by Osborn—in which she played Liat, the daughter of "Bloody Mary" (Juanita Hall). Nuyen had no previous stage experience and her command of the English language was, at best, limited. Even before the show's premiere, Logan and Merrick impressed upon Shatner the responsibility he bore for the play's success; he was eight years older than Nuyen, had a decade's worth of acting experience, and was something of a "name," which was important to the show's backers looking to recoup their Broadway investment.

There was trouble from day one. Following four weeks of rehearsals in Manhattan, *The World of Suzie Wong* embarked on its test runs in New Haven, Connecticut, and in Philadelphia. Logan and Osborn retooled and rewrote the play constantly—not an unusual occurrence during out-of-town dry runs. But there was a growing tension between Nuyen and Logan, which reached a boiling point when Logan refused to attend rehearsals at a critical juncture. Nuyen, who wasn't a trained actress, learned her lines phonetically and was often unable to absorb their deeper emotional meanings. "The feud between Logan and France was very dramatic," Shatner said. "She was a lovely young lady. She had this beautiful face, and when acting in films—for the immediacy—she was wonderful. But having the discipline of a theatre actor is different. She'd never been onstage. She wasn't an actress."[10] She would often forget her lines onstage and needed prompting from her costar. The script, Bill said years later, "was cut to shreds and became a ghastly apparition of what it was."[11]

The World of Suzie Wong opened on October 10, 1958, to mixed reviews. It didn't help the show's cause that some theatergoers thought they were going to see an Asian-themed musical similar to *Flower Drum Song*, which was playing across the street at the St. James Theatre with stars Larry Blyden and Myoshi Umeki. "France Nuyen, an attractive Eurasian, plays Suzie with considerable charm and validity," noted the *New York Times*. "Her accent is pleasantly naïve, and her style of playing is simple and affecting. As the bemused painter, William Shatner gives a modest performance that is also attractive—a little too wooden perhaps, which is one way of avoiding maudlin scenes."[12] "William Shatner . . . plays the artist with gratifying restraint and a strong note of sincerity," the *Washington Star* opined.

"Its manly hero is played with an oddly melodramatic gloss and many a deep-seated sigh by the normally interesting Canadian actor," noted the *Herald Tribune*.

Bill's hometown newspaper, the *Montreal Star*, lauded both the play and Shatner's performance. "How can it miss? It doesn't . . . William Shatner, product of Montreal's acting groups . . . plays the artist with gratifying restraint and a strong note of sincerity. France Nuyen is very fetching, and also effectively sincere as the Chinese call-girl with the heart of gold."[13]

But ticket sales were lagging, and it didn't take long for the Broadway rumor mill to kick into overdrive. There were gossipy stories about tension between Bill Shatner and France Nuyen and between Shatner and Ron Randell, with the two costars exchanging backstage blows one night during a performance. Shatner didn't deny any of it. "It's true. France Nuyen and I have had differences of opinion since the show opened last October," he said. "But what's unusual about that? She's a very sensitive and highly skilled performer. She also has some very definite ideas on how a scene should be played."

He also fessed up to the fistfight with Randell. "Ron and I had a misunderstanding backstage one night some time ago and I suppose it's correct to say a few punches were thrown. But the fact is no punches landed," he said. "We're much better actors than boxers. Because of what happened, Ron and I are better friends than ever."[14] In a later version of their fight, Shatner claimed that Randell took a swing at him, missed, and clocked an eighty-six-year-old prop man in the face.[15]

(In Shatner's autobiography, *Up Till Now*, he claimed that Randell, who was playing ex-sailor Ben Jeffcoat in the show, had a habit of putting his hand on Shatner's shoulder in their scene together onstage; if he got a laugh, he would lay his hand on Shatner's shoulder. If he didn't get a laugh, he "pounded" Shatner's shoulder. Shatner complained to Logan to no avail and then confronted Randell about the situation. When it happened again at the next performance, Shatner punched Randell onstage and their brawl continued once the curtain came down.)[16]

What *The World of Suzie Wong* did have in its favor were local suburban theater groups, which would purchase tickets in large blocks, ensuring that the money would continue to roll in and keep the show going, at least for the immediate future. Shatner claimed that audiences hated the show and that he once heard an audience member whisper loudly to their significant other, "Will you still love me after this?"[17]

"We were panned universally. It was a very turgid drama . . . people were screaming 'kill this play,' but the producers were not going to give the money back—the largest advance ticket sales of a straight play up until that time—so they ran the play," he said. "Over the next few months we cut fifteen minutes from the running time and changed the reading of the lines from being a turgid drama to essentially a comedy."[18]

Behind the scenes, things got worse before they got better. France Nuyen was still angry at Logan, and she would stop what she was doing onstage if he entered the theater in her sight line. Shatner claimed that on other nights she would stare into space instead of delivering her lines, leaving him to improvise dialogue. He said that Nuyen had fallen in love with Marlon Brando, and, attempting to get out of her contract, she had stood in the pouring rain one night during intermission and then appeared onstage, soaking wet, hoping to catch pneumonia. On it went. Offstage, she refused to speak to her costar. "For a while she wasn't speaking to me, or anyone else, at all," he said. "She'd go onstage hating me and I was afraid it would hurt her performance and the play. Things have improved lately. We're now exchanging a few civil words—but it's not a war as it used to be."[19]

Slowly, though, ticket sales picked up, and whatever bits of stage "business" Shatner undertook because of his truculent costar—including comic asides to the audience and straying from the dialogue—engaged theatergoers.

"People kept getting up and leaving, so in one performance I said, 'Sit down . . .' and then I said '. . . Suzie', and the guy getting up sat down," he said. "I tell the story of forcing people to sit down, talking in a staccato fashion, to make sure nobody got up and left. Then I say, 'And you wonder why I talk like this,' which gets a big laugh."[20] Shatner and Nuyen caught the attention of CBS, and on November 16, 1958, they appeared together on *The Ed Sullivan Show*, performing a scene from *The World of Suzie Wong* in an episode that also featured Lou Costello, the Canadian comedy team Wayne and Shuster, comic actor Arnold Stang, and Dody Goodman.

By the end of October, advance ticket sales had reached $1 million, ensuring that *The World of Suzie Wong* would run through at least the beginning of the next year. It did better than that—in the end, when all was said and done, the show ran for 508 performances before closing on January 2, 1960. Shatner was awarded the 1958–59 Daniel Blum Theatre World Award (along with Nuyen and others, including Tammy Grimes and Rip Torn). Still, the bad feelings generated by *The World of Suzie Wong* persisted with him, even years after the show was a distant memory. "That turned out to be one of the great mish-mashes of our time," he said. "My part was sliced to virtually nothing and, while I worked steadily for two years, I tend to look on it as two years out of my life."[21,22]

Maybe, but not only did *The World of Suzie Wong* put Bill Shatner on the Broadway map, it reintroduced him to the American television industry. While costarring on Broadway he'd kept his toe in the television waters, appearing on Sunday-morning shows such as *Look Up and Live* and in prime time on NBC's *Sunday Showcase* (as Senator Thomas P. Gore). He said he was offered the lead role in a planned television series production of *Ellery Queen* but turned the role down. "I like TV," he said at the time. "I'm an actor, not a property."[23] (*The Further Adventures of Ellery Queen* aired on NBC from 1958 to 1959 with both George Nader and Lee Philips in the title role.)

In 1959, CBS signed Shatner and portly actor Kurt Kasznar to costar in a pilot that would be the basis for a television series based on Rex Stout's *Nero Wolfe* detective stories. (Sydney Greenstreet starred in an NBC radio adaptation, *The New Adventures of Nero Wolfe*, which ran from 1950 to 1951.) CBS, which was enjoying success in the legal mystery courtroom genre with *Perry Mason*, starring Raymond Burr, was eyeing *Nero Wolfe* for a potential Monday-night time slot (10 p.m.); the series would be shot in New York City, with Kasznar, starring on Broadway in *Look After Lulu!*, as the titular armchair detective and Shatner playing Archie Goodwin, his eager young colleague and the narrator of Nero Wolfe's exploits. (The role was played in the radio series by several actors, including Lawrence Dobkin and Harry Bartell.)

A brownstone in Gramercy Park was used in the pilot episode to replicate Wolfe's lair from the Rex Stout novels. The episode, "Count the Man Down," was shot in March 1959 with guest star Alexander Scourby and revolved around the mysterious death of a guided-missile scientist during a launch at Cape Canaveral. CBS, though, passed on turning the pilot into a series. Television critic Donald Kirkley of the *Baltimore Sun* thought that *Nero Wolfe* with Kasznar and Shatner was a victim of its own success, declaring in June 1959 that it was considered "too good" for a half-hour show.

But television pilots come and go, and *Nero Wolfe* was only a blip on Bill's radar screen. The television roles continued to roll in like a tsunami, and the twenty-eight-year-old actor found himself highly in demand and barely able to take a breath between acting jobs—many on top-shelf series. He returned to *Alfred Hitchcock Presents* as a creepy mama's boy in the 1960 episode "Mother, May I Go Out to Swim?" and made the first of his two starring appearances on Rod Serling's classic CBS sci-fi/thriller anthology series *The Twilight Zone* in "Nick of Time," playing strapping newlywed Don Carter, who visits a small-town diner in Ohio with his wife, Pat (Patricia Breslin), to kill some time while their car is being repaired. (They're on their way to New York City.) Don grows obsessed with a coin-operated napkin holder/devil-headed fortune-telling machine that accurately predicts his future (including a job promotion); as he spirals into mania, dropping coin after coin into the machine and asking questions about his future, a distraught Pat finally convinces him to wrest himself away from the diner. They get their car and triumphantly drive away—just as another, older couple sits in the same booth, the man obviously held in sway by the bobble-headed napkin holder as Don had been. That led to a role on the *Twilight Zone*-ish ABC series *One Step Beyond*; other television roles for Bill that year included *The DuPont Show of the Month*, *Outlaws*, and *Moment of Fear*. Perhaps out of fear, he continued to write; he was given a "Story by" credit for a 1961 episode of the CBS detective series *Checkmate* starring Anthony George, Sebastian Cabot (as a college professor), and Doug McClure, Shatner's future *Barbary Coast* costar.

Bill hoped to star in the *Checkmate* episode, but CBS had other ideas. "You'll get a kick out of this," he told columnist Hal Humphrey. "I just sold a script to the CBS *Checkmate* series and naturally figured I'd play the lead guest part. Then comes word from the sponsor that they want a bigger name. They're trying to get Bob Newhart, the comic, but I understand he's never done any acting." CBS eventually cast Tony Randall as an egomaniacal killer who vows revenge on the man who helped send him to prison: Dr. Carl Hyatt (Cabot). "It's a tough game to lick," Bill said. "If you do a TV series it's got to be for the money, because it's impossible to get quality from it. There is never enough time for rehearsal or for the writer to work on the script. If you don't do a series, then there's the waiting between jobs. It doesn't leave much choice for the actor today."[24]

He considered himself a "real actor" who couldn't be tied down to one particular show, since "a real actor did not sign to do a series because then he couldn't accept the starring role in the Broadway play or Hollywood film that was going to make him a star."[25] He turned down the chance to star in a new television series, *Dr. Kildare*, which premiered on NBC in 1961 and turned Richard Chamberlain, the show's handsome young intern, into a household name. (James Franciscus also turned down the lead role.) *Dr. Kildare* ran for five seasons and 191 episodes; Bill settled for appearing on the series six times as a guest star.

He also declined an offer to star in *The Defenders*, which was based on a two-part 1957 *Studio One* episode, written by Reginal Rose, called "The Defender," in which Ralph Bellamy and Bill costarred as a father-and-son lawyer team trying to prove a nineteen-year-old (played by newcomer Steve McQueen) innocent of murder charges. Four years later, CBS resurrected the episode as a series, with E. G. Marshall and Robert Reed taking over the roles played by Bellamy and Shatner in the *Studio One* episode. *The Defenders* ran four seasons and won thirteen Emmy Awards (including one for Marshall and three consecutive Emmys for Outstanding Drama Series). If Bill was chagrined at turning down starring roles in two groundbreaking television shows, he wasn't admitting it. "There were few roles that I wanted and didn't get," Shatner wrote in his autobiography. "It was magical. I learned to love doing live television."[26]

He had his integrity. What he *didn't* have, after nearly five years since his last big-screen appearance in *The Brothers Karamazov*, was a hit movie.

CHAPTER 4

A Man for All Seasons

William Shatner's acting career had come a long way in the nearly ten years since his graduation from McGill and Joseph Shatner's worries about his son's career path. He was firmly entrenched in the television industry in both the United States and Canada as a highly sought-after actor. While most of his television roles were airing on American networks, he hadn't forsaken the CBC. He returned to Toronto several times a year to star in television productions including *Julius Caesar* (as Mark Antony) and *The Well*, appearing alongside Corinne Conley and future *Star Trek* castmate James Doohan.

Nineteen sixty-one was a milestone year for Shatner. He turned thirty in March and, in April, signed on to costar with Julie Harris and Walter Matthau for his Broadway return in *A Shot in the Dark*, Harry Kurnitz's adaptation of Marcel Achard's farcical stage comedy *L'Idiote*. The show was scheduled to open in October at the Booth Theatre on West Forty-Fifth Street. That spring, he was involved in an automobile accident, a two-car collision while driving on Sepulveda Boulevard in Los Angeles, and was "shaken up." According to newspaper reports, the accident occurred when, trying to make a left turn onto Oxnard Street, he collided with a car driven by a Sherman Oaks realtor. "Neither driver was given hospital treatment," a local newspaper reported.[1]

In June, Gloria gave birth to their second child, daughter Lisabeth, who joined big sister Leslie in the growing Shatner family. Bill kept himself in good physical shape and was fit and trim; his hairline, receding since his mid-twenties, was camouflaged with a succession of artfully placed hairpieces.

Nineteen sixty-one was also the year in which Bill returned to movie-making on both ends of the production spectrum—snaring a starring role in the low-budget Roger Corman drama *The Intruder* and a supporting part in *Judgment at Nuremberg*, a splashy big-budget Hollywood feature with an all-star cast.

Filmmaker Roger Corman, five years older than Shatner, was carving out a niche for himself with his no-frills approach to producing and directing starting in 1954 with *The Monster From the Ocean Floor*, which he produced for $12,000. By the time he became interested in *The Intruder*, Corman had an impressive track record for filming on the cheap yet always turning a profit, partly by hiring little-known actors (who would eventually become big stars)—including Charles Bronson and Jack Nicholson, who starred in *Machine Gun Kelly* and *Cry Baby Killer*, respectively, both produced by Corman and released in 1958. He was said to have shot *Little Shop of Horrors* (Nicholson had a cameo as a masochistic dental patient) in two days and one night.

"I had developed the script for *The Intruder* from Chuck Beaumont's novel about this racist demigod who comes to a small town where they're about to integrate the local high school," Corman said. "I didn't have a great deal of money, so I knew I was going to have to go with an unknown, and somebody had told me about Bill, who was new to Hollywood but had built a very good reputation in New York on Broadway."[2] Corman reportedly considered Tony Randall, among others, for the lead role of Adam Cramer "when [he] thought [he] was going to have a bigger budget." He was partnering on *The Intruder* with his younger brother and frequent collaborator, Gene. "But I never even made an offer to [Randall or the others] when I realized that my brother and I had to finance the film ourselves—that the usual companies we worked with, which financed our films, wouldn't finance this one," he said.[3] Bill recalled that he was paid the "Corman salary" for his starring role (read: not very much). "He thought he was getting me for a good price," he said. "He didn't realize . . . I'd have paid *him* to play this role."[4]

Charles Beaumont, a prolific writer, had penned nearly twenty episodes of *The Twilight Zone* and wrote *The Queen of Outer Space,* a campy science fiction movie. *The Intruder*, Beaumont's second novel, published in 1959, told the tale of a charismatic, smooth-talking white supremacist named

Adam Cramer, who arrives in the small Southern town of Caxton just after the Supreme Court has ordered an end to school integration.

Corman figured he could shoot the movie on location in Southeast Missouri, mostly in the town of Sikeston, in three and a half weeks and for under $100,000. (Some reports cite the movie's budget as $80,000.) "I brought only, I think, four actors from Hollywood and [for the rest] I got local people because I thought they would have the right accents and look and act Southern, which they did," Corman said. "Bill was going to have to come in completely prepared because there was not a great deal of time on the set for rehearsals and so forth, so most of Bill's preparation was done before the picture. He understood what he was doing and came in very well prepared and actually helped the local actors, taking them to the side, talking with them." Frank Maxwell, Beverly Lunsford, Jeanne Cooper, Robert Emhardt, and Leo Gordon joined Shatner in the cast; Beaumont, fellow *Twilight Zone* writer George Clayton Johnson, and author William F. Nolan appeared in smaller roles (Beaumont most prominently as the town's high school's principal). For the part of Joey—the black high school student (wrongfully) accused of raping a white classmate—Corman chose local resident Charles Barnes, a nineteen-year-old high school honors student who went on to study engineering at the University of Missouri.[5]

It was a difficult shoot that stretched over July and August under the hot Missouri sun; Corman said the production was "run out of a couple of towns" by local authorities who didn't care for its subject matter. There were death threats against Corman, the actors and the crew. Corman settled on Sikeston, located in the "boot heel" of Missouri between Kentucky and Tennessee, to shoot most of the movie. "Everything looks Southern," he said. "It was the perfect location. I was under the laws and protection of a Midwestern state, even though it's this little area in the South. Everything worked out according to plan—except the 'protection' of a Midwestern state was essentially zero."

Bill and the film's cast and crew stayed in a motel just outside of Sikeston; upon their arrival, a local policeman arrived to brief them on their "escape route," since the town had learned what *The Intruder* was about—and the townspeople were not happy. Shatner claimed later, in a likely apocryphal tale, that the town's only integrated group was a prison gang whose sole job was to kill everyone involved with the movie.[6]

The Intruder opens with Adam Cramer stepping off the bus in Caxton in his shiny white suit and tie (which he wears throughout the movie). Before too long, the smiling, charismatic hatemonger is flirting with the teenage daughter (Lunsford) of the town's fair-minded newspaper publisher (Maxwell) and sleeping with Vi (Cooper), the sultry wife of Sam (Gordon), his traveling-salesman neighbor. Cramer, "a charlatan who earns money out of the terrible business of fomenting hate,"[7] has one purpose: to rile up the townspeople of Caxton in the days leading up to the local high school's integration. He claims to be a member of the Patrick Henry Society; when asked about his line of work, he answers "social reform."

In a pivotal scene early in the movie, Cramer whips the mob into a frenzy with an impassioned speech on the courthouse steps—a hate-filled rant against the NAACP, "headed by a Jew who hates America!" Bill came down with a case of laryngitis two days before filming the scene and, the day before his big speech, spoke to no one for twenty-four hours in order to protect his voice. Corman needed reaction shots from the crowd for the rally scene; trying to save Bill's raw vocal chords, he fooled the extras who turned up for the scene by getting them to cheer with talk of their hometown St. Louis Cardinals—and inciting their anger by mentioning the hated University of Alabama football team. While Bill gesticulated histrionically (and mutely) to the crowd, Corman shot him from behind. It wasn't until around midnight, when most of the crowd had gone home, that Bill delivered his lines for the camera.

"He came through with a raspy quality in his voice [that] actually helped the sequence and he was able to say what he did not say in the long shots," Corman noted.[8] A local newspaper publisher told Shatner and Corman the next day that many of the extras in the crowd scene had witnessed a lynching in a nearby tree; waiting for them to leave before Cramer spewed his incendiary lines was a smart move, he told them.[9]

The Intruder was a daring film for its time; the Civil Rights Act had been passed four year earlier, in 1957, but was largely unenforced in the South, and the year before, four young African American college students in Greensboro, North Carolina, refused to move from a Woolworth's lunch counter without being served. Segregation was a way of life; tensions in the region were high.

In *The Intruder*, Adam Cramer whips those tensions into hysteria—a black church is bombed, killing its minister; Caxton's pro-integration newspaper publisher, Tom McDaniel (Maxwell), survives a brutal attack but loses an eye and breaks several ribs; and Joey—who's falsely accused of rape by McDaniel's confused daughter, Ella (Lunsford)—is chained to a schoolyard swing and nearly lynched by the mob. Corman ran into trouble shooting that scene, which closes the movie. Recounting the trouble, he said:

> I remember one day, toward the end of filming, Adam puts Joey on a swing outside a school. I was supposed to shoot two days for that sequence, and when we shot the first day, everything was fine. We came back the second day, and the chief of police and a couple of cars met us at the city limits. He said, "If you come into the city, you're all going to be arrested. Just turn around and go home."
>
> My brother, who was producing, took him aside and started talking nonsense so that I could keep shooting. So, we turned around and went back to Sikeston; I remembered there were some swings in a public park there. The only problem was the height of the swings, which were different in each place and I had to allow for that. Each time I showed something that showed the height of the swings, I would cut away to somebody in the crowd. Nobody has ever noticed that they were different heights.

*   *   *

Bill's second movie of 1961, filmed earlier that year in Berlin and Hollywood, promised another kind of oppressive, tense atmosphere—but also the promise of a handsome payoff: a career boost for the young actor.

For *Judgment at Nuremberg*, veteran producer/director Stanley Kramer had assembled an all-star cast featuring Spencer Tracy, Burt Lancaster, Marlene Dietrich, Judy Garland, Montgomery Clift, Maximillian Schell, and Richard Widmark. Kramer would direct the movie, a fictionalized, melodramatic take on the Nuremberg trials, which brought Nazi officials high and low to justice between 1945 and 1949 under a four-country Allied military tribunal (the United States, Britain, France, and Russia). Bill was hired by Kramer for a small role after flying to Los Angeles and meeting with the director.

Judgment at Nuremberg, written by Abby Mann, focused on the trial of four Nazi-era judges. Tracy played American Chief Trial Judge Dan Haywood, overseeing the Nazi judges' trial; Lancaster and Werner Klemperer played defendants Ernst Janning and Emil Hahn, while Schell took the role of German defense counsel Hans Rolfe. (Klemperer and Schell reprised their roles from the 1959 *Playhouse 90* episode "Judgment at Nuremberg," which aired on CBS.)

Bill had acted in several television productions written by Mann, who might have helped land him his *Judgment at Nuremberg* role as West Point graduate and US Army Captain Harrison "Harry" Byers, Dan Haywood's clerk/liaison. (Martin Milner, who was starring with George Maharis on CBS's *Route 66*, played the role in the *Playhouse 90* production.) Bill's role wasn't very big but gave him the chance to share screen time with the great Spencer Tracy, who was considered by many to be the finest actor of his generation.

Tracy, then sixty-one and a lifelong alcoholic, was suffering from kidney problems during the shoot and was nearing the end of the line. (He died six years later.) But he still commanded the screen and would garner an Oscar nomination for his performance as Dan Haywood in *Judgment at Nuremberg*. If the film's large cast was unaware of or unschooled in the extent of the Nazi-era atrocities when they signed on to the project, that was soon rectified: Stanley Kramer and Abby Mann required everyone to watch the movies filmed by Allied soldiers liberating concentration camps in Germany and Poland and throughout Eastern Europe. The horrific images, which had yet to be seen by the general public, were projected on two screens set up on either side of a stage.[10] Bill remembered the "absolute silence" once the images began to flicker on the screens,[11] followed by the occasional gasp and audible sobbing. "A lot of the cast and crew were Jewish, so this picture had an even deeper impact on us," he said. "Every day I went to work feeling like I was doing something important."[12]

In the movie's most gripping scene, Judge Haywood delivers a rousing eleven-minute summation of his verdict—a scene the great Spencer Tracy did in one take, astonishing everyone on the *Judgment at Nuremberg* set, including Bill Shatner. (His Harry Byers announces to the courtroom that Judge Haywood has made his decision.) "He was so intimidating to me that . . . trying to ingratiate myself I said to him, 'Oh, Mr. Tracy, that was really wonderful. I didn't know film actors memorized things like that.' And he never spoke to me after that. He went back into his dressing room and never talked to me again."[13]

*   *   *

"If the show is good it all won't mean a thing," Harry Kurnitz said of *A Shot in the Dark*, his adaptation of Marcel Achard's comedy *L'Idiote*. The show marked Bill's return to Broadway; it had been though several titular iterations (*The Naked Truth*, *The Maid's Room*) on its journey from Paris to New York City before producer Leland Heyward made the final decision. He rounded out the cast of *A Shot in the Dark* with Julie Harris, Donald Cook, Gene Saks, and Louise Troy.

Bill was looking forward to his return to the New York stage following a busy winter and summer shooting *Judgment at Nuremberg* and *The Intruder*. In September, *A Shot in the Dark* kicked off its pre-Broadway, out-of-town tour at the Shubert Theater in New Haven, Connecticut, under the watchful eye of veteran stage director Harold Clurman. Bill was convinced, from the very start of rehearsals, that the venerable Clurman, a cofounder of New York's Group Theatre and the second husband of venerated actress/acting teacher Stella Adler, was gunning for him. He was convinced, for reasons unknown to him, that Clurman never wanted him in the play—and that he was out to make the actor's life as difficult as possible. "He seemed to get a perverse joy out of insulting me," Bill said, noting that Clurman questioned his every stage move, mannerism, and even his acting ability.[14] It was an inauspicious start.

The out-of-town run was further darkened by the sudden death of sixty-year-old star and Broadway veteran Donald Cook, who suffered a heart attack and died in New Haven in early October. Clurman suggested Walter Matthau as a possible replacement, and an urgent call went out to the actor, who was twenty years younger than Cook, to see if he was interested. Matthau, who'd turned forty-one the day Cook died, had appeared in a few movies (most notably opposite Andy Griffith in 1957's *A Face in the Crowd*); his Broadway resume boasted roles in *Will Success Spoil Rock Hunter?*, *Guys and Dolls*, and a 1959 Tony Award-nominated turn in *Once More, with Feeling!* He was interested. Cook died on a Sunday; his understudy, Joel Thomas, replaced him when *A Shot in the Dark* opened the next day in Philadelphia. Matthau went to see the show, signed a contract, and rehearsed for two days before appearing onstage with his new costars that Friday. The role was a turning point for Matthau, earning him a Tony Award the following April and launching his Oscar-winning career.[15]

Julie Harris, who was already a Broadway veteran at age thirty-six, with two Tony Awards under her belt (for *I Am a Camera* in 1952 and *The*

Lark in 1956), took center stage in *A Shot in the Dark* as its protagonist, Josefa Lantenay, a vibrant, impulsive, lusty chambermaid (she rarely wears underwear) who's discovered—naked, unconscious, and with a gun by her side—with the body of her murdered Spanish lover, Miguel. Josefa admits to killing Miguel, though her story continues to change, and we learn that she's protecting her secret lover—eventually revealed as her boss, wealthy French banker Benjamin Beaurevers (Matthau). Examining Magistrate Paul Sevigne (Shatner), who's handling his first big case since being promoted to Paris from a small town, is charged with putting all the pieces together. He's eager to please both his bosses and his status-hungry wife, Antoinette (Diane van der Vlis). As events unwind, he discovers that Beaurevers's jealous wife, Dominique (Louise Troy), is the real killer—thinking that she'd shot and killed her husband, and not Miguel.[16]

A Shot in the Dark opened at the Booth Theatre on October 18, 1961, to middling reviews. The *New York Times* wrote that Paul Sevigne was "played attractively by William Shatner" and noted the show's "fresh lines" but claimed they were "intermittent."[17] Bill's hometown newspaper, the *Montreal Star*, raved about its favorite son and his new stage venture: "It is a neatly contrived crime mystery, enlivened by comedy that is full of surprises, situations and dialogue whetted to razor sharpness . . . Prominent in the cast is William Shatner, product of McGill University and the Canadian Stratford Festival, who performs admirably as a young investigating magistrate."[18]

Despite its lukewarm reviews, *A Shot in the Dark* proved to be a bona fide Broadway success, playing to packed houses as the calendar turned to 1962. But if Bill hoped that *A Shot in the Dark* would be his big break, he was sorely disappointed. He was pleasant enough in the role and was always mentioned in reviews, but his costars, Walter Matthau and Julie Harris, received the lion's share of critical attention as *A Shot in the Dark* finally completed its journey in September 1962 after a run of 389 performances. "Fourteen months was enough," he said tersely. He might have felt differently had he even been considered for the play's big-screen Hollywood adaptation, which opened in 1964. The movie, directed by Blake Edwards, who cowrote the script with William Peter Blatty (future author of the 1971 novel *The Exorcist*), removed Paul Sevigne from the plot completely, replacing him with clueless Sûreté Inspector Jacques Clouseau—Peter Sellers's breakout character from *The Pink Panther*. *A Shot in the Dark* launched Sellers (and Clouseau) into cinematic history.

Bill, who turned thirty-one in March, was growing frustrated with the arc of his career. While he was working steadily in television, the movies, and now on Broadway, the big break was eluding him. What else could he possibly do? "I know I'm a good actor. But I'm not a star and I'm no longer a supporting player," he said knowingly at the time. "For me the big leap forward never came. I keep plugging away and hoping for the best."[19]

Judgment at Nuremberg opened in theaters in December 1961 to critical acclaim; Bill's supporting performance as Harrison Byers was largely overlooked and rarely mentioned in reviews of the film—which was understandable, given the movie's megawatt stars (Spencer Tracy, Marlene Dietrich, Montgomery Clift, Burt Lancaster et al.) It was almost as if he'd never even appeared in the movie.

The reviews for his starring role as Adam Cramer in *The Intruder*, which also opened for an early release in December, were mostly positive—*when* anyone bothered to pay attention to the low-budget Roger Corman flick. Despite its incendiary subject matter, the movie made little lasting impact despite several bold critical assertions. "William Shatner masterfully plays the bigot," *Variety* noted in its brief review. The *New York Herald Tribune* called it "a major credit to the entire motion picture industry," while the *Los Angeles Times* lauded *The Intruder* as "the boldest, most realistic depiction of racial injustice ever shown in American films."[20]

Part of the problem with *The Intruder's* release was that Corman was having trouble finding a distributor for the movie. "It was totally about the subject matter," he said. "They told me, 'This film won't make any money.' And they were right. It got wonderful reviews. Bill got brilliant reviews."[21] The *New York Times*, which finally got around to reviewing *The Intruder* in May 1962, thought the movie's "highly explosive material is handled crudely and a bit too clumsily for either conviction or comfort" but praised Bill's performance as "unctuous and deceitful in a provokingly superficial way."[22] His costar, William F. Nolan, said: "[Shatner's] performance as Adam Cramer was one of the outstanding acting performances of the year. If the movie had been a mainline movie distributed by a mainline company, I think Shatner certainly would have at least been nominated for an Academy Award. He certainly deserved it. I don't think to this day he's done as well [in the movies] as he did in *The Intruder*."[23]

∗   ∗   ∗

At this point in his career, Bill Shatner could look back at the "what ifs" and wonder if he had let too many good opportunities slip through his fingers. While he was preparing for *A Shot in the Dark* on Broadway, both *The Defenders* and *Dr. Kildare* premiered in September 1961 on CBS and NBC, respectively, launching memorable runs with stars Robert Reed and Richard Chamberlain. Was Bill kicking himself for passing up both television roles to chase a dream of movie and theatrical stardom that was growing more distant with each project? He claimed not to care whether he worked in movies, television, or the theater—as long as he was *working*. "There is crass commercialism in all three media," he told columnist Dusty Vineberg in his hometown *Montreal Star*. "There are still some idealists in all media. Acting's all the same. You take a deep breath and say the words and that's acting."[24] He did admit to dream movie roles—a drama directed by Elia Kazan, a musical scored by Richard Rogers. Those hopes, at this point, were receding into the rearview mirror of his career.

He was still a marketable, in-demand television actor, and now he turned his attention to the small screen, more out of necessity than obligation. The live television productions in New York on which he'd thrived from the mid-'50s to the early '60s were scarcer now as the industry migrated toward filmed and videotaped productions and moved west to Los Angeles. Bill had plenty of work, including appearances on popular television shows such as *The Dick Powell Theatre*, *77 Sunset Strip*, *Route 66*, and *Burke's Law*—and on lesser-known series. He costarred on *Lamp Unto My Feet*, an ecumenical religious series that aired Sunday mornings on CBS. Bill made several *Lamp* appearances, including a two-part episode, "The Cape," about parents coping with a mentally challenged child. It aired in September 1962 with costar Jerry Stiller.

The work was steady, but it still wasn't enough to instill confidence in him vis-à-vis his ability to support his growing family. "I had kids, a wife and a dog and $1,800 seemed to be the glass ceiling for me," he said of his per-episode fee at the time. "I could get well below that, but I could never get above it and I remember thinking, 'I've got to get more than $1,8000 ahead here,' so art and commerce were vying with each other even at that moment."[25]

In the midst of shuttling back and forth between television studios, Bill was hired by producer Selig Seligman to star in *Alexander the Great*, a weekly series created by Robert Pirosh, whose resume boasted cowriting credits on two Marx Brothers movies (*A Night at the Opera*, *A Day at the Races*) and a 1949 Oscar for writing the screenplay for the World War II movie *Battleground*. Pirosh envisioned *Alexander the Great* as a retelling of the historic Battle of Issus in 333 BC, in which the Macedonian army, led by Alexander the Great, defeated the much larger army of the Persian Empire. Bill would play Alexander the Great; the cast included future *Batman* star Adam West, Joseph Cotten, Simon Oakland, and John Cassavetes.

The two-hour pilot for *Alexander the Great* was filmed over a six-month period in the Utah desert (St. George) in 1963 at a reported cost of $750,000. Bill spent a year preparing for his role, getting himself into top physical shape (he was thirty-two years old—the same age Alexander was when he died), and learning how to shoot a bow and arrow and "to ride a horse at a gallop bareback" as Alexander had done.[26] The cast was outfitted in lavish period costumes "in which the men wore little loincloths and the women carried trays of grapes and wine and wore as little as permissible."[27] West, who was playing Alexander's merrymaking sidekick, Cleander, recalled that he and Bill were supposed to switch leading roles each week. "Four o'clock in the morning out in the desert of St. George, Utah, where it was mighty cold, they were putting body makeup on us so we could wear our little thongs and ride around on Arabian studs and fight the Persians," he said. "You had to see this thing. It was like 'Land of the Lost.' But Bill was remarkably effective. I think he's always good. If you're one of those people who have presence and poise and that aura, whatever you want to call it, things work, and it entertains people."[28] But *Alexander the Great* failed to entertain any buyers and Seligman could not sell the pilot. It was shelved until five years later, when ABC aired *Alexander the Great* on its children's anthology series, *Off to See the Wizard*, in order to capitalize on the success of its homegrown *Batman* star West and Bill Shatner's newfound fame on *Star Trek*.

So, the television work continued. Bill returned for a second visit to Rod Serling's CBS series *The Twilight Zone* in an episode entitled "Nightmare at 20,000 Feet". The half-hour episode, written by Richard Matheson and directed by Richard Donner, centers around jittery salesman Bob Wilson (Shatner), who's just been released from a six-month stay in a sanitarium after suffering a nervous breakdown during a cross-country flight. Now, Bob is returning home, on an airplane, with his empathetic wife, Julie (Christine White). He's determined to put his past behind him and get his life back—until he looks out of his window and, in the rain outside, sees a furry, gremlin-like creature trying to destroy one of the airplane's wings. (The gremlin was played by acrobat/stuntman Nick Cravat, who'd worked closely with Burt Lancaster.)

But since this is *The Twilight Zone*, Bob is the only person who sees the creature, and as his hysteria ramps up, everyone else on the plane, including his wife, thinks he's having another meltdown. Unable to convince anyone that the gremlin exists, Bob grabs a passenger's gun, smashes out his window, and shoots at the creature, nearly getting sucked out of the airplane as he fires off a few rounds in the driving wind and rain. Cut to the runway. The plane has landed, and Bob is taken away on a stretcher in a straitjacket. "I know," he says to no one in particular. "But I'm the only one who does know . . . right now." The camera then pans to an aerial view of the plane's metal wing—which is severely twisted and damaged.

The mythology surrounding the *Nightmare at 20,000 Feet* episode has grown exponentially since it first aired in 1963, in what was then *The Twilight Zone's* penultimate season. (It ended its five-year run in June 1964 after 156 episodes.) *Nightmare at 20,000 Feet* is considered one of the anthology series' best installments and has been spoofed multiple times, including on the animated Fox television series *The Simpsons*, on NBC's *Saturday Night Live*, and by Jim Carrey in the movie *Ace Ventura: When Nature Calls*. The episode was revived in 1983 for *Twilight Zone: The Movie*, with John Lithgow playing John Valentine, a version of Bob Wilson (who has a fear of flying). In 1999, Bill guest-starred on Lithgow's NBC sitcom, *3rd Rock from the Sun*, where their characters referenced the *Twilight Zone* episode.

At the time, though, it was just another acting job. "I probably wouldn't have remembered too much about it a month and three or four other shows later," Bill said.[29] He recalled the "claustrophobic" set, of being "pinned in the seats and being unable to move," and he believed that the episode struck such a resonant chord by tapping into "a twinge of some universal nightmare."[30] "Nightmare at 20,000 Feet" director Richard Donner recalled having fun on the set, particularly when Edd "Kookie" Byrnes, starring in ABC's *77 Sunset Strip*, stopped by to see his wife, Asa Maynor, who played the put-upon, flustered stewardess in the episode.

"It was late at night and Bill and Edd and she planned this little game behind my back where they staged what looked like a fight between Bill and

Edd on the wing of the airplane, which was twenty feet off the ground," Donner said. "I heard the commotion, turned around to see what it was, and I see Edd Byrnes hitting Billy and he fell from the wing to the floor. And I said, 'Oh my God, that's it. He's as good as dead.' And as I ran over, Bill stepped out of the plane. They had a dummy rigged to look like Bill in his [Bob Wilson] outfit."[31]

CHAPTER 5

The Captain's on Deck

It was around this time that the Shatners bought a house in the Los Angeles suburb of Sherman Oaks so Bill could be closer to the studios. They also needed a bit more space, since there was another baby on the way: Melanie Shatner arrived in August 1964, joining big sisters Lisabeth, three, and Leslie, six. Bill's television career was going great guns, with guest-starring roles in shows including *The Outer Limits* and *Burke's Law* and a 1964 episode of the NBC series *The Man from U.N.C.L.E,* which also featured a thirty-two-year-old actor named Leonard Nimoy. (They appeared briefly onscreen together.) While the work was lucrative, it was growing monotonous, and Bill wondered (and worried) about where his acting career was headed. "The dream was hollow, all the things I thought went along with it—good parts, money and acclaim—weren't happening," he said. "As a star I was one step down from Paul Newman—a good actor, but not popular enough to bring in big audiences."[1]

He would lie awake in bed at night, wondering how he would support his family or pay the mortgage: "I was living from job to job with no security, and talent didn't seem to make any difference between success and failure."[2] Several years earlier he'd passed up the opportunities to star in *The Defenders* and *Dr. Kildare*, but he didn't burn his creative bridges, guest-starring on both series (five times on *The Defenders*, six times on *Dr. Kildare*).

In his memoir, *Up Till Now*, Bill spoke of that time as one in which he was "no longer even being offered parts that were going to make [him] a star." He recalled how his parents would come to visit him, Gloria, and the girls at the house in Sherman Oaks "with the requisite pool" and how his father would ask him how he was doing—and whether he needed some financial help. "I'd gotten many superb reviews and even won awards—but I wasn't earning enough money to support my family. Had I been single, with few responsibilities, I would have been fine. So, I began to wonder if this was the time to find another career."[3]

But it was all about to come full circle. Bill's nose-to-the-grindstone work ethic had not gone unnoticed by *The Defenders* executive producer Herbert Brodkin, who was working on a new legal drama series for CBS called *For the People* and was searching for a leading man. This time, Bill didn't hesitate at the possibility of starring in a weekly series, and when Brodkin offered him the role of Assistant District Attorney David Koster in *For The People*, he immediately accepted (despite reports that he was in deep negotiations with MGM to star in a pilot for an NBC series called *The Mayor*, which never came to fruition). In addition to *The Defenders*, Brodkin's strong industry track record included his producing work on the acclaimed television anthology series *The Alcoa Hour*, *Goodyear Television Playhouse*, and *Studio One*. "It was Herbert Brodkin and all the resources he had available to him," Bill said about accepting the role. "I leapt at the chance and left LA and went back to New York and stayed in New York for the months that required me to shoot the series."[4] Gloria stayed behind in Sherman Oaks to take care of Leslie, Lisabeth, and Melanie.

For the People was created by Joel Katz, a Columbia Law School graduate who was working for Brodkin. ("Brodkin always got the credit" for creating the series, he said.) Katz's relationship with Bill Shatner dated back several years; they'd met when Katz was working as a general counsel for the talent agency Ashley-Steiner, which counted Bill as a client. When Shatner was starring on Broadway in *The World of Suzie Wong*, he lived in Katz's apartment on Fifty-First Street in Manhattan while Katz, his wife, and small child decamped to Westport, Connecticut, for the summer. "I cast around for the district attorney, who was newly married and was trying to do more than just convict people," Katz said. "So, I thought of Bill and interviewed him. He must have read for the part."[5] Katz came up with the show's title, which reflected its moral ethos. "Our show takes a different point of view," Bill explained in one of the many newspaper and magazine interviews he gave while promoting *For the People* before its launch. "Our point of view is that of the men dedicated to preventing crime and catching the lawbreaker." Of his new character, Assistant District Attorney David Koster, he said: "[He's] too mature to be a fast-flitting fighter pilot who thinks he's indestructible . . . and he's too young to be a slow, lumbering bomber pilot. He's in between . . . but he's always eager for another mission."[6]

Bill had high hopes for his first starring television series role. Stuart Rosenberg, who'd directed multiple episodes of *The Defenders* (none with Shatner guest-starring), was brought on board as the series' director; Jessica Walter was hired to play David Koster's idealistic wife, Phyllis; and veteran actor Howard Da Silva would play David's politically connected boss, Anthony Celese. (Da Silva was blacklisted in the '50s during the McCarthy-era hysteria and returned to television on *The Defenders*.) Lonny Chapman rounded out the cast as Det. Frank Malloy of the NYPD. "I've been in a lot of shows headed for Broadway, and there's a smell of success about the hit ones," Bill said. "I sense the same about this TV series, an excitement on the set, a feeling of victory."[7]

That might have been the vibe on the set, or maybe it was just Bill's promotional hyperbole, but he and everyone else involved with *For the People*, including Herbert Brodkin and Joel Katz, knew the show's chances were slim to none. It was replacing *Mr. Broadway*, a drama series starring Craig Stevens as a New York public relations man that had lasted only thirteen weeks on CBS the previous fall. Midseason replacement series rarely succeeded and were, more often than not, considered prime-time placeholders for more important series coming down the pike (at least in the minds of the network executives). The brain trust at CBS didn't help the cause, driving an early nail into the coffin of *For the People* by scheduling it to air on Sunday nights opposite NBC's *Bonanza*, the top-rated show on television starring Lorne Green—Bill Shatner's old pal from their Stratford Festival days. "*Lamp Unto My Feet* had a better time slot . . . Test patterns had a better time slot," Bill cracked.[8] Brodkin talked the network into delaying the show's premiere one week due to its complicated shooting schedule, which forced CBS to air a rerun of *For the People* only a few weeks after its premiere.

In hindsight, it didn't make a difference.

For the People premiered on January 31, 1965, and, as expected, was trounced by *Bonanza*. The New York newspapers were not pleased with the show; the *New York Times* called it a "ridiculous series" with "a banal meld of every trite situation in every series about prosecuting attorneys,"[9] while the *New York Post* critic opined that "it looks at first glance as if the people are in trouble."[10] *TV Guide*, however, thought *For the People* was "more compelling" than *The Defenders* and lauded Bill's performance. "The ratings have not been great so that you can take the tack that, 'What the devil do they know?'" Shatner told CBC interviewer Clement Fuller in an interview in early March. "We're up against the number one show Sunday nights at nine o'clock following *The Ed Sullivan Show*, I might add. Hopefully we will build by word of mouth and by publicity where we will become a popular show as well."[11]

CBS officially cancelled *For the People* in late March, two months after its premiere, announcing it would end its run of thirteen episodes in May— along with Herbert Brodkin's two other shows on CBS: *The Defenders* and *The Nurses* (on which Bill guest-starred as a doctor in 1963).

*   *   *

The final episode of *For the People* aired on May 9, 1965. By that time, Bill was back in California, in and around the area of Big Sur, starting work on his next project and his fourth big-screen role in *Incubus*.[12] He didn't need a cancelled television series to remind him how far his once-bright star had fallen; *Incubus*, a low-budget horror movie filmed in black-and-white, was only the second big-screen movie to be shot entirely in Esperanto, the fabricated international language created in the late nineteenth century by Polish ophthalmologist Dr. L. L. Zamenhof. (The first movie filmed in Esperanto, *Angoroj*, which translated into *Agonies* in English, hit French movie screens the year before and died a quick death.)

No one on the *Incubus* set, including Bill Shatner and his costars, spoke Esperanto, understood it, or had any idea of why they were speaking it (though Bill claimed to have a "vague awareness" of the language[13]). *Incubus* writer/director Leslie Stevens penned the original script in English but changed it to Esperanto before shooting began. "Strangely enough, it didn't seem that big a deal," said producer Anthony M. Taylor. "In retrospect, it seems more so. If the film wasn't going into the drive-ins, we felt our best chance would be getting it into an art house, where the audience would accept the idea of having another language and subtitles."[14]

The cast would have to learn their lines phonetically, and the actors who had speaking parts were given tutorials in Latin and Greek so they could correctly pronounce the words. (Stevens insisted that even the crew speak in Esperanto. Good luck with that one.) What could possibly go wrong? Four years earlier, Bill Shatner shared the big screen with Spencer Tracy in

Judgment at Nuremberg; now his best-known costar was Allyson Ames, an under-the-radar actress with a string of television credits to her name (including guest-starring roles of varying importance on *Maverick, Burke's Law, 77 Sunset Strip,* and *Perry Mason*) who was romantically involved with Stevens at the time.

Incubus did have three saving graces: Stevens, composer Dominic Frontiere, and cinematographer Conrad Hall. Stevens produced the ABC Western *Stoney Burke,* which ran for one season with star Jack Lord, and followed that with *The Outer Limits,* a *Twilight Zone*-inspired science fiction/fantasy series that aired for two seasons on ABC. (Shatner guest-starred in the 1964 episode "Cold Hands, Warm Heart.") Frontiere scored the music for *The Outer Limits* and for many other television series, most famously for *The Fugitive* (on which Bill guest-starred in 1966). Hall would eventually win three Oscars (for *Butch Cassidy and the Sundance Kid, American Beauty,* and *Road to Perdition*).[15]

Unfortunately, their combined talents couldn't save *Incubus* from its predetermined fate. Bill plays Marc, a young soldier who arrives with his sister (Ann Atmar) in the small village of Nomen Tuum, renowned for its magic well, which can both heal the sick and enhance one's looks. Nomen Tuum is also inhabited by evil spirits called succubi, who lure the sick and vain into their version of hell, which is lorded over by Incubus, the God of Darkness. Kia (Ames) is a rebellious succubus who falls in love with Marc. It does not end well.

Incubus was shot in two weeks and rushed through the post-production process. When Stevens premiered the movie months later at the San Francisco Film Festival (Sharon Tate and Roman Polanski were in attendance), its soundtrack was missing; an estimated five thousand people sat through another short film while producer Anthony M. Taylor rushed into an adjacent projection room to grab another copy of *Incubus* that had an actual soundtrack. It didn't get much better from there; an audience of around one hundred Esperanto speakers, invited to screen *Incubus* at the festival, jeered both the movie and the actors' unintentionally hilarious pronunciations of Esperanto dialogue. Not surprisingly, Stevens and Taylor had trouble finding a distributor—Big Band great Artie Shaw showed some interest (through his new movie distribution company)[16]—and the movie disappeared quickly in the United States. It found an appreciative audience in France (with a nod to the movies of comedian Jerry Lewis) and didn't resurface until thirty years later.[17]

*   *   *

Back in Los Angeles, Gene Roddenberry was in a fix, and reached out to Bill about his new project, a television series called *Star Trek* that he was hoping to sell to NBC.

Roddenberry, who was thirty-five, had a colorful background, even for Hollywood. Born in Texas in 1921 and raised in Los Angeles, the son of an LA police officer, Roddenberry studied police science (with an interest in aeronautical engineering) at Los Angeles City College. He earned his pilot's license and, in 1941, enlisted with the United States Army Air Corps, flying nearly ninety combat missions during World War II. After the war ended, he became an airline pilot for Pan Am from 1945 to 1948 before deciding to leave the aeronautics business to chase his passion for writing. He joined the LAPD in 1949 and eventually became police chief William H. Parker's main speechwriter while simultaneously selling various radio and television scripts as a freelance writer. Roddenberry resigned from the LAPD in 1956 to dedicate himself to writing for television, churning out scripts for series including *Highway Patrol, Bat Masterson, Have Gun—Will Travel, Jefferson Drum, The Kaiser Aluminum Hour,* and *Dr. Kildare.* He also wrote pilots for several television series, none of which made it to the air.

But *Star Trek* was different.

The pilot that Roddenberry wrote for the futuristic space series was called "The Cage" and took place on board the huge intergalactic ship USS *Enterprise* under the watchful eye of Captain Christopher Pike. "The Cage" was produced by Desilu Productions, the television studio created in 1950 by *I Love Lucy* star Lucille Ball and her then husband, Desi Arnaz. Desilu, with Ball as its president (Arnaz left the company in 1962), had a big hit with the ABC/CBS series *The Danny Thomas Show* (also called *Make Room for Daddy*), starring comedian Danny Thomas, and a moderate success with *The Untouchables*, which aired on ABC from 1959 to 1963, with Robert Stack as crime-fighting Prohibition-era agent Eliot Ness. The studio was intrigued by Roddenberry's concept of *Star Trek* as "*Wagon Train* to the stars"; it also needed another promising television project to assuage its anxious shareholders.

"The Cage" pilot was shot at the Desilu studios in Los Angeles from late November to mid-December 1964, with Robert Butler directing and handsome, strapping actor Jeffrey Hunter, known primarily for his movie roles (including Jesus Christ in *King of Kings*), starring as Captain Christopher Pike. He commanded the USS *Enterprise* along with his support crew: Number One (played by Majel Barrett, who married Roddenberry in 1969); Mr. Spock, the half-human/half-Vulcan officer played by Leonard Nimoy, a guest star on Roddenberry's earlier NBC series, *The Lieutenant*; and ship doctor Phillip Boyce (veteran actor John Hoyt). Thirty-two-year-old actress Susan Oliver played Talosian beauty Vina, who sets Captain Pike's heart aflutter.[18]

But NBC executives were not overly impressed with "The Cage." Its pacing, they thought, was too slow; its tone too serious and cerebral. "Jeff Hunter played Pike as a thoughtful, much more introverted person," Nimoy said. "And I think my tendency, when I was in a scene with him, was to try to provide energy, because I thought if he's playing 'introspective' and I'm playing 'introspective' . . . it could be a dull scene. So, my tendency was to be more energetic around him." The suits at NBC also thought that Susan Oliver's exotic, sexy Vina (who was painted green) wouldn't play in the South; neither would Mr. Spock's pointy ears, which gave him a Satanic look. There were other reasons. "The connections weren't being made—the doctor was perhaps a little too old and too wise and he was always counseling the captain, and that wasn't quite the relationship Gene [Roddenberry] wanted," said *Star Trek* writer Dorothy "D. C." Fontana. "The captain changed . . . largely because there were some problems with the actor's wife, who insisted he should be shot in this direction, he could only be shot in that direction, maybe there are days he's not going to work."[19]

The network rejected "The Cage" in February 1965 but was willing to give Roddenberry the chance to shoot a second pilot, an almost unheard-of indulgence in the television business. (Lucille Ball, who was a fan of Roddenberry's work, was said to have pushed NBC to commission the second pilot.) Jeffrey Hunter had a six-month option for *Star Trek* and wasn't interested in returning for another go-round. He decided to opt out of the project in order to pursue his movie career. "Jeff Hunter is a movie star," his wife, Dusty Bartlett, told Herb Solow, the executive in charge of Desilu's television production.[20] That was the official version; Shatner claimed in *Star Trek Memories* that Hunter was fired due to his wife's constant demands and unhappiness over the first pilot.[21]

Star Trek needed a new captain for the USS *Enterprise*. Roddenberry reached out to Jack Lord, who starred in the 1962 ABC series *Stoney Burke*, but he reportedly wanted a fifty percent ownership stake in the show. No dice. Three years later, Lord signed on to star in *Hawaii Five-0*, which ran for twelve seasons on CBS. Gene said Jack Lord took his name too seriously," Fontana said. "That would have been a different Captain Kirk."

Enter William Shatner.

CHAPTER 6

Star Trek

Years later, Herb Solow recounted how Bill Shatner ended up on the *Star Trek* pilot. "We needed a star, and an agent named Ina Bernstein called and said, 'We have a client in New York named William Shatner, who's just finished doing this little low-budget movie, [*Incubus*]," Solow said. "Gene and I saw the movie and we'd seen Shatner on that episode of *The Twilight Zone*, with the gorilla on the wing [*Nightmare at 20,000 Feet*]."[1]

The opportunity for the *Star Trek* pilot arrived at a serendipitous time for Bill, who was still working steadily but was keenly aware that his chance at big-screen stardom was more and more remote as he turned thirty-four in March 1965. "There even came a point when I thought, I don't know whether I'm ever going to break through, to get those roles that I think I should be playing," he said. "But I was in a financial bind and had to accept a lot of things that I wouldn't have done in an earlier day."[2] The television roles were still being offered to him; following the cancellation of *For the People*, Bill guest-starred on *12 O'Clock High*, *The Fugitive*, *The Big Valley*, *Bob Hope Presents the Chrysler Theatre*, *Dr. Kildare*, and *Gunsmoke*. But the one-off television roles were stretching him financially—he had a mortgage to pay and a wife and three young children to support. It kept him up at night. "[I was] thrashing in bed wondering how I was going to support my wife and our children," he said.[3] Committing to the second *Star Trek* pilot was a no-brainer. What did he have to lose?

Gene Roddenberry invited Shatner to screen the first pilot. "I was in New York doing [*For the People*] . . . when Gene [Roddenberry] called me," he said. "Would I come to Los Angeles to look at a pilot he had made and hadn't been able to sell? I flew to LA and saw the pilot and thought, 'It's deadly serious. Everyone is taking themselves so seriously.'"[4] Robert Justman, the assistant director on "The Cage," would also be the assistant director for the second pilot. He'd worked with Leslie Stevens on *The Outer Limits* and was the assistant director for the 1964 episode "Cold Hands, Warm Heart," in which Bill costarred with Geraldine Brooks as an astronaut just back from a colonizing trip to Venus who can't figure out why he's always so cold. "Gene was very happy that he was able to get Bill Shatner, who was highly thought of in the industry," Justman said. "I had worked with Bill on *The Outer Limits* and he had a good reputation in the television and entertainment industries even at that time . . . He was someone to be reckoned with, and we certainly understood that he was a more accomplished actor than Jeff Hunter was, and he gave us more dimension."[5]

Bill watched "The Cage" and thought Jeffrey Hunter was fine but that the episode itself was "deadly serious" and could use a little levity. Roddenberry agreed and hired Shatner as his new captain with input from Solow, James Goldstone—who was directing the second pilot—and NBC. This time around, the network and Desilu weren't taking any chances, and three scripts were considered for the second pilot: Roddenberry's *Omega Glory*; *Where No Man Has Gone Before*, written by Sam Peeples; and *Mudd's Women*, penned by Stephen Kendal. But Kendal's subsequent illness meant that his episode would be delayed; the choice was narrowed down to Roddenberry and Peeples—and Peeples's *Where No Man Has Gone Before* was chosen to be Shatner's hoped-for *Star Trek* launching pad. (Bill was paid $10,000 for the pilot, compared to Hunter's $5,000 fee.)

In May 1965, Roddenberry sent a memo to researcher Kellam DeForest with a list of possible surnames for the new captain, among them January, Thorpe, Raintree, Boone, Hannibal, and Neville. The second-to-last name on the list was Kirk—and Captain Christopher Pike morphed into Captain James Kirk. Majel Barrett's Number One was dropped from the pilot (Barrett reappeared on *Star Trek* as Nurse Christine Chapel), while Leonard Nimoy's Mr. Spock was elevated to Science Officer and the ship's second in command. Several new faces were brought into the mix, including Bill's fellow Canadian James Doohan as Scottish Chief Engineer Montgomery Scott; George Takei as the ship's Japanese American physicist, Lt. Sulu (Roddenberry's surname homage to Desilu's Herb Solow); and Mark Piper as *Enterprise* doctor Paul Fox. Paul Carr, Lloyd Haynes, and Andrea Dromm rounded out the cast as Navigator Lee Kelso, Communications Officer Alden, and Yeoman Smith.

Where No Man Has Gone Before began filming at the Desilu Culver studio on July 19, 1965. The episode's plot revolves around the USS *Enterprise*, with Captain James Kirk at the helm, searching for the SS *Valiant*, an Earth spaceship that disappeared two hundred years earlier and is believed to have been destroyed by its captain. During the search, the *Enterprise* crosses the edge of the galaxy and hits a barrier that kills nine crew members and severely damages the ship's internal operating systems. Lt. Commander Gary Mitchell (Gary Lockwood) and the ship's psychiatrist, Dr. Elizabeth Dehner (Sally Kellerman), are knocked unconscious.

Upon awakening, Mitchell's eyes have a silvery glow and he's imbued with psychic abilities. He grows increasingly arrogant and hostile, believing he has God-like powers; the analytical Mr. Spock believes that this same fate befell the captain of the SS *Valiant* and tells Captain Kirk he thinks Mitchell should be killed before he harms the rest of the crew. Kirk disagrees but decides to maroon Mitchell on the remote planet of Delta Vega—a plan that goes awry when Mitchell kills Navigator Lee Kelso, knocks out both Kirk and Spock, and flees with Dr. Dehner, whose eyes have now taken on the silvery glow. Dehner eventually attacks Mitchell and weakens him before Kirk uses a phaser rifle to create a landslide that kills Mitchell to end the episode.

Shooting on *Where No Man Has Gone Before* wrapped on July 28, 1965, at an estimated cost of $300,000, about half the cost of the Jeffrey Hunter pilot. There were a few snafus along the way; during filming, a wasp nest in the rafters at Desilu studios was disturbed and several of the actors, including Bill, were stung. (He wore extra makeup during filming to hide his swollen eyes.) Lockwood had problems with the special contact lenses he wore to simulate Mitchell's eyes and their silvery glow. Wearing the lenses, for only minutes at a time, was "agonizing," he said, and he went without them during rehearsals. Adding insult to injury, Lockwood's pants split wide open during Mitchell's fight scene with Kirk, exposing his private parts to Kellerman (who took it all in stride).[6]

One of the most important elements of *Where No Man Has Gone Before* was the interplay between Captain Kirk and Mr. Spock. Even before the pilot rounded into its finished form, Leonard Nimoy, who was playing Spock, recalled feeling more comfortable acting alongside Shatner than he had alongside Jeffrey Hunter's Captain Christopher Pike. Nimoy and Shatner, who first met in 1964 on set of NBC's *The Man From U.N.C.L.E.*, discovered that they had a lot in common; they were almost exactly the same age (Nimoy was four days younger), and they were both were raised in Jewish households. (Nimoy's parents were immigrants from the Ukraine; he grew up in Boston's West End and was fluent in Yiddish.) "I didn't know where I was with Jeff Hunter," Nimoy said. "I was floundering when I was working with him. Jeff was playing Captain Pike as a very thoughtful, kind of worried, kind of angst-ridden, nice guy, thinking his way through a problem, and I, as Spock, couldn't find a space."[7]

"When Bill came on board and when Dee (DeForest Kelley) came on, it became much clearer to me what the possibilities were of how we could interact with each other," he said. "Bill with this very energetic and very kind of proactive type . . . creates opportunities for other people to find their place around that."[8]

NBC executives were eager to see what they had in the second pilot, but various delays that summer impacted its post-production schedule. Roddenberry was being pulled in several different directions and was laser-focused on *Police Story*, a half-hour cop show (different from the Joseph Wambaugh-inspired series that aired in the mid-'70s on NBC) that counted among its cast DeForest Kelley—soon to join the USS *Enterprise* as Dr. Leonard "Bones" McCoy—and Grace Lee Whitney (Yeoman Rand on *Star Trek*). He was also directing a Western called *The Long Hunt of April Savage* that was earmarked for ABC with stars Robert Lansing and Rip Torn.

Roddenberry was finally able to turn his attention to *Where No Man Has Gone Before* in the fall, and by the New Year it was ready to be screen-tested at Preview House, a three-hundred-seat facility on Sunset Boulevard in Los Angeles where people were invited to watch screenings and react to what they saw. (They pressed "like or dislike" buttons and their reactions were logged—by sex, age, etc.—for research purposes.) But the first screening of *Where No Man Has Gone Before* was held in the afternoon, with an audience, Solow remembered, largely comprised of "little old ladies with blue hair." To no one's surprise, they disliked what they saw. Solow complained to NBC and demanded that the pilot be screened again, this time in the evening, with a more demographically balanced audience. NBC caved, and the results the second time around were much more positive.

Solow's next step was to fly to New York to present both *Where No Man Has Gone Before* and the *Mission: Impossible* pilot to NBC executives—who, in early March, gave the green light to both series for inclusion on the network's 1966 fall schedule. "I got a call from my agent the next day telling me that *Star Trek* was a go," Shatner recalled, and after phoning Roddenberry, he took his daughters out for hot dogs and soda to celebrate the big news.[9] There were no guarantees, of course—*For The People* lasted only thirteen episodes—but maybe, finally, *this* was Bill Shatner's big break.

Meanwhile, while Bill and his *Where No Man Has Gone Before* costar George Takei waited on the fate of their new series, they appeared together in an episode of NBC's *Chrysler Theater* called "Wind Fever," in which Takei played an Oxford-educated barrister in Southeast Asia defending a jungle missionary/doctor, Ely Harris (Shatner), against charges of malpractice. Takei was taken aback when he greeted Bill before filming began and there didn't seem to be a glimmer of recognition on Bill's part—even though they'd just filmed *Where No Man Has Gone Before* in the recent past. Takei chalked it up to Bill not recognizing him in his barrister's getup (complete with a white wig) yet found his behavior toward him strange. Later, when Takei wanted to talk about the pilot, Bill seemed "disengaged." Still, he praised Shatner's performance in "Wind Fever." "Bill was crafting a fascinating portrait of an idealist with a dark underside . . . Bill broke the tension with his jokey banter and lighthearted pranks. His silly giggles were bubbling up constantly." But Takei's feelings toward Bill were a harbinger of things to come, and their relationship took a darker turn on *Star Trek*.[10]

Bill returned to the stage, briefly, when he signed on to costar in *The Hyphen*, a comedic play written and directed by legendary radio scribe Norman Corwin on commission from the University of Utah. (Corwin won an Oscar in 1956 for adapting Irving Stone's novel, *Lust for Life*, into the big-screen movie starring Kirk Douglas in his Oscar-winning role as artist Vincent van Gogh.) The play was produced at the university's Pioneer Memorial Theatre, with Bill playing the lead role as a scientist grappling with his "empirical facts"—and with love in the form of costars Sherri Sailer and Joan Payne. "Mr. Shatner demonstrated a flexible sureness in ranging from outrage to amused repartee to philosophical musing to outright eloquence," noted the *Salt Lake Tribune*. "Almost constantly onstage, he meets the demands of the role with energy to throw away." Bill reprised the role in "The Discovery," a 1972 episode of the CBC series *Norman Corwin Presents*.[11]

*   *   *

Production on *Star Trek* kicked into high gear in late May 1966 at Desilu's Gower Street lot (the original home of *I Love Lucy*) as filming started on "The Corbomite Maneuver" (which aired in November as the series' tenth episode). Leonard Nimoy, James Doohan, and George Takei were back— Lt. Sulu now as the ship's helmsman—while DeForest Kelley and Nichelle Nichols joined the series as USS *Enterprise* doctor Leonard "Bones" McCoy and Lt. Uhura, the ship's communications officer. Roddenberry made a concerted effort to showcase the cast's diversity: Takei's Japanese American family was sent to internment camps in Arkansas and California during World War II; Nichols, as Lt. Uhura, was one of the first African American women to be featured in a television series in an authoritative, crucial role—and not as a servant or second-class citizen.

"I still feel, to this day, that Bill Shatner was the perfect casting [choice] for that role," Justman said. "Everything was fated to happen that way. Leonard [Nimoy] and Bill and kindly Dr. Bones McCoy were a wonderful combination. They were friends, yet at times they would be at odds with each other. It was like the real thing. What was important was the human equation—that's what the show was about."[12]

Bill whipped himself into top physical shape for the grueling *Star Trek* shooting schedule and could often be seen walking around the Desilu lot with twenty-pound weights attached to his waist, ankles, and wrists—"[so] I can take my shirt off on camera," he said.[13] (It's also been speculated that he shaved his chest for the role.) Bill needed his stamina; *Star Trek* filmed on a frenzied schedule in order to be ready for the fall. Each episode took around six days to film, and episodes were shot out of sequence in order to maximize locations; Captain Kirk was in nearly every scene and Bill was memorizing reams of dialogue, sometimes for several different scenarios simultaneously.

"It was an enormous task," said Justman. "For the leading man of a show, if a script is fifty-two to fifty-four pages, you had the star having to know the dialogue for anywhere from twenty to forty pages and shooting a show in six days—that's a lot of stuff to memorize and deliver it and make it believable."[14] Bill would say that his onerous dialogue burden on *Star Trek* contributed to the breathy, halting-delivery style of acting he often used, since he was often trying to remember his next line . . . which caused him . . . to pause . . . and think of what . . . to say next. He's been mercilessly lampooned for that acting style ever since.

The days on the Desilu lot stretched from the early morning into the evening; Bill was up at dawn, often arrived at 7 a.m., and didn't leave until 10 p.m. On the weekends he relaxed at home in the San Fernando Valley with Gloria, the girls, and the family dog (usually a Doberman Pinscher, Bill's favorite breed—his Dobermans over the years have included Kirk, Morgan, China, Heidi, Paris, Royale, Martika, Sterling, Charity, Bella, and Starbuck). Their four-bedroom, two-bathroom house had a pool in the backyard, and Bill taught his girls how to swim. He bought a motorcycle and would often roar off to ride the dirt trails in the nearby hillside.

With *Star Trek* slated to premiere in September, the NBC publicity machine went into overdrive promoting the network's new series. Color television was making big strides; the 1966–67 television season would be the first time all three networks (ABC, CBS, NBC) aired their entire prime-time lineups in color, and *Star Trek* was, to NBC, an important cog in its color machine. Its special effects and costumes, and the often-bizarre makeup of its alien characters (and creatures) the USS *Enterprise* encountered during its intergalactic travels, would, NBC hoped, be enhanced by the network's superior color quality—the standard to which the other networks strove to equal or surpass. The color of NBC's shows (including top ratings-grabber *Bonanza*) was vibrant and crisp; the network was owned by RCA, which manufactured color cameras for television studios and for the home market and was way ahead of the industry game vis-à-vis color technology. NBC made sure the public knew the shows on its fall schedule were airing in color and spent millions of dollars on advertising in the months leading up to the fall premieres.

"Color all the way on NBC-TV4 . . . sneak previews of three of the great new shows," blared a Macy's advertisement in the *New York Times* in August. "Watch *Tarzan, Star Trek, The Hero* on your Magnavox color TV from Macy's . . . Kicking off the evening, *Tarzan* comes to NBC in blazing, tropical color. Ron Ely stars as the greatest Tarzan ever. See tigers! Elephants! Cheetah, the chimp! *Star Trek* follows with the space adventures of the USS *Enterprise*. William Shatner captains this 400-man space ship for exciting missions to worlds beyond imagination."

Bill made the publicity rounds, sitting for a slew of newspaper interviews to enthusiastically promote the launch of *Star Trek*. "There'll be lots of jeopardy and character conflict among the crew on the ship," he told one reporter. "It was the lack of these elements that made *For the People* fail, I believe. Philosophical conflict is not enough these days."[15] He would describe Kirk as "an amalgam" of Alexander the Great from the failed television pilot and Henry V, his onstage alter ego from his Stratford days. "For me the Kirk character was classical. He was noble. So, I thought of him with the 'look of eagles' on his face, that look of nobility that one thinks of on a stamp, a coin, or a statue."[16]

Robert Justman noted that Gene Roddenberry told *him* that Captain James Kirk was a combination of Hamlet and Captain Horatio Hornblower, the fictional early-1800s Royal Navy officer and hero of the popular C. S. Forester novels that first appeared in 1937. "This is an imperfect hero," Justman said. "The Captain has fears and doubts about his capability, yet he's faced with the responsibility of protecting the lives of everyone on board and possibly other life forms on other planets—and it was a responsibility that weighed heavily on him. And he found a receptive ear in 'Bones' McCoy."[17]

The first episode of *Star Trek*, "The Man Trap," premiered on Thursday, September 8, 1966, at 8:30 p.m. The series was competing against *My Three Sons* and the *Thursday Night Movie* on CBS and ABC's *The Tammy Grimes Show* and *Bewitched*. Initial reviews were mixed; the *New York Times* called the show an "astronautical soap opera that suffers from interminable flight drag," while *Variety* predicted it wouldn't last, that it was a "dreary mess of confusion . . . a long hour with hardly any relief from violence, killings, hypnotic stuff, and a distasteful, ugly monster." Bill, it noted, was "wooden." The *San Francisco Chronicle* thought "the "opening yarn was a breath-catcher" while the *Washington Post* critic wrote that "the plots may be space opera, but the show has been produced with care and lots of money." The *Boston Globe* thought *Star Trek* was "too clumsily conceived and poorly developed to rate as an A-1 effort"; the *New York Post* critic Bob Williams was more direct: "One may need something of a pointed head to get involved."

Critics in the South were harsh; the *Houston Chronicle* branded *Star Trek* a "disappointingly bizarre hour," while the *Memphis Press-Scimitar* critic opined that it was "one of the biggest disappointments of the season." Even Gene Roddenberry's father wasn't impressed: "He sat there the first night *Star Trek* was on the air and he waited and saw the whole thing and went out and apologized to all the neighbors."[18]

The *Hollywood Reporter*, meanwhile, predicted *Star Trek* "should be a winner," noting that its "suspense and tricks with gadgets" would please sci-fi fans. Even science fiction guru Isaac Asimov got into the act, criticizing the fact-based veracity of *Star Trek* (and *Lost in Space* on CBS) in an article for *TV Guide* magazine published in November 1966 (and titled "What Are a Few Galaxies Among Friends?").[19] He did note, though, that *Star Trek* "seems to have the best technical assistance of the current crop." Asimov eventually came around and bought into *Star Trek* as one of the show's biggest boosters, developing a close friendship with Roddenberry and talking the show up in subsequent interviews and articles.

The show's initial ratings reflected its critical reception: mixed and mediocre. In mid-October, Nielsen released its analysis of the first two weeks of the new fall prime-time schedule. *Star Trek* ranked far behind the CBS sitcom *My Three Sons* at 8:30 p.m. Thursdays but was comfortably ahead of *The Tammy Grimes Show* on ABC. The better news for NBC was that, according to Nielsen, *Star Trek* ranked as the number-one series—in all of network television—for people who were watching it in color. But Nielsen's competitor, Trendex, also commissioned a study regarding shows airing in color, and *Star Trek* was not among the top ten in color-television households. (NBC's *I Spy* claimed the top spot.) NBC, did, however continue pushing the color aspect of *Star Trek* in television and newspaper advertisements. "When you're first in Color TV, there's got to be a reason," exclaimed an ad that ran in *TV Guide* in October 1967. The ad showed a picture of Kirk and Mr. Spock, with Kirk pointing his finger; below that was an RCA color television set with Spock and Kirk on its screen.[20]

It was obvious, early in the show's run, that Mr. Spock, the half-human/half-Vulcan character with the pointy ears, was becoming a *Star Trek* fan favorite—despite NBC executives' apparent dislike of the character's Satanic appearance (those pointy ears!). The NBC offices in Burbank and in New York, and the Desilu studios in Los Angeles, were deluged with fan mail regarding Spock. Grassroots fan clubs devoted to the character sprang up around the country. Network executives demanded that the episodes in which Spock was heavily featured air as quickly as possible to capitalize on fan reaction.

"Bill's energy was very good for my performance, because Spock could then be the cool individual," Nimoy said. "Our chemistry was successful right from the start. [We were] very competitive, with a sibling rivalry up to here, and after the show had been on the air a few weeks and they started to get a lot of mail about Spock, then the dictum came down from NBC: 'Oh, give us more of that guy! They love that guy!' Well, that can be a problem for a leading man who's hired as the star of the show."[21]

Bill was not pleased; he got along well enough with Nimoy, who kept his distance from Bill and the rest of the cast in order to remain in character. (He was also, admittedly, drinking heavily after the breakup of his first marriage; although he never showed up to work drunk, it added a veneer of sullenness to his dour demeanor.) Bill thought that it was Captain Kirk, and not Spock, who was the show's de facto lead star and its prime protagonist—that it was Kirk, and not Spock, who carried the dramatic bulk of each episode on his broad shoulders. That it was Kirk, and not Spock, who got the girl, stared down the bad guys, and nobly commanded the USS *Enterprise*—with Spock as his loyal second in command.

"To be perfectly honest, this really began to bother me," Bill recalled. "Once the show had been on the air for a couple of months, although Captain Kirk was still the lead character, all of the sudden Spock's popularity began increasing exponentially . . . I was now faced with no longer being the only star of this show. And to be unflatteringly frank, it bugged me."[22]

Robert Justman, the show's associate producer, noted the difference between Bill Shatner and Leonard Nimoy's personalities on the set that first season: Shatner, always well prepared, came in, did his job, and was "likable, and industrious"—but had "a tendency to ride roughshod over the 'lesser' performers," a situation that would be revisited years later when Takei, Doohan, and other *Star Trek* cast members wrote their memoirs. Nimoy, by comparison, "had great empathy" for struggling actors. "Bill is a dynamic presence. He enjoys being the center of everything, and when he's on the set, he dominates," Takei said. "But Captain Kirk is Bill Shatner's creation. It's his metabolism. He vibrates Captain Kirk. It's Bill's unique talent, energy, and persona that made Captain Kirk the kind of character he was . . . he was fascinating to watch, sometimes difficult to work with."[23]

"Bill Shatner's problem was that he wasn't given as interesting a character to play as Nimoy was," said Norman Spinrad, who wrote the Season 2 *Star Trek* episode "The Doomsday Machine." "He was the lead character, but he couldn't be the most interesting. That led to all the line stealing and all the crazy lunatic stuff."[24]

Nimoy considered himself an equal with Shatner in terms of *Star Trek* billing, and before too long, friction developed between the actors. Some of that involved their salaries. As the show's presumptive star, Shatner was earning $5,000 per episode (plus a "secret" percentage of its profits, according to Solow); Nimoy's weekly salary came to $1,250 per episode, presumably with no percentage of its profits. The growing tension between Shatner and Nimoy erupted into a full-blown war of egos one morning when *Life* magazine sent a photographer to snap photos of *Star Trek* makeup artist Fred Phillips as he went through the grueling process of affixing Spock's pointy ears to Nimoy, sitting patiently in a makeup chair.

"Bill's hairpiece was being applied. The top of his head was a lot of skin and a few little odd tufts of hair," James "Scotty" Doohan recalled. "The mirrors on the makeup room walls were arranged so that we could all see the laying on of his rug."[25] Desilu chief Herb Solow also witnessed the scene as Bill entered the makeup room and saw the scene unfolding before him. "Bill Shatner became annoyed. He was being totally ignored . . . I watched as he sprang from his makeup chair and announced in true Captain of the USS *Enterprise* fashion, 'From now on, *my* makeup will be done in my trailer.'" Shatner them stormed out of the room.[26]

Bill remembered the interaction differently, admitting that he and Nimoy "didn't really get along" at that stage of the game; the makeup showdown only added fuel to the simmering competitive fire. "I was concerned all of my little makeup secrets were going to be revealed," he said (omitting any mention of a hairpiece).[27] In Bill's version, he asked why the *Life* photographer was in the room, and then watched him "quietly" leave. Nimoy was "furious," Shatner remembered, and confronted his costar, telling him, in no uncertain terms, that the photo shoot was approved by Gene Roddenberry, Herb Solow, and the show's publicity department. Nimoy then refused to come out of his trailer until Roddenberry stepped in to keep the peace.[28]

They were competitive in other ways, too. One of the stories both Bill and Nimoy would repeat in later years, alone or together at *Star Trek*-related events (often with a smile on their faces), revolved around the bicycle Nimoy used to tool around the *Star Trek* set and to race to the studio commissary to ensure he got a spot in the front of the lunch line.

"Leonard had this bicycle," Bill recalled. "He always had to be the first one into the studio commissary for lunch. Always . . . So, one day I put his bike in my trailer . . . for safekeeping. I told him where it was, but I forgot to mention that one of my Dobermans was in there with it. Dobermans are very territorial, you know." Other variations on the story have Shatner hiding Nimoy's bicycle in the trunk of Nimoy's car—and then having the car towed away—or chaining it to a fire hydrant or even using rope to hang it from the studio rafters.[29]

As Leonard Nimoy's fan mail grew exponentially with Spock's popularity, it created yet another sore spot between the two actors. (Kirk just wasn't as popular a character, at this point, in the *Star Trek* mythology.) Various figures vis-à-vis the number of fan-mail letters Nimoy received each week were leaked to consumer and trade magazines; Shatner was not pleased, nor was Roddenberry. He sent a pointed letter to the publicists handling Nimoy, Shatner, and DeForest Kelley—not accusing anyone per se of leaking inflated fan-mail numbers, but making his point: "We simply won't have it and would cease to cooperate in publicity with any actor who gave out such information."[30]

Roddenberry took it one step further, writing a letter to *TV Week*, claiming: "Shatner's extraordinary dramatic ability and talent which often sets up the scene and gives Leonard a solid foundation and contrast which makes Mr. Spock come alive. Bill was trained in the old Canadian Shakespeare school with all its discipline and both his work and professional attitudes reflect this rich background."[31] He even wrote to Isaac Asimov, asking his advice on how to make Captain Kirk a more popular character. "Mr. Shatner is a versatile and talented actor, and perhaps this should be made plain by giving him a chance at a variety of roles," Asimov replied. "In other words, an effort should be made to work up story plots in which Mr. Shatner has an opportunity to put on disguises or take over roles of unusual nature."[32]

It didn't help Bill Shatner's ego that, following the first season of *Star Trek*, Leonard Nimoy was nominated for an Emmy Award as Outstanding Supporting Actor (as he would be the next two seasons—he never won); the series itself was nominated for Outstanding Dramatic Series. It also garnered nominations in several technical categories as well as an NAACP Image Award by way of Nichelle Nichols's Lt. Uhura. "The difference between Bill and Leonard was simple enough," said *Star Trek* actor David Ross. "Leonard was calculating. He thought before he said a word. Shatner, being real, said what he was feeling, and it sometimes got him in trouble."[33]

Star Trek became a family affair of sorts in its first season when two of Bill's daughters—eight-year-old Leslie and five-year-old Lisabeth—appeared briefly in the show's eighth episode, "Miri," which aired in late October 1966. The girls spent two days on the *Star Trek* set in late August, which was not an entirely happy experience for either of them. "My dad thought it would be wonderful for my sister Liz and I to experience what acting was about so we would never want to become actresses," Leslie recalled. "After about three days I just remember breaking out and crying, 'I don't want this anymore! I want to go home!' and they were about to do a big scene with all the kids. So [my father] took me back behind the set and calmed me down and once the cameras started rolling he came over and put his hand on my head—so I got my semi-close-up and after that I got to go home."[34] The episode also included the children of other *Star Trek* personnel in small roles, including Grace Lee Whitney's son, Scott, and Gene Roddenberry's daughters, Darleen and Dawn. Phil Morris, the son of *Mission: Impossible* star Greg Morris (that series also premiered on NBC in 1966), appeared briefly along with his sister, Iona; Greg went on to a busy acting career. (He memorably played the Johnnie Cochran-like lawyer, Jackie Chiles, on NBC's *Seinfeld*.)

As *Star Trek* flew into uncertain terrain in that first season, Bill suffered a personal loss when his father died in Florida in early 1967, four months into the show's run. Joseph Shatner was sixty-nine and lived long enough to see his only son carve out a successful career in show business (which was always Joseph's biggest concern). He passed away in Miami, and Bill heard the news around noon in Los Angeles while he was shooting the *Star Trek* episode "Devil in the Dark." He booked a late flight to Miami and, with hours to kill before his flight, decided to go ahead and continue filming the episode—which he did with some difficulty as his emotions overcame him. Nimoy, he recalled, helped to console him, not so much with words but by being around and letting Bill know he was there for him. It was a Thursday; on Friday, he picked his mother up in Miami and they flew back to Montreal with Joseph's body. The funeral took place over the weekend, and by Monday, he was back in Los Angeles to shoot the show. Ann Shatner remained a widow for two years, marrying Robert Lichtenstein in Montreal in 1969.

In March 1967, NBC announced it was renewing *Star Trek* for a second season despite the show's sluggish ratings. Whether or not the network's decision had anything to do with *Star Trek*'s popularity among the households watching it in color is anyone's guess; there were reports of a letter-writing campaign undertaken by the show's fans when rumors of its cancellation began circulating in the press. Herb Solow claimed, perhaps apocryphally, that during the closing credits of "Devil in the Dark," the last episode of Season 1 (shot while Shatner grieved his father's death), an NBC announcer intoned: "'Star Trek' will be back in the fall. And please don't write any more letters."[35] But it didn't really matter. The news was a relief to everyone involved with the show.

*   *   *

The daily grind of shooting a weekly television series began to infiltrate Bill's private life—or what little private life he had after spending up to sixteen hours a day at Desilu working on *Star Trek*. "It was such an onerous burden," he said. "The learning of the words. Sometimes there would be a two-page speech and I'd have to learn it like that night or during the day. So, I was doing ten pages in a day of dialogue and trying to learn ten pages of dialogue for tomorrow—I was right back to doing a play and rehearsing a play. That kind of work takes you out of the broad picture."[36]

He was spending less time at home with Gloria and the girls; he loved his daughters, and tried to be the best father he could, but he just wasn't around very much. "He appeared only once or twice a week" at home once he began shooting *Star Trek*, Lisabeth said.[37] He and Gloria had drifted apart, even before *Star Trek*, and the increased workload and his time at the studio drove a further wedge into their decade-long marriage. "I wasn't good at being married," Shatner admitted in his memoirs. "I didn't know how to make a real commitment to another person."[38] While he worked hard to pay the bills, his relationship with Gloria began to fade into the background.

They had started married life in 1956 as two young actors both working steadily and hoping for the big break. Bill was now starring on a network television series while Gloria's acting ambitions had been on hold for some time while she raised Leslie, Lisabeth, and Melanie. "The person you fell in love with slowly disappears, replaced by . . . frustration, anger, disenchantment, and tremendous resentment," Bill said, perhaps summing up both his and Gloria's feelings. "And then you get angry at them for no longer being the person you married."[39]

Gene Roddenberry's vision for *Star Trek* included a lot of beautiful women, particularly in guest-starring roles—including Bill's *The World of Suzie Wong* costar France Nuyen (in the Season 3 episode "Elaan of Troyius"), Barbara Bouchet, Marianna Hill, Sherry Jackson, Nancy Kovack, and Joan Collins, further blurring the lines between Bill's work life and his domestic situation. Gloria, he said, resented him "for probably many reasons," though it's impossible to say if he's referring to any extracurricular activities that might have unfolded behind closed doors at the Desilu studio. He and

Gloria eventually separated, and he moved out of their Beverly Hills home while *Star Trek* was still in production. Their divorce played out quietly over the final two seasons of the series.

"He was extremely charming, very humorous, and loved to make jokes on the set and the crew would love that," said Joan Collins, who played Edith Keeler in the penultimate Season 1 episode of *Star Trek*, "The City on the Edge of Forever," considered by many of the show's fans as one of its best.

> He was quite tall and we did our first scene, I think it was in the mission, and I had very short, cropped hair that I had just styled in London by the very famous Vidal Sassoon, who was a friend of mine and had done [my hair] in a very modern style of the '60s. And Bill commented that he liked my haircut. The next day I was sitting in the makeup chair and this voice said, "I thought our scene went rather well yesterday, didn't you?" and I didn't recognize him or the voice and I sort of rumbled something and then I looked over and he said, "You don't recognize me, do you, without the makeup and the hair?" I said, "Of course I do, sorry." He was very tan on the show and he was quite pale [in the makeup room]; he had hair, but he didn't have a lot of hair like Captain Kirk.
>
> So, Captain Kirk fell in love with Edith Keeler and our love scenes were apparently quite sizzling and the crew were taking bets, apparently, of when I would succumb, as he was quite a bit of a ladies' man. . . . I did not—I was married at the time, I had two children and I passed.

So Bill tried to seduce her?

"A little bit yes, he did," Collins said. "But that was before the #MeToo generation when actors with pretty actresses, they all did that."[40]

Grace Lee Whitney, who played Captain Kirk's yeoman, Janice Rand, in the first half-season of *Star Trek*,[41] said there was a "strong physical attraction" between them, chalking it up (on her part) to "lust, not love." Their relationship was never consummated. "I would like to think that the reason I never became involved with Bill Shatner was that I was moral and virtuous, and I wanted to be a good girl," she said. "But I don't know if that's altogether true."[42] Celeste Yarnall, who played Yeoman Martha London in the 1967 *Star Trek* episode "The Apple," described Bill's on-set flirting as "relentless."[43] Bill apparently didn't chase after all the actresses who appeared in guest-starring roles on *Star Trek*. Over the show's seventy-nine-episode run, Captain Kirk locked lips with nineteen women (yes, someone counted), including Nancy Kovack, a thirty-two-year-old actress and television veteran (including roles on *Perry Mason*, *I Spy*, *The Man from U.N.C.L.E*, *Batman*, *Honey West*, and *I Dream of Jeannie*) who guest-starred in the Season 2 episode "A Private Little War," an anti-Vietnam parable in which Captain Kirk returns to a planet on which he'd lived for thirteen years to battle the encroaching Klingons. Kovack played Nona, a witch doctor who saves Kirk's life with a remedy that enables her to control his will, and later uses that control to kiss Kirk.

"It's very boring for you to hear that he's wonderful," said Kovack, who married internationally acclaimed conductor Zubin Mehta in 1969. (They celebrated fifty years together in 2019.) "I've heard that people say that on the set he wasn't wonderful, but for me, on the set, he was a wonderful human being—highly professional and deeply kind, and I don't know how much better you can get than that. But he was all of that, and wonderfully amusing. He loved laughter and humor and innuendos and all kinds of things and was very quick in his mind. It was a joy to talk to him because of that. He was always ready for something." They kept their relationship strictly professional, Nancy recalled, though they were photographed in public—Nancy with coiffed hair and wearing a nice dress and Bill in a tuxedo—at what appears to have been the Hollywood opening for the big-screen movie *The Shoes of the Fisherman*. (Bill is holding a program with the movie's title on its cover.) The movie, starring Laurence Olivier and Anthony Quinn, opened in November 1968, nine months after "A Private Little War" first aired on *Star Trek*. "Canadian-born actor William Shatner, wearing a tuxedo, talks to his date, Nancy Kovack, while standing under a tent at a formal event," reads the photo's official caption. "I remember he once said something to me that put everything into perspective," Nancy said. "That, in Canada, as a very young boy, I believe he had blondish hair, and he was perceived as a 'golden boy,' a 'golden child,' and that clicked with me. I could see immediately how that propelled his life and I've never forgotten that. I don't know why, it's not important to anything, but I believe it's factual."[44]

Thirty years later, James Doohan recalled how, during a party attended by most of the *Star Trek* cast, Bill tried to hit on Diana Muldaur, who was guest-starring on the Season 2 episode "Return to Tomorrow." "Bill was at the other end of the table propositioning Diana. We know because we all heard her say, 'Oh, you little man. If I wanted to fuck anybody, it'd be

Jimmy Doohan.'"[45] Years later, in an interview for the Archive of American Television, Muldaur seemed to confirm Doohan's story about Shatner. "He was very nice, but he would hit on you, of course. Some of them did and some of them didn't. William Shatner evidently hit on them all; at any rate, it didn't do him any good."[46]

The second season of *Star Trek* premiered at 8:30 p.m. on Friday, September 15, 1967, with the episode entitled "Amok Time." *Star Trek* was competing on its new night against the Jim Nabors sitcom *Gomer Pyle, U.S.M.C.* on CBS, and *Hondo*, a Western, on ABC. Walter Koenig joined the cast in Season 2 as USS *Enterprise* navigator Pavel Chekov. (In his Chekov wig, Koenig looked suspiciously like teen idol Davy Jones from *The Monkees*, entering its second and final season on NBC.) As the season progressed and the calendar turned to 1968, *Star Trek* found itself running (or flying) in place; its ratings were mediocre, and its loyal fan base was not translating to particularly solid viewership numbers. The series was popular among college-age students, professionals, and sci-fi fans, who appreciated its intelligent, well-written episodes and its under-the-radar social commentary. (A future episode in Season 3, "Plato's Stepchildren," featured an interracial kiss between Captain Kirk and Lt. Uhura—virtually unheard-of on television in 1968.)

In late 1967, as rumors abounded that NBC would cancel the series, Gene Roddenberry surreptitiously funded a "Save *Star Trek*" fan-mail campaign organized by superfan Betty Joe Trimble and her husband, John. In January 1968, two college students—Wanda Kendall from Pasadena, California, and Devra Langsam, who was attending Brooklyn College—picketed NBC's studios in Midtown Manhattan, handing out bumper stickers urging the network not to cancel the show. Kendall's classmates at Cal-Tech funded her cross-country trip. "Mr. Neilsen [sic] never asks us," she said, alluding to the company used by the three networks to measure television ratings and its viewership vis-à-vis *Star Trek*.[47]

"I knew nothing about the letter-writing campaign. I knew nothing about any of the intrigues until years later," Shatner said. "Suddenly there's intrigue and I don't know anything about it. I didn't have any time. The letter-writing campaign was micromanaged by Gene Roddenberry and might have helped in the staying of our execution."[48]

Shatner and Leonard Nimoy gamely sat for press interviews to promote the series, including one chat with *Los Angeles Magazine* columnist Burt

Prelutsky in October 1967, in which Prelutsky noted that Shatner "is about thirty-five and wears a hairpiece." Asked to compare this second season of *Star Trek* to its maiden voyage on NBC, Shatner cited better scripts and more "finely tuned" shows. "Last year there were too many problems still to be solved," he said. "How do you make what's essentially a military adventure the basis for a sympathetic story?"[49] [50]

While Bill was busy at the Desilu studios shooting *Star Trek*, giving interviews and dealing with his dissolving marriage, he somehow found the time to record a spoken-word album for Decca Records.

It was called *The Transformed Man*, and it featured Bill reciting lines from famous pop songs (including "Mr. Tambourine Man" and "Lucy in the Sky with Diamonds"), which were transposed onto ersatz, Top 40 versions of those songs sung by faceless studio voices. Bill sung and spoke (and sometimes shouted) the words in his inimitable dramatic START . . . PAUSE . . . START vocal style. The album also included him reciting passages from *Hamlet* and *King Henry V*—harkening back to his Stratford theater days. *The Transformed Man* was produced by arranger/composer Don Ralke, who'd previously worked with Bill's Canadian cohort Lorne Greene on his number-one spoken-word ballad "Ringo" (about Wild West outlaw Johnny Ringo). The cover of *The Transformed Man* featured a photograph of Bill staring straight ahead, half of his face darkened. Above the photograph were the words "WILLIAM SHATNER: Captain Kirk of Star Trek. THE TRANSFORMED MAN."

Listening to Shatner's bizarre recitations, it's impossible to say whether he was playing along with the joke or taking it all very seriously. (Ben Folds told actor Kevin Pollak on a podcast that, when he was recording his 2004 album *Has Been* with Bill, he told Folds how he "didn't know what he had done" while recording "Mr. Tambourine Man.")

Bill wrote the album's liner notes, mentioning his "thrill" at the overture when attending a theatrical performance as a kid and his work "as a producer, actor, writer" at McGill: "So you see, music and I are old, familiar friends. Looking back in retrospect, I've always had a secret ambition to do something with the spoken word combined with the magic of music." Mission accomplished. Bill recorded the album at Gold Star studios on Santa Monica Boulevard and, upon its release in the fall of 1968, was a guest on *The Tonight Show Starring Johnny Carson* (on *Star Trek*'s home network, NBC), where he crooned part of "Mr. Tambourine Man." The album landed among critics with a resounding thud, but Bill would have the last laugh.

Despite its sketchy viewership, *Star Trek* was renewed for a third season in March 1968. "We are pleased to tell you that *Star Trek* will continue to be seen on NBC Television," an NBC announcer informed America following the March 1 episode, "The Omega Glory." "We know you will be looking forward to seeing the weekly adventure in space on *Star Trek*." The letter-writing campaign spearheaded by Betty Joe Trimble helped the cause—some estimates put the number of letters sent to NBC at over 110,000, and while that's likely spectacularly inflated,[51] it certainly didn't hurt. New York's governor, Nelson Rockefeller, and Isaac Asimov also gave *Star Trek* ringing endorsements, and there was even a *Star Trek* comic book, published the previous summer by Gold Key, that likely factored into NBC's decision to renew the series.[52]

Bill spent part of the winter of 1968 out in the Pacific Ocean, shooting his role as Steve Monroe in *The Revolution of Antonio de Leon*, a television movie slated to air that fall on NBC. It told the tale of a desperate (and alcoholic) South American guerilla (played by Michael Parks) who hijacks a ship carrying arms and holds its passengers (including Steve Monroe) hostage. Shatner told a story about an actual fire aboard the boat during filming, which was extinguished before the fog rolled in. The cast and crew were stranded without a radio (strange, given the typical technical support on a Hollywood production). "Finally, many hours later, we heard faint sounds of rescue boats in the distance," he recalled. "Through the use of a walkie-talkie, we called them in by the sound of their engines. Once we were rescued, the engine started immediately, of course."[53] *The Revolution of Antonio de Leon* did not air until eight years later under the new title, *Perilous Voyage*, during a low point in Shatner's career.

Bill also discovered the joys of flying—he played Captain James Kirk, after all—and earned his pilot's license, using his hours in the air, on weekends, to help him relax. "There is something not only thrilling about it but exhilarating to the utmost degree," he said of flying an airplane. "When in the air, I feel that the plane and I are one."[54] His newfound *Star Trek* fame had its perks; in the spring of 1968, he was invited to visit Cape Kennedy in Florida, where he was given "royal treatment" by NASA scientists and astronauts, who were big fans of the show, and was allowed to sit inside an Apollo spacecraft: "I was looking out the window at the simulated atmosphere on a

TV screen when a replica of the *Enterprise* floated by." Asked to sign a replica of the *Enterprise*, he wrote, "When you get to the moon, I'll see you."[55]

*   *   *

Horses, too, became another of Bill Shatner's lifelong passions, hearkening back to his boyhood in Montreal. There was a riding stable not too far from the house on Girouard Avenue, and he would often go there as a teenager. "I remember going there all the time and having this sort of innate interest in riding, which I couldn't fulfill at the time because of the expense involved," he said. "But I was just drawn there anyway."[56] "My parents became aware of my newfound love because of the way I smelled. I'd ride my bike to the stable three or four times a week, sandwiching these trips between football and acting. Even those mongrel horses appealed to me. I was good at riding them, and they responded. I would often daydream about having a ranch, with my own horses."[57] Bill's love of the saddle—or lack thereof—was tested while he was preparing for his failed television pilot, *Alexander the Great*. He spent six months learning how to ride bareback for his starring role—and once filming commenced, he was instructed to rear a horse on its hind legs. The story goes that, afterward, he was told by Glen Randall Jr.—Gene Autrey's trainer and noted Hollywood horse trainer—that he had "more natural ability as a horseman" than anyone Randall had ever seen.[58]

In March 1967, after wrapping production on the first season of *Star Trek*, Bill was back on a horse when he flew to Spain for the "paella Western" *White Comanche* (also called *Comanche Blanco*), playing the dual roles of drifter Johnny Moon and his bare-chested Native American twin brother, Notah, who leads Comanche war parties. (Hollywood veteran Joseph Cotten was the movie's only other notable actor.) The warring brothers eventually have a showdown, riding at each other at full gallop in the middle of town; Bill rode two horses for the role(s), one called "El Nervioso" (for the charging scenes) and "El Tranquilo" ("who would be calm when the clapboard clacked in his face and I had to wheel the horse away and ride off into the sunset").[59]

Back home, he bought his first horse while attending a quarter-horse auction in Visalia, California, where he was introduced to a local horse owner and his ten-year-old son. "I had no plans whatsoever of buying a horse that day, but I was sitting there with them and suddenly the horse owner's kid points at some gelding and says to me out of the blue, 'That's the horse you should buy,'" he said. "And I raised my hands in mock horror, like, 'Me, buy a horse?!' And then I hear the auctioneer saying, 'And Shatner buys the horse at . . .'"[60] It was no passing fad; Bill eventually bought a horse farm in Lexington, Kentucky, and his love of horses continues to this day. (He still rides.)

*   *   *

The renewal of *Star Trek* in the spring of 1968 was thrilling news for all concerned, but there were subtle problems lurking beneath the surface. Gene Roddenberry was unhappy over NBC's plan to move the show to Fridays at 10 p.m.—dubbed the "suicide hour" for its historically low viewership levels; several newspaper items (probably generated by Roddenberry himself) noted the series would be better off airing Fridays at 7:30 p.m. (allotted to the Western series *High Chaparral*, starring Leif Erickson and Cameron Mitchell).

As filming commenced on the new season, Roddenberry was also concerned about Bill's weight gain and sent a confidential memo to the show's associate producer, Edward Milkis, noting that Shatner "appeared very heavy" at the Emmy Awards in May. "Even though he has taken off a little poundage since the end of last season, if he follows his usual pattern of putting it on again, we are likely to have him heavier than ever before long," Roddenberry wrote to Milkis. Shatner didn't have to be told twice; he went on a crash diet after seeing himself onscreen while shooting the first episode of Season 3.[61]

Bill and Leonard Nimoy had grown closer over the course of the show's first two seasons, but there was still an undercurrent of competition between Captain Kirk and Mr. Spock over who was the real *Star Trek* protagonist. Spock was, anecdotally, the more popular character, and Nimoy went through several salary disputes with Roddenberry and Desilu, eventually getting his per-episode fee boosted in Season 2 (and, by default, garnering more screen time for Spock as the series progressed). Fred Freiberger was brought in to produce Season 3 of *Star Trek* and, sensing the competition between Shatner and Nimoy and hoping to avert problems, had an idea. He called a meeting with Shatner, Nimoy, and Roddenberry and asked the *Star Trek* creator directly who the series' real star was: Shatner or Nimoy? Roddenberry deliberated before giving his verdict: "Shatner." That only exacerbated the tension between the two actors.[62]

Bill had other problems to deal with and costly legal bills to pay when Gloria filed for divorce after thirteen years of marriage. They'd lived apart for some time—and Bill spent as much time as he could with his three young daughters—but he and Gloria both knew the marriage could not be saved. "I was working so hard to support my family and resented Gloria because I was getting so little joy out of my marriage," he said, adding diplomatically, "She resented me for . . . for probably many reasons."[63]

The divorce was finalized in March 1969 in Santa Monica, California. Gloria, now thirty-four, testified that her husband was absent from home—often for months at a time—and that he rarely told her where he was going, which made her "nervous and depressed." Under the divorce settlement, she was granted custody of Leslie, Lisabeth, and Melanie, monthly alimony of $2,500 for child support, the family home in Beverly Hills, and half of the couple's community property, which was estimated at $500,000.[64]

"My marriage to Gloria didn't simply end, it was ripped apart," Bill said. "It left only sharp edges. And poverty."[65] It would take years for him to recover financially and emotionally from the breakup. "I was lost and lonely. I got divorced in the middle of the series and took affection wherever I could find it. Not every week from every one of the beautiful girls that was on the show, but there was always someone around who, uh, had needs to be fulfilled and who needed to fulfill."[66]

The third season of *Star Trek* premiered on Friday, September 20, 1968, at 10 p.m. with the show's fifty-sixth episode, "Spock's Brain," in which Captain Kirk hunts for Kara (Marj Dusay), an alien female who boards the *Enterprise* and surgically removes Mr. Spock's brain. (Mr. Spock's half-Vulcan physiology enables him to stay alive for twenty-four hours minus his most vital organ.) The episode was written by former *Star Trek* producer Gene Coon under the alias "Lee Cronin," probably for a good reason: "Spock's Brain" is considered by many *Star Trek* fans the worst and dumbest episode in the show's three-season history. Shatner attributed its lameness to cost-cutting and NBC's indifference to the series, which was drifting along aimlessly. (Roddenberry, by this point, had checked out and was working on *Pretty Maids All in a Row*, a movie he was producing with stars Rock Hudson and Angie Dickinson.) "Frankly, during the entire shooting of that episode, I was embarrassed," Leonard Nimoy wrote in his autobiography, "a feeling that overcame me many times during the final season of *Star Trek*."[67] Bill

SHAARE ZION GRADUATING CLASS 1945

Can you recognize William Shatner from Star Trek?
Which one is he? Answer on page 16

Bill (top row, third from right) with his Hebrew school graduating class at Shaare Zion Synagogue in Montreal, 1945. (*Alex Dworkin Canadian Jewish Archives*)

TH KRAMINER and BILL SHATNER are seen above Abbott and Jimmie McBride in the Children's Theatre of "Daddy Long-Legs," wh will be presented all, Westmount on Saturd rnoon

A newspaper clipping, probably 1944 or '45, of Bill and co-star Elizabeth Kraminer in a Montreal Children's Theatre production of *Daddy Long-Legs*. Bill played Jimmie McBride. (*Alex Dworkin Canadian Jewish Archives*)

Bill, fifteen years old, in the summer of 1946. (*Photofest*)

Front and center, with fellow members of McGill University's Radio Workshop. Bill was president of the organization. (*Students' Society of McGill University*)

SHATNER, WILLIAM
"There is not a fiercer hell than the failure in a great object."
Born March 22, 1931, in Montreal. Attended West Hill High School. Entered McGill, 1948. Activities: Radio Workshop, 1948-50; President of Radio Workshop, 1951; Red & White Revue, 1949; Producer and Director of Red & White Revue, 1950; Players' Club, 1948-51; Intramural Sports; Freshman Reception, 1950-51.

William Shatner, McGill University, Class of '52. He graduated with a degree in economics for a career path he had no interest in pursuing. (*Students' Society of McGill University*)

**Bill (top) with William Hutt and Doris Chillcott in a 1952 Canadian Reper-
tory Theatre production of *Castle in the Air*. (*Library and Archives Canada*)**

Bill sporting a shiner in "The Black Eye," a 1954 episode of CBC's *General Motors Theatre* anthology series. (*CBC Still Photo Collection*)

1955: Co-starring on the CBC opposite Basil Rathbone in *Billy Budd*. Rathbone praised Bill's use of "universal English." (*CBC Still Photo Collection*)

Bill and Steve McQueen in *"The Defender,"* a two-part episode of *Studio One* that aired live on CBS in 1957. (*CBS Photo Archive/©CBS/Getty Images*)

Bill and Lee J. Cobb in the *Studio One* episode "No Deadly Medicine." (*CBS Photo Archive/©CBS/Getty Images*)

Goin' Hollywood: As Alexey in *The Brothers Karamazov* with Richard Basehart (Ivan) and Yul Brynner (Dmitri). (*Photofest*)

Bill and France Nuyen on Broadway in *The World of Suzie Wong*. They did not get along. (*Photofest*)

Bill returned often to Canada for television work, including these 1960 CBC appearances on *The Well* (top, opposite future *Star Trek* co-star James Doohan) and in *Julius Caesar*. (*CBC Still Photo Collection/Albert Crookshank and Dale Barnes*)

Sharing a scene with Judy Garland in *Judgment at Nuremberg* (1961). The movie's all-star cast featured Spencer Tracy, Marlene Dietrich and Burt Lancaster but did little to further Bill's movie career. (*Photofest*)

Back on Broadway with Julie Harris and Walter Matthau in *A Shot in the Dark*, which ran for nearly a year and garnered Matthau a Tony Award. Bill's role as Paul Sevigne morphed into Inspector Jacques Clouseau (Peter Sellers) in the 1964 movie adaptation. (*Bettmann/Getty Images*)

Believe him or not: Hysterical Bob Wilson (Bill) and the furry gremlin no one else can see in "Nightmare at 20,000 Feet," the classic episode of Rod Serling's *The Twilight Zone,* which aired in 1963 with co-stars Christine White and Nick Cravat (as the gremlin). (*CBS Photo Archive/©CBS/Getty Images*)

Bill as white supremacist Adam Cramer, stirring up trouble in Roger Corman's critically acclaimed (but little-seen) movie *The Intruder*, shot on location in the Deep South. Leo Gordon (right) co-starred. (*Photofest*)

Bill and Jessica Walter in the short-lived CBS legal series *For the People*. Its cancellation opened the door for Bill to star in the second *Star Trek* pilot. (*CBS Photo Archive*/©*CBS*/*Getty Images*)

You don't say? Bill and Allyson Ames in the 1966 horror movie *Incubus*—inexplicably shot in Esperanto, a language none of the cast or crew understood. (*Photofest*)

The classic *Star Trek* lineup on NBC: Bill, Leonard Nimoy and DeForest Kelley as Capt. James T. Kirk, Spock and Dr. Leonard "Bones" McCoy. (*CBS Photo Archive/©CBS/Getty Images*)

refused to let his acting guard down, despite the show's ratings woes. "Bill was a different kind of actor than Leonard, a different kind of actor than DeForest," noted *Star Trek* director Ralph Senensky. "Bill was glib. Bill just did it, but he did it fine and there were occasions . . . the fine scene he does in 'Metamorphosis' [directed by Senensky], when he's talking with that translator to the cloud and he does a remarkably good job on that scene. When we saw the dailies the next day, Gene Coon, after Bill's take, said, 'That's why we pay him the big money.'"

As *Star Trek* floundered (again) in its new time slot, the writing was on the wall. The show rebounded from "Spock's Brain" and successive episodes were a little better (depending on whom you asked). Season 3 highlights included the interracial kiss between Kirk and Uhura ("Plato's Stepchildren," which aired November 22, 1968) and "The Paradise Syndrome," which aired October 4. In that episode, Kirk spends three months on a planet after his memory is erased. (It's a long story—he now refers to himself as "Kirok.") He falls in love with the beautiful Native American tribal priestess Miramanee (Sabrina Scharf) and they marry. She gets pregnant with Kirk's child but is eventually stoned to death—and dies in Kirk's arms—after the *Enterprise* swoops in to rescue its captain, whose memory is restored by Mr. Spock's Vulcan mind fusion.

It didn't really matter how good or bad *Star Trek*'s episodes were in that third season since no one was watching the show, which was handicapped by its lack of affiliate power. Entering the 1968 television season, NBC had 210 affiliates; of those, only 181 stations aired *Star Trek* (compared to the 222 affiliates and independent stations airing NBC's top-rated show, *Bonanza*).[68] The odds were stacked against the USS *Enterprise*, and in February 1969—a month after *Star Trek* wrapped its seventy-ninth episode—NBC officially cancelled the series. The final episode, "Turnabout Intruder," was moved to 7:30 p.m. and aired on June 3, 1969 (a Tuesday). It was originally slated to air March 28 but was preempted by the death of former president Dwight D. Eisenhower and missed the deadline for a possible Emmy nomination.[69] The *Star Trek* cast and crew threw a farewell party for the show and for themselves. George Takei noted the "faint sound of melancholy" in Shatner's "raucous merriment and loud hilarity" that night.[70]

CHAPTER 7

The Wilderness Years

The cancellation of *Star Trek* left Bill Shatner at a crossroads in his life. Within a three-month period, he'd lost both his marriage and his network television show—and he entered a period of professional and financial uncertainty from which it would take him years to recover.

On the other hand, the end of his marriage, and of *Star Trek*, freed Bill from the constraints of the network publicity machine—and of maintaining the image of the happy husband. He didn't have to play that game anymore. Never the easiest of interview subjects, his attitude grew ornery, sometimes downright hostile, in the years that *Star Trek* was still airing on NBC—particularly when the attention was focused on his personal life. This was apparent in an interview with Bill that ran in the *Los Angeles Times* in May 1968.

His date of birth? "I tell you, sweetheart, that's unimportant." According to the clips he is thirty-seven. One attempts to talk about his early years—and with some diffidence, saying, "If one may ask . . ." "You may not . . . I prefer not to tell you." When did he graduate? "It doesn't matter . . . After I graduated, I did sixty plays in two years." Today the Shatners live in Beverly Hills with their three daughters: Leslie Carol, nine; Lisabeth Mary, six; and Melanie Ann, three. "No, I don't want to talk about my wife or [my kids] at all. They're involved too much at this point."[1]

He was free now to date whomever he pleased without calling undue attention to the state of his marriage or to the network paying his salary. "I took affection anywhere I could find it," he said of that time. "It seemed like there was always someone around who had her own needs to be fulfilled, so lust and romance and passion all began playing a more important role in my life . . . During much of this period I was single, and I certainly had opportunities to be with many women, and I grasped a great many of those opportunities."[2]

Bill's newfound sexual freedom was dampened somewhat by his professional opportunities. While it was liberating to be single and unfettered and partaking in the dating scene, Hollywood is a cruel mistress that does not take kindly to perceived failure. Doors that were opened just months before to William Shatner, Television Star, were quickly closing. Captain Kirk was just another forgettable lead character on a forgettable television show. In the immediate aftermath of the *Star Trek* cancellation, a few small guest-starring roles trickled in for Bill—*The Virginian, Medical Center, The FBI, The Name of the Game*—but it was getting tougher for him to pay the bills and fork over his monthly alimony payments to Gloria.

There was no quick fix for Bill's precarious financial health, and there would be no injection of cash vis-à-vis residuals for any of the *Star Trek* cast when the series was launched into syndication in a handful of markets in 1969—including New York City (on WPIX, in September) and Philadelphia (on WKBS). The money would have helped, but it wasn't until four years later, in 1973, that the Screen Actors Guild—under its president, actor Dennis Weaver (then starring in *McCloud* on NBC)—ensured that its members received residual checks in perpetuity for shows airing in syndication.[3] Bill claimed (perhaps apocryphally) that his financial situation became so bad that he couldn't even cash a check for fifteen dollars. "I was able to put together enough money to make the down payment to buy a little house," he said. "And I furnished it with used furniture and damaged furniture from downtown Los Angeles. I furnished the house I bought for three hundred dollars. With a sofa and a bed that had a torn mattress—that had come from a damaged crate."[4]

As the calendar turned to 1970, Bill, now turning thirty-nine, was virtually homeless—at least when he was on the road acting in local dinner-theater productions and living in the back of his pickup truck. "I had three kids and was totally broke," he said. "I managed to find work back East on the straw-hat circuit—summer stock—but couldn't afford hotels, so I lived out of the back of my truck, under a hard shell. It had a little stove, a toilet, and I'd drive from theater to theater. The only comfort came from my dog, who sat in the passenger seat and gave me perspective on everything. Otherwise, it would have just been me counting my losses."

Bill crisscrossed the country in his pickup truck, starring in locally produced stage productions such as *The Tender Trap* (which included short runs
at the Bergen Mall in Paramus, New Jersey, and at the Westport Country
Playhouse in Connecticut) and *There's a Girl in My Soup* opposite British
actress Jill Haworth. (Stops included the Paper Mill Playhouse in Millburn,
New Jersey, and the Playhouse in the Park in Philadelphia.) "That was
probably the time where he was the most frustrated and the most dejected,"
recalled his daughter, Lisabeth. "It was hard for him to get work because *Star
Trek* had been so iconic. It was hard for people to look at him as an actor
with a lot of facility, which was really what he was."

He also directed; his July 1969 production of *There's a Girl in My Soup*
at the John Drew Theater in East Hampton, New York (on Long Island),
received a "cold, laughter-less opening night reception" according to *Newsday* critic Barbara Delatiner. She spent the next day with Bill as he met
with a group of local (mostly bored) children who didn't know why they
were dragged to an elementary school on a rainy day until "Captain Kirk!"
and "the boss of the *Enterprise*!" walked into the room. "I'm out among the
people for the first time since *Star Trek* success," Bill, wearing "celebrity-
sized sunglasses," told Delatiner afterward. "It's my first summer-stock tour,
and I really can't get over it. The impact of television. Old ladies giggling at
the sight of me. Little girls shaking with fear when they're brought backstage.
It's remarkable." The article noted that Shatner would be on the road for six
more weeks, "and then it's cross-country in his economical camper, in which
he sleeps parked outside the theater."[5]

He chugged along in his truck, joined by his "dumb-as-a-brick" Doberman, Morgan, who disrupted a performance of *Travels with Charley* by
somehow getting into the theater and walking down the center aisle—right
after being sprayed by a skunk.[6] Sometimes the jobs were closer to home,
but the results were the same. In December 1970 he costarred opposite Anne
Francis in a stage production of *Remote Asylum* at the Ahmanson Theatre in
Los Angeles. There were high expectations for the show, which was written
by Mart Crowley, whose first play, *The Boys in the Band*—about a group
of homosexual friends—opened off-Broadway in 1968 and ran for over
one thousand performances. *Remote Asylum*, which took place at a resort in
Mexico, didn't fare as well.

Bill played a tennis star named Tom, and Francis (replacing original
costar Dina Merrill) was Tom's mistress, Dinah, an ex-film actress in danger

of losing her two children to her ex-husband. "William Shatner is lost and out of place, both physically and spiritually, as the tennis player," sniffed one critic, adding: "[He] needed about a week in the steam room before his next match . . . The part appears to have been written for Farley Granger—probably another example of misplaced cinematic influence."[7]

"Imagine Honey West and Captain Kirk as uneasy lovers in a plush retreat in a faraway country, a sort of Mexican Shangri-La with electricity," critic Robert C. Wylder sniped, alluding to names of Bill and Ann Francis's best-known television characters. "Sound interesting? Well, it isn't, really."[8] He fared better in a 1972 dinner-theater production of *The Seven-Year Itch* in suburban Chicago. "Shatner is extremely innocent, even impish . . . he has expertly caught the flavor of the part," a critic noted—before scolding "the inconsiderate people who clink their glasses and talk out loud and cigarette and cigar smokers who litter the air with a blue haze."[9]

Bill wasn't always such a hit with his costars on the dinner-theater circuit, one of whom described him as "toxic" when they appeared together in *The Seven-Year Itch*, which ran for about two weeks at the Pheasant Run Theater in suburban St. Charles, Illinois. She recalled:

> Shatner shouldn't have tried to do comedy because he's not funny and he directed the show, too, and you need to have a sense of humor to do comedy. There was an actor in the cast (Douglas Mellor) who had a drinking problem and he was very nervous . . . and from the moment this poor guy would arrive at the theater, Shatner would be giving him notes and you can't function like that, you have to be free to be able to perform . . . and he was so tied up in knots by these constant notes that he got onstage and he couldn't function. There are certain people who like to feel superior by making other people feel like they can't do their job, and that's what I found with Shatner.

Bill, she said, "came across as a nice guy" when he first arrived.

> I went out to dinner with him the first Monday night—I was very young and naïve and I thought, "Oh, it's a nice thing, you take your leading lady out to dinner." It could have turned into something but I got out of it.
>
> I was also doing a children's theatre production of *The Wizard of Oz* so I'd go out matinee days and bring in a sleeping bag.

There was a couch in the hallway of the dressing rooms and I would take a nap between the two shows and Shatner would come in and bother me. It was harassment. I didn't know the word then. He'd kind of say "come on" and I said, "Please, somebody might come," and he said, "Yeah, you might."

There was another girl in the cast just out of acting school and playing a small role. On the second day of rehearsal she came in and said, "Last night, Bill made me your understudy," and the next day she came in and said, "Bill made me assistant director." You kind of roll your eyes at that.

She recalled that the actress playing Bill's wife in that production of *The Seven-Year Itch* had to carefully orchestrate her movement onstage, because "every time her hand got up toward the toupee, it was kind of crazy—he would kind of work her arms down."[10]

"I took jobs—unbelievable jobs," Bill recalled of those days. "I took jobs for two hundred fifty dollars that took me out someplace to . . . I did everything. I did some game shows that were demeaning. I went places, did things, night after night—I'd travel—two or three jobs in one day, if I could—just to make money to get this thing together again. I became frantic, obsessed."[11]

He talked about being "insane, the way an animal is insane," during this time, having lost his wife, his family, and his television show. He wasn't suicidal, he said, but he met people and embarked on relationships with women in the early 1970s that he blocked out in his emotional fog. "People come up to me—I see people I met then and knew, in fact I had a whole relationship with them, with a beginning, a middle, and an end, and those relationships, those people—I see them now and I don't *remember* them," he said. "I don't remember what I did. I don't remember what I felt . . . I was scrambling, clawing to get everything back and put it together again."[12]

His frenzied work schedule didn't help him escape the shadow of Captain Kirk in what he called his "lowest ebb" as an actor. "Typecasting became the real hero," he said. "The bad part was being identified with the role continually."[13] The constant traveling impacted his relationship with his three daughters, who wouldn't see him for long stretches at a time. "He was gone like the whole summer, almost, and I remember when he returned, I'd gotten so used to not seeing him we had to kind of reestablish our relationship again," Leslie said. "That was a difficult time."[14]

Bill wasn't winning many new fans back in Canada, either. "American show biz (not as mild as Canadian) does funny things to people and it has certainly worked its evil wonders on Montreal's own," John P. Hardy noted in a 1971 interview with Bill in the *Montreal Gazette*. "Shatner may smirk at the cliché, but he carries himself and seems to enjoy being a personality . . . perhaps it twists the abused adage to conclude that 'stardom is in the eyes of the beholder.'"[15] The article noted, as an afterthought, that Bill Shatner would be seen more on Canadian television screens in a few months: *Star Trek* was making its debut in syndication on Montreal's CFCF-TV.

It didn't help that his television appearances were, for the most part, undistinguished and forgettable. The *New York Times* criticized his "unenthusiastic" performance opposite "an overworked" Elizabeth Ashley in the NBC movie *The Skirts of Happy Chance*, and he took a shot at NBC's cancellation of *Star Trek* in an interview about the movie with the *New York Daily News*: "What would be amusing to me is if the reruns of the series, which are being slotted in Jerry Lewis's Tuesday night 7:30 time period on the network, would wind up pulling down big ratings. Imagine how the NBC executives would feel once they've cancelled the show and dismantled the sets."[16] He didn't realize at the time the prescience of that scenario.

He fared better in *Shadow Game*, a *CBS Playhouse* presentation about the cutthroat world of advertising, which aired in May 1969 and was written by Loring Mandel, one of the shining lights of TV's "Golden Age" in the 1950s. While the *New York Times* singled out star Daniel Massey's "warmly intelligent performance as the one decent young executive in this advertising zoo," it noted that "he is overshadowed by the gritty, stinging performances of William Shatner as the glandular and brutal Peter Hoyt, a man for whom betrayal is the most intriguing game of all."[17]

There were some bright spots amid the professional gloom. In 1970, he was cast opposite Cameron Mitchell, Jack Cassidy, Martin Sheen, Richard Basehart, and Buddy Ebsen in *The Andersonville Trial*, a television adaptation of the hit 1959 Broadway drama. Directed by George C. Scott, it told the story of the 1865 war-crimes trial of Henry Wirz (Basehart), who commanded the notorious Confederate POW camp in Andersonville, Georgia. Bill played Chief JAG Prosecutor Norton Parker Chipman (the role George C. Scott played in the Broadway production). "William Shatner as the Judge Advocate, and Jack Cassidy as the civilian defense attorney, found mutuality of doubt over the proceedings," the *New York Times* opined in its review of the special.[18]

The Andersonville Trial aired on PBS in May and went on to win three Emmy Awards for "Outstanding Single Program," for technical direction and camera work and for writer Saul Levitt's adaptation. It also earned a Peabody Award for its "mounting tension and, ultimately, a numbing impact. This extraordinary production . . . probed deeply into man's continuing dilemma of the conflict between duty and conscience."[19]

* * *

The Andersonville Trial had an even bigger impact on Bill Shatner's life.

He met Marcy Lafferty during rehearsals for the PBS production. Marcy, a twenty-four-year-old actress, had been hired by director George C. Scott as a production assistant to help the cast rehearse their lines. "Apparently I was the only member of the cast who took advantage of her—to rehearse my lines," Bill later joked.[20] They grew close and began a romantic relationship, despite their fifteen-year age difference, though it took him two weeks to call her after filming on the show ended. "I fell for him, hook, line, and sinker," Marcy said. "Bill had just been through a terrible divorce and a folded series. He didn't want to get involved. But I hung in there and wormed my way into his heart."[21] Marcy was no stranger to show business; her father, Perry Lafferty, had worked in radio since the 1940s as a producer and director and was married to radio actress Frances Carden. In 1965, he was hired by CBS as its West Coast programming president and oversaw hits including *All in the Family*, *M*A*S*H*, *The Mary Tyler Moore Show*, and *Maude* before moving to a similar job at NBC in 1976.

Marcy graduated from the University of Southern California and pursued an acting career. She landed small roles on television series, including *Hawaii Five-O*, *Dan August*, *The New People*, and *Medical Center*. She also acted on the stage; in February 1967, she was mentioned, by name, in a *New York Times* review of *A Coney Island of the Mind*, a collection of works by poet Lawrence Ferlinghetti that was hammered into a television production by NBC's Los Angeles affiliate, KNBC. (It aired on WNBC in New York City.) The production featured actors, including Marcy, from USC's School of the Performing Arts "and underscored how television working in conjunction with an outstanding university drama school has an exciting role to play in publicizing and encouraging new artists."[22]

Marcy admitted to having a "schoolgirl crush" on Bill after they met on the set of *The Andersonville Trial* and their relationship slowly unfolded. "It's really not one of your great romantic beginnings, because he was going with someone else at the time," she said. "It was a pretty low time in my life. It was about two weeks after the show, and I had really given up hope he would call—and then the phone rang." She noted a sadness and a bitterness in Bill that seemed to lift when he talked about his children. "I just turned to jelly," she said after their first kiss, shared over a hamburger. "As they say in all those terrible books, my knees buckled, and I couldn't think of a thing to say."[23]

Marcy thought her new boyfriend was selling himself short by saying yes to nearly every role that was offered to him and accepting those jobs at a discounted rate. "He had children to support, houses to support," she said. "And he didn't do what so many actors have done after a series—in fact— price himself too high. He couldn't say no. He literally could not afford to."[24] Marcy got along famously with Bill's daughters—Melanie called her "the most beautiful, perfect caretaker imaginable"[25]—and she often joined Bill and the girls on their weekend jaunts to the ski slopes or to the woods on camping expeditions.

Bill was still a fairly marketable commodity as a veteran, dependable actor who could be hired for an episode or two, learn his lines, and nail the role. Following his costarring turn on *The Andersonville Trial*, the television floodgates opened once again—provided his appearances were one-offs or short-lived guest-starring roles: *Men at Law*, *The Sixth Sense*, *Hawaii Five-O*, *Mission Impossible* (two episodes in 1971 and '72), *Marcus Welby, M.D.*, *Owen Marshall, Counselor at Law*, *The Bold Ones: The New Doctors*, *Kung Fu*, *Barnaby Jones*, *Mannix*, *The Six Million Dollar Man*, *Ironside* (four episodes) . . . the list goes on. He showed up on time, did his best with the material given to him, and left—in some cases jumping from one series to another within a matter of days.

There were television movies, too, including *The Horror at 37,000 Feet* (1973). "Terrible doesn't begin to express how truly awful some of those movies were," he said. "I knew what they were; the reality is when you open a script entitled *The Horror at 37,000 Feet* you can be certain you're never going to hear those magic words, 'The nominees for Best Picture . . .'"[26] In 1973, he spent twelve days in Tampa, Florida, filming his role as grifter/ serial killer Matt Stone, who preys on elderly women, in the low-budget (read: schlocky) big-screen movie *Impulse* (originally titled *Want a Ride, Little Girl?*).

Bill broke a finger during the filming of *Impulse* in a scene gone wrong, in which Matt Stone tries to hang Karate Pete, played by Harold Sakata, the actor best-known as "Odd Job" from the James Bond movie *Goldfinger*. Sakata almost died because the rope was too tight; he was saved by a quick-thinking crew member—and by Bill, who broke his finger trying to support Sakata's substantial girth. Marcy had a small role in the movie as a hotel clerk. "I've forgotten why I was in it," Bill said later. "I probably needed the money. It was a very bad time for me. I hope they burn it." *Impulse* went on to gross $4 million.

He started appearing in commercials to help pay the bills. In 1974, he was hired as the spokesman for Promise Margarine and starred in a series of ads. ("Promise tastes like butter," he'd say, holding up his hand in a Spock-like gesture, "Promise.") He shot a series of television commercials in Canada for Loblaw's, the country's biggest grocery chain. ("Don't get left out in the cold, come on in and stock up that freezer!") "The money is very good, and I think the commercials are very good," he said, noting that John Wayne, Lucille Ball, and Arthur Godfrey had all appeared in commercials. "It's all part of the total picture surviving in the business today."[27]

*   *   *

William Shatner's role as white supremacist Adam Cramer in Roger Corman's 1962 movie *The Intruder* was one of his biggest triumphs (and his best acting) in the years leading up to *Star Trek*.

In 1974, hoping, perhaps, to reclaim some of his big-screen mojo, Bill reunited with Corman on *Big Bad Mama*, a cheesy, Depression-era shoot-'em-up action flick starring Angie Dickinson as Wilma McClatchy, who takes over her lover's bootlegging business in Texas after he dies and embarks on a crime spree with her two comely daughters, Polly (Robbie Lee) and Billy Jean (Susan Sennett). Wilma falls in love with bank robber Fred Diller (Tom Skerritt), who joins her gang; Bill played William J. Baxter, a dishonest gambler who beds Wilma and tangles with Diller.

All of the Roger Corman calling cards were on full display in the movie: soft-core sex, nudity, and plenty of cleavage. Bill's sex scene with Angie Dickinson was uncomfortable in more ways than one. (She bared all, he didn't.) They'd worked together shortly before filming *Big Bad Mama* on the ABC television movie *Pray for the Wildcats*, in which Bill played Warren Summerfield, a disgruntled advertising executive who's forced by sociopathic executive Sam Farragut (Andy Griffith) to take a dangerous dirt bike trip to Baja, California, in order to compete for Farragut's business. He's joined by colleagues Paul McIlvain (Robert Reed) and Terry Maxon (Marjoe Gortner); Dickinson played Paul McIlvain's wife, Nancy, who's having an affair with Summerfield. She and Bill "got along great" during the filming of *Pray for the Wildcats*, she said.

> We were very attracted to one another—not necessarily [in a] sexual [way] but we just got along great. . . . So, then a couple of years later, *Big Bad Mama* comes up and I remember saying to [director] Steve Carver on our first meeting, "Do we have to do all that nude stuff?" And he said, "Yeah." Because I really think if they took three things out of that movie, one being Tom Skerritt with the young rich girl, one where he's chasing my two girls and they're all going to sleep together and the one of Shatner and me making stupid love with the camera—oh God, it's just so embarrassing, awful, and stupid . . . it's a total ripoff of *Bonnie and Clyde*. They even used the same getaway car—and yet, it's a very good movie.[28]

Big Bad Mama was shot over twenty-one days on a Roger Corman-like budget of under $750,000; Bill arrived on the set on the eleventh day of production, eventually clashing with costar Tom Skerritt and irritating several other cast members while shooting his scenes with them. "We had readings of the script and Bill was in Canada or somewhere where he wasn't available, and this is one of the problems that I think created the animosity on the set," said director Steve Carver. "He wasn't there for the reading, and when he showed up on the set, he was basically an outsider to the camaraderie that we created on those first ten days of shooting between Tom and Angie and the girls [Robbie Lee and Susan Sennett].

"Bill had developed that technique of talking during shots, and actually, if he was off-camera in some of the close-ups, he talked to the actors," Carver said. "So, when you're rolling the camera, if he flubs a line, rather than cut the camera and do another take he says, 'Keep rolling.' And it infuriates actors because then they have redo everything and rekindle the whole thing. They didn't like that . . . And his whole approach was very irritating and frustrating to a lot of the actors, because he would talk during the take as if the camera wasn't rolling. It created a little tension."[29]

Carver also noticed some bad blood between Skerritt and Shatner, which escalated as the shoot progressed and tempers flared. "I noticed something was going on between Tom and Bill. I thought it was part of the characterizations at first, where there's an animosity because that's what's written into the script, and these guys [Diller and Baxter] don't like each other," he said. "But off-camera they didn't like each other. I noticed this and words were said."

The situation between the two actors came to a head four days later in a scene shot at a racetrack. "That's when it all blew up," Carver said.

> That's when the physical fights happened. We were in this car, and Bill was supposed to stay in the car while Tom and Angie and the girls go into the racetrack office to rob it. And Tom gets up out of the back seat, Bill is sitting in the passenger seat, and his elbow purposely hits Bill's hat and knocks his wig askew while the camera is rolling. Bill jumps out of the car, tackles Tom to the ground, and they're wrestling and throwing punches and the whole crew is in shock and I jump in there and I try to pull them apart. Here's these two guys just beating the hell out of each other. From then on it was a war. They were not pulling punches as far as the dialogue was concerned, as far as their physical nature, their attitude, their body language. Everything was real. There was no love between them.[30]

Bill's relationship with Skerritt was awkward enough, but the atmosphere on the set of *Big Bad Mama* grew downright strange when it came time for Bill to shoot his sex scene with Angie Dickinson. "Steve Carver should be hung by the balls for that," Dickinson said nearly forty-five years later. "It was just the worst scene in the world from all points of view. It ruined sex for everyone, ever."[31]

According to Carver's recollections, Bill wanted to film the scene a certain way, much to Dickinson's chagrin. "He told Angie what he wanted to do [in the love scene] and Angie said, 'No way,' I'm not doing that,'" Carver said. "I remember to this day [during the scene] he would wet his fingers and run them on her shoulder or back or wherever and she hated that. She said no. And she would try to coax him into something that was more subtle.

One would call it erotic, but to me it was kinky. So in any case the love scenes were awkward." .

Dickinson, who was six months younger than Shatner, was topless during their bedroom scene; Bill, for reasons known only to him, took a more modest approach. Initially, he walked onto the set wearing only his underwear, much to Dickinson's amusement. Carver told Bill that his underwear would be visible on camera and would ruin the shot and asked him to remove his skivvies. "I tried to talk around it a little bit. I was even embarrassed a little. I don't know how to talk to guys about being nude," Carver said. He said, 'I'll use a little tape.'" According to Carver, Bill disappeared into the makeup room—and reappeared a few minutes later wearing thick gaffer's tape over his private parts. "He used the heavy-duty stuff," he said.

> He came in with all this silver tape on him and boy, it looked like it hurt, you know, just to put it on, let alone take it off.
> So Angie made another joke or said something, and he got real pissed off and he started ripping [the tape] off. I was just cringing from watching that. But then he demanded everyone leave the set and Angie said, "No, I want everybody on the set. Don't go." So, we compromised, and we got most of the people off [the set] and we shot the scene. I tried to make Bill feel comfortable, telling him exactly how we were shooting it. We were shooting it waist up and we weren't shooting full masters and we were lighting it subtly. We weren't doing any pornography, although with Roger it was, "Shoot as many breast shots as possible."[32,33]

Big Bad Mama was the last time Carver worked with Bill Shatner, and he remembers him fondly—despite the Shatner–Skerritt contretemps and Bill's awkward sex scene with Angie Dickinson. "I had no problems with him," he said. "We had a lot in common as far as religion and background . . . I would sit down with him over lunch and chat. He would tell me about stuff. I would talk to him about *Star Trek*, and he was very pleasant. I thought he was a really good guy."[34]

The movie opened to scathing reviews. "*Big Bad Mama* is mostly rehashed *Bonnie and Clyde*, with a bit more blood and Angie Dickinson taking off her clothes for sex scenes with the crooks in her life," *Variety* sniped. But through the years it has achieved a cult-like status and even inspired a 1987 sequel, *Big Bad Mama II*, once again produced by Roger Corman (Jim Wynorski directed) and once again starring Angie Dickinson as Wilma

McClatchie. Dickinson, though, never worked with Bill again. "I have read about him and I've watched him and everything else," she said. "He is a difficult man. There is no real explanation. But he is difficult. I don't want to say he's not a pushover, because that's not what I mean, but he brings difficulty to the room. I admire him tremendously and he's had quite a career and he's a real icon, but I think it's the Aries in him—he's got that power that they can carry. He's not an easy fella to have fun with."[35]

*   *   *

Bill's romance with Marcy Lafferty culminated in a marriage proposal, and they were wed in Brentwood, California, on October 20, 1973, in the home of Marcy's father, Perry Lafferty. Bill went public with the wedding four days later. "I was perfectly happy with the way things were for a long time," Marcy said. "He made me happy. It wasn't ideal, but nothing is. I had no grand marriage scheme—there just came a time that I didn't feel I could continue to give so much of myself if he didn't share deep-laid feelings."[36] Bill was forty-two and Marcy was twenty-seven; she was fine knowing that he didn't want to have any more children. She shared her new husband's love of horses and Doberman Pinschers and she continued to act sporadically, snaring small roles in television series (*The Sandy Duncan Show*, *The FBI*) and in television movies (*Tell Me Where It Hurts*, *Coffee, Tea or Me?*). Bill and Marcy eventually bought a ranch house on McConnell Drive in the Hillcrest area of Los Angeles, south of Beverly Hills.

*   *   *

A funny thing happened to *Star Trek* on its way to the television graveyard: it became an unexpected hit in syndication.

The series that most American television viewers didn't care about the first time around was finding a second life in reruns that began airing on local stations in the fall of 1969, mostly as cheap filler for the stations' late-night or early-evening time slots. Before too long, the number crunchers at those stations, including WPIX in New York City and KTVU in San Francisco, discovered that a surprising number of people were tuning into the repeats— and that *Star Trek* was finding the audience in local markets that had proven elusive during its original run on NBC. "*Star Trek* did great on independent stations at eleven o'clock at night, because it ran against the news," said Richard Block, the vice president and general manager of Kaiser Broadcasting Corp., which was syndicating the series in the early 1970s. "The news skews old, and *Star Trek* got younger viewers."[37]

There were several theories for this resurgence. One was the show's underlying message of diversity and acceptance, of peace and love in Gene Roddenberry's "Can't we all just get along?" vision of humanity. Then there was Bill Shatner/Captain Kirk's ham-fisted, staccato delivery . . . Of. His. Lines. Or Leonard Nimoy's King of Cool Mr. Spock. Or Dr. "Bones" McCoy's (DeForest Kelley) self-righteous exclamations ("I'm a doctor, not a flesh peddler!" "I'm a doctor, not a scientist!"—it's a long list) or his most-quoted line: "He's dead, Jim." Maybe it was James Doohan's cranky chief engineer, Montgomery "Scotty" Scott ("I've given her all she's got captain, and I can't give her no more!"). As the *Star Trek* reruns caught on, "Beam me up, Scotty" crept into the nation's parlance—a jokey reference to situations gone awry or awkward. Others found the show's cheesy, low-budget special effects particularly intriguing.

"I think the thing people dug was that *Star Trek* was one show that was optimistic about the future," Roddenberry said in 1972 about the show's resurgence. "The series constantly asked, is this good, is this bad, is this beautiful? *Star Trek* emphasized that we shouldn't interfere in the lives of other people. Maybe the kids saw something about Vietnam in that."[38]

"We never had a gigantic audience [and we] were never one of the top ten shows," Nimoy recalled. "What we had was a very dedicated and vocal audience, smaller than what we would have hoped for but an intense audience . . . that really, really cared about the show a lot."[39]

Star Trek also had Bill Shatner's unique acting style—at turns hammy, overblown, understated, combative, and sensitive. A young Jason Alexander, later to star as Jerry Seinfeld's obnoxious friend George Costanza on NBC's acclaimed series *Seinfeld*—considered by many to be the best sitcom in television history—cited William Shatner as the biggest influence on him as an actor. (They became chummy in later years, and Alexander served as Roastmaster for Shatner's Comedy Central roast in 1986.)

"I know it sounds like a joke. I became an actor because I wanted to be William Shatner commanding the *Enterprise*," Alexander said. "And before I had any training or lessons or anything, I would basically do William Shatner. I just thought if you . . . broke . . . sentences . . . down, that you could play any . . . role," he said, imitating Captain Kirk. "It worked for many years. I did Shakespeare as William Shatner. I once played Nathan Detroit in *Guys and Dolls* as William Shatner. Who knew? I thought that was great acting."[40]

The first *Star Trek* convention, *Star Trek Con*, was held in the Newark (New Jersey) Public Library on March 1, 1969, while the original series was in its death throes on NBC. It was organized by superfans Shema Comerford and Devra Langsam, who coedited *Spockinalia*, the show's original fanzine, which appeared during the show's inaugural season. *Star Trek Con* was free and was reportedly attended by over three hundred people. Langsam, in the grassroots pop-culture groundswell following the show's cancellation, also helped to organize *Star Trek Lives!*, which was held at the Statler Hilton in New York City from January 21 to 23, 1972—and, this time, featured celebrity guests, including *Star Trek* creator Gene Roddenberry, costar Majel Barrett (who'd married Roddenberry in 1969), series writer D. C. Fontana, Isaac Asimov, and noted science fiction writer Hal Clement. *Star Trek Lives!* was attended by over four thousand people and proved so successful that four more iterations of the convention were held in New York City, one each year through 1976. Guests included Leonard Nimoy, George Takei, Nichelle Nichols, and Captain Kirk himself (in 1975).

The *Star Trek* revival started to pick up steam as the series was syndicated to more and more local television stations in the United States (125 stations by the spring of 1972) and was sold to sixty foreign countries. Students attending Emerson College in Boston during the 1971–72 academic year could attend screenings of *Star Trek* at graduate seminars, while other colleges and high schools around the country followed suit. "A few hospitals show certain episodes to mental patients," an Associated Press story noted in April 1972.[41] There were community theaters staging *Star Trek*-inspired plays, and over one hundred privately published fan magazines devoted to the series sprung up nationwide. "Fans write episodes, poetry, and music," one report noted. "One fan created a Vulcan musical scale, a Vulcan book of songs, and a Vulcan dictionary."[42]

In February 1973, the *Star Trek Lives!* convention attracted over seven thousand people (each paying a five-dollar admission fee) and featured twenty-five stalls selling everything from *Star Trek* play money to fortune-telling equipment to a twenty-five-foot-wide replica of the USS *Enterprise*. The press started comparing the fervor of the newly minted "Trekkies" or "Trekkers" (both terms were used) and their devotion to all things *Star Trek* to the hysteria of Beatlemania in the 1960s. "We're into what you could call speculative reality," said a twenty-four-year-old Hunter College psychology major attending the second *Star Trek Lives!* convention. "If you feel the world outside is too constraining, this is a way to remove the restrictions of here and now." Earlier that year, *Star Trek* was voted the most popular series among viewers aged fourteen to eighteen . . . in West Germany.[43]

* * *

Star Trek's growing postmortem popularity in the early to mid-seventies did little to impact Bill Shatner's career. The residuals, which eventually rolled in, helped a bit, but he was having a tough time escaping the long shadow of the USS *Enterprise.* If anything, the *Star Trek* resurgence and the series reruns airing worldwide only underscored the Shatner-as-Kirk connection in the minds of the public and Hollywood executives (as it did for Leonard Nimoy as Mr. Spock and, to a lesser extent, the supporting cast members). "There are Trekkies, kind of spaced-out groupies who follow me wherever I'm doing a play in summer stock," he said at the time. "They want to know all about the show but everything I can remember has been distilled into one long hiccup."[44]

Star Trek's rebirth in syndication did, however, reteam Bill with Nimoy, DeForest Kelley, Nichelle Nichols, George Takei, and James Doohan when *Star Trek: The Animated Series* launched on Saturday mornings in the fall of 1973 on NBC.

(Walter Koenig's Pavel Chekov was missing from the cartoon version; the role was cut for budgetary reasons, but Koenig was assuaged by the offer to write an episode for the series, "The Infinite Vulcan," which aired in Season 1.)

The Animated Series hewed as closely to the live-action original as possible; in addition to Shatner et al. voicing their *Star Trek* characters, it brought back several of the show's original writers, including D. C. Fontana, David Gerrold, and veteran *Star Trek* director Marc Daniels. "The joy was in the fact that we didn't have to worry about where the zipper was on the costumes," said Fontana, who was an executive producer (along with Roddenberry). "We could do what we couldn't do on the live-action show . . . we did not talk down to our audience and we did not write down to our audience. We were doing *Star Trek.*"[45]

What *was* different about the Saturday-morning cartoon version was that Shatner and company recorded their parts separately, which was standard operating procedure for an animated series. Shatner called it "the strangest form of acting" he'd ever done; he would record his lines—usually in the nearest bathroom—on whichever movie or television set he happened to be working at the time ("Apparently the acoustics in a bathroom are particularly good," he said).[46] The series' animation was crude by today's standards—"It was limited in motion and [in some character] expression," Fontana said—but its writing, and the cast's commitment to the series and to their characters, appeased the majority of the show's fan base. "NBC's new animated *Star Trek* is as out of place in the Saturday morning kiddie ghetto as a Mercedes in a soapbox derby," noted the *Los Angeles Times*. "It is fascinating fare, written, produced, and executed with all the imaginative skill . . . that made Gene Rodenberry's famous old science fiction epic the most avidly followed program in TV history."[47]

Star Trek: The Animated Series aired a total of twenty-two episodes through mid-October 1974. Perhaps its most notable achievement was revealing that the "T" in James T. Kirk stood for "Tiberius" (in an episode written by Gerrold).

As Bill Shatner approached his mid-forties, the slog of the mind-numbing guest-starring roles continued apace, offset by the occasional movie or game show appearance (sometimes with Marcy in tow). *Petrocelli, Kodiak, Police Surgeon* (two episodes), *Police Story, Amy Prentiss* (starring his *For the People* costar Jessica Walter), *Police Woman* (headlined by his *Big Bad Mama* lover Angie Dickinson), *The Rookies* . . . they all seemed to blend together into one indistinguishable mass.

In 1974 and '75, Bill and Marcy appeared on a handful of episodes of *Tattletales* ("The game of celebrity gossip!"), a CBS daytime television game show hosted by Bert Convy, in which celebrity couples—one better half on camera and the other backstage (wearing large headphones)—answered personal questions about each other. (The Shatners competed against the likes of *Kojak* star Kevin Dobson, Phyllis Diller, Elke Sommer, Orson Bean, George Hamilton, and Scoey Mitchell, all joined by their spouses.) Bill retained his Canadian citizenship, just in case the Mother Country came calling with an opportunity. "But it hasn't," he said. "It's as if my country doesn't want me."[48]

His movie career was also flatlining—with one notable exception (for all the wrong reasons). In late 1974, Bill flew to Mexico to start shooting on *The Devil's Rain*, directed by B-movie horror maven Robert Fuest, best known for directing Vincent Price in the 1971 underground classic *The Abominable Dr. Phibes*. Bill's costars on *The Devil's Rain* included Ernest Borgnine, Eddie Albert, frenemy Tom Skerritt, Ida Lupino, Keenan Wynn, Joan Prather, and future *Welcome Back, Kotter* star John Travolta, making his big-screen debut at the age of twenty. The movie's technical advisor was Anton LaVey, founder of the Church of Satan. He had a small onscreen role as (what else?) the High Priest of the Church of Satan. (The film's tagline: "The 300-year search for the power to damn mankind is over—and the towering of a devil on earth is now unleashed!")

Bill played Mark Preston, whose family is cursed after betraying the Satanic priest Jonathan Corbis (Borgnine). Corbis has harassed the Preston family for decades regarding a Satanic book that holds great power. Ida Lupino played Mark's mother, Emma; Skerritt and Prather played Mark's older brother, Tom, and his wife, Julie, who search for Mark while he battles the evil, shape-shifting Corbis (who takes the form of a goat-like demon). Travolta played Danny, one of Corbis's minions. In the canon of unverifiable pop-culture lore, Travolta is said to have been exposed for the first time to the Church of Scientology, by Joan Prather, while filming *The Devil's Rain*. The movie opened in August 1975 to poor reviews; Roger Ebert, writing in the *Chicago Sun-Times*, called it "painfully dull," while the *New York Times* branded it "as horrible as watching an egg fry."[49]

But *The Devil's Rain* lived on and achieved a modicum of notoriety among hard-core horror fans (and trivia buffs). Following the release of John Carpenter's 1978 big-screen horror classic *Halloween*, it was revealed that the creepy mask worn by the movie's serial killer, Michael Myers, was produced from a mold of William Shatner's face taken during the production of *The Devil's Rain* (for use as a special effect in a scene where Mark Preston's face melts away). The mask was made by Don Post Studios and was purchased by the *Halloween* production team from a magic shop on Hollywood Boulevard and then spray-painted white. It was donned by actor Nick Castle for his scenes playing the knife-wielding maniac Michael Myers.

*   *   *

After six years in the television wilderness, Bill finally got the chance to star in another series when he was offered *Barbary Coast*, a hybrid of *The Wild, Wild West* and *Mission Impossible* that first aired in May 1975 as a two-hour *ABC Sunday Night Movie* directed by actor Bill Bixby and starring Bill and Dennis Cole in the lead roles. Viewership for the movie was promising, and ABC rubber-stamped *Barbary Coast* as a weekly series set to premiere on its fall schedule. Cole was replaced by veteran television actor Doug McClure, with whom Bill had worked ten years earlier on an episode of McClure's NBC series, *The Virginian*. McClure, appearing on his sixth series, hadn't seen the *Barbary Coast* pilot. He won the role after calling his friend, series creator Douglas Heyes, to say hello—and Heyes hired him for the series. He also hired several writers from *Mission: Impossible*, including Harold Livingston, who later wrote *Star Trek: The Motion Picture*.

Bill adopted a number of quick-change disguises for his role as 1870s government agent Jeff Cable, who teams with con man/gambler Cash Conover (McClure). Conover owns the Golden Gate Casino, located in San Francisco's rough-and-tumble red-light Barbary Coast district, and together Jeff and Cash tangle with criminals and foreign spies, often in a light-hearted vein; McClure said Heyes et al. tried to tone him down because, he claimed, "I can go too far. If it goes overboard, it's not funny."[50]

The series was created by veteran television producer/director Douglas Heyes, who hired several writers from *Mission: Impossible*, including Harold Livingston, to write scripts for *Barbary Coast*.

Filming on the series, originally called *Cash & Cable*, started in the summer of 1975. Bill got off to an inauspicious start on his new series when he broke the tibia and fibula in his right leg while filming a scene on a muddy, slippery street and the "falling horse" (a horse trained to take a spill) on which he was riding took a spill and landed on him. The horse was uninjured, but Bill needed a fiberglass cast on his leg and was unable to work for several weeks. (The fiberglass cast broke several times, delaying production even further.)

In the run-up to the show's September 8 premiere on ABC, Bill downplayed comparisons between *Barbary Coast* and *The Wild, Wild West* and also the show's violence, or lack thereof, which was an offshoot of its 8 p.m. time slot—the so-called "family hour" in prime time. "I wear a hell of a lot of disguises," he said. "I pose as an organ grinder in one story, an Oriental in another and you name it."[51] He managed to wrangle a role for his wife;

Marcy appeared as "Tranquility Smith" in the episode entitled "The Ballad of Redwing Jail."

Jeff Cable's clever disguises didn't help *Barbary Coast* attract a sizable viewership, nor did ABC's decision to schedule the series opposite two CBS spinoffs from *The Mary Tyler Moore Show*: Valerie Harper's hit sitcom *Rhoda,* starting its second season, and *Phyllis* (starring Cloris Leachman), which premiered that fall and found an instant audience. "*Barbary Coast* is half adventure, half spoof, and all complicated," *TV Guide* noted in its review. "The plots are so involved that it takes someone with nothing else on his mind to understand them. If there's anything that makes a spoof go poof, it's not knowing what's going on—before they start making fun of it." The relationship between Jeff Cable and Cash Conover didn't work because it was "too vague," noted the *Los Angeles Herald-Examiner* critic.

The *New York Times* ripped the show and its "two man-boys, the types who will spend the rest of their lives joshing one another with undisguised love and admiration" and disdained its production values: "*Barbary Coast* is the type of program in which, when bagpipes are playing in an adjacent room, a character goes to the doorway, pulls some heavy curtains across it, and the sounds of the bagpipes are totally silenced." Bill and Doug McClure were spared the paper's critical wrath.

The ratings for *Barbary Coast* were bad, and before too long, television veteran Cy Chermak (*The Virginian, Ironside, Kolchak: The Night Stalker*) was brought on board as the show's executive producer. "I assumed they wanted me to try to save the show," he said. "Comedy Westerns never worked well. I invented a watchword logo, 'Good, clean, dirty fun.' We never used it. I soon realized that they didn't want a [show] doctor, they wanted hospice care. They kept cutting back on the budget and soon the show was cancelled."[52] Still, not all was lost: one of the supporting players who appeared on *Barbary Coast* was a twenty-six-year-old actor named Leslie Moonves. "That was my first role where I delivered a telegram to William Shatner and literally said, 'This is your telegram, sir.' He gives me a tip and I leave and that's how I got my Screen Actors Guild Card," Moonves recalled. "He was very nice. You remember when you're a young actor the guys who are very nice to you." Moonves's acting career stalled, but he found enormous success in other areas of television, eventually rising to Chairman and CEO of CBS where, thirty-five years later, Bill would star in the short-lived sitcom *$#*! My Dad Says.*[53]

ABC pulled the plug on *Barbary Coast* in late 1975, and its final episode aired on January 9, 1976. ABC eventually replaced the series with the sitcoms *On the Rocks* and *Good Heavens* (the latter starring Carl Reiner). It would take Bill seven years to return to television as the star of another series.

In a way, though, shooting *Barbary Coast* on the Paramount lot turned out to be fortuitous for Bill since he had the chance to revisit the sound stages and sets that had been his home while shooting *Star Trek*. As he was walking around the studio one day, he heard the *clackety-clack-clack* of typewriter keys and, following the sound, he discovered Gene Roddenberry in his office, sitting in a corner and pecking away at his typewriter.

He told Bill that he was working on a *Star Trek* movie.[54]

CHAPTER 8

Fanning the Flames

The previous year, Bill attended two dueling *Star Trek* fan conventions in New York City in January and February 1975, marking his first organized interaction with fans since the show's cancellation. "I vaguely knew these conventions were taking place, but I really didn't want anything to do with them," he said. "That was my past, I'd done that."[1] Or not. With the series' rebirth in reruns, and with Gene Roddenberry talking about a new *Star Trek* project, Bill was taking baby steps toward accepting that—at least in the pop-culture universe—he was inexorably linked to Captain James T. Kirk.

In his first appearance at a *Star Trek* industry event, Bill visited Al Schuster's International Star Trek Convention at the Hotel Americana in January 1975, where he was joined by James Doohan and Walter Koenig and science fiction writers Isaac Asimov, Harlan Ellison (who'd written the *Star Trek* episode "The City on the Edge of Forever"), and Hal Clement. Bill walked onstage and was greeted with "thunderous applause" and proceeded to engage the audience in a question-and-answer session. He showed up a month later at Devra Langsam's renamed Star Trek Convention at the Commodore Hotel with other guests including George Takei, Gene Roddenberry, Majel Barrett, and Isaac Asimov. The crowd there was estimated at eight thousand (very enthusiastic) people. Roddenberry told the audience that Paramount was seriously considering a big-screen *Star Trek* movie, and Shatner once again answered questions from the audience, including this exchange:

> Fan: "In the episode 'A Piece of the Action' when you played the game 'Fizzbin,' did you ad-lib it, or was it written beforehand?"
> Shatner: "'A Piece of the Action?'"

Fan: "The Chicago gangster thing."

Shatner: "Oh, the Chicago gangster thing. I . . . only remember these things by the girls in them—why didn't you tell me which girl was in it?" (laughter)

Fan: "Because there wasn't any in it!" (cheers and applause)

Shatner: "There was no girl in it? No wonder I can't remember!"[2]

Thom Anderson, one of the event's organizers, noted that there was a "sexually charged" atmosphere when Bill appeared onstage; he also said that Leonard Nimoy, in his appearances at *Star Trek* conventions, was treated like "the Pope," with rapt Trekkies hanging on his every word.

All the attention and interest that was showered upon Bill by the rabid *Star Trek* fans, in those first few public appearances, gave him an idea: why not take his act out on the road? The cancellation of *Barbary Coast* freed up his schedule, and in early 1976 he embarked on a whirlwind one-man lecture tour—forty-five college campuses in forty-five days to coincide with his forty-fifth birthday in March. He talked about the "cosmic and universal implications" of *Star Trek* with students at schools including Cornell University, Rowan University, the University of North Carolina, and the University of Pittsburgh.[3]

"It was quite sensational," he said. "I spoke to 100,000 people in all. In the first half [of the lecture] I sketched the origins of science fiction, with readings from Greek mythology, Rostand, Brecht, and of course H. G. Wells, and in the second [half] answered questions, which were almost always about *Star Trek*."[4] His opening show, at Texas A&M, drew over 3,500 people; he read from the works of Ray Bradbury—and Shakespeare—and walked off the stage to a rousing standing ovation. "I wasn't sure I knew, or how it would go," he said later. "I could have been laughed off the stage in five minutes."[5]

He took it one step further by recording the lectures, which were edited and transformed into the album *William Shatner Live*, which he sold from a post office box in Hollywood (for $8.50) the following year under his Lemli Productions banner (Lemli combining his daughter's first names). "What probably started out as a friendly guest appearance has turned into a major act by Shatner," the *New York Post* noted in its review of the album. "This album was recorded at Hofstra University in New York . . . It is basically only a novelty item, but a must for those who are obsessed with the old TV series." There were plans for a second one-man tour in 1978, which would be written by science fiction author Robert Silverberg. Bill ventured he would open the show with "a poem by D. H. Lawrence and the sound of whales— very bizarre and strange—veering toward rock and roll in a prose way." That project never came to fruition.

The timing of Bill's one-man tour coincided with the now-legendary *Star Trek* parody that aired on NBC's *Saturday Night Live* in late May 1976, at the end of the show's first season—with John Belushi as Captain Kirk, Chevy Chase as Mr. Spock, and Dan Aykroyd as Dr. McCoy. The sketch, "The Last Voyage of the Starship *Enterprise*," was written by Michael O'Donoghue, who spent a month with Belushi, a hard-core *Star Trek* fan, as he tried to perfect his Shatner-as-Kirk mannerisms, including his by-now-familiar staccato, halting delivery of dialogue.

In the skit, the USS *Enterprise* is being chased through the galaxy by a 1968 Chrysler Imperial. Captain Kirk orders the car to be destroyed; when that fails, "Bones" McCoy races onto the deck to tell Kirk the "aliens" are boarding the ship. The "aliens" turn out to be NBC executives Herb Goodman (guest host Elliott Gould) and his assistant, Curtis (Garrett Morris), who are there to inform William Shatner and his crew that *Star Trek* has been cancelled. Mr. Spock tries a Vulcan mind-meld on Goodman to no avail, and Spock/Nimoy is dragged off the set, sobbing. As the *Star Trek* set is dismantled (and Spock's pointy ears are removed), Belushi's Shatner/Kirk remains seated defiantly in his captain's chair. "And except for one television network, we have found intelligence everywhere in the galaxy," he says, holding up his hand in Spock's "live long and prosper" Vulcan salute. "Promise." (A jokey reference to Shatner's margarine commercials.)

Four months later, in September, NASA announced that its first space shuttle would be called *Enterprise* in honor of *Star Trek*. DeForest Kelley, George Takei, James Doohan, Nichelle Nichols, Leonard Nimoy, Walter Koenig, and Gene Roddenberry were on hand when the shuttle prototype rolled out of the manufacturing plant in Palmdale, California. Bill was noticeably absent.

He did find the time to star in *American Enterprise*, a series of five educational films that were shown in schools nationwide. The project, financed by Phillips Petroleum Company, only underscored how low Bill's bar was set at this point in his career. The 1976 *American Enterprise* series was produced in conjunction with America's bicentennial celebration; Bill, usually dressed in a suit and wearing glasses (to make him appear more "official"?), walked stu-

dent viewers through five twenty-eight-minute-long films covering the top-
ics of "Land," "People," "Innovation," "Organization," and "Government."
"Each looks back on history, explaining how and why we grew," according
to the series' promotional materials. "Viewers will have five opportunities to
come to your own conclusions about how America happened."

Had the show-business stars aligned properly at this point in his career,
Bill might have gone from hosting *American Enterprise* to hosting the daytime game show *Family Feud*. The new show was produced by television
game-show titans Mark Goodson and Bill Todman—and they were, apparently, considering William Shatner in the role that eventually went to British-born comedian Richard Dawson. "He was on the leading edge of getting
it," Dawson said of Shatner. "I went to see Mark Goodson with my manager
and said, 'You said I could try out for your next pilot. The guy you've already
given the nod to is married to Perry Lafferty's daughter, Marcy. [Perry Laf-
ferty] was the one who was going to make a decision on whether this show
would go or not. Mark said, 'The problem being?' I said, 'He doesn't have
any more daughters I can marry. Give me a break.' I wasn't against William
Shatner getting it, but he was married to Perry Lafferty's daughter."[6] *Family Feud* breathed new life into Dawson's career following years of middling
movies (*The Devil's Brigade*) and supporting television roles (most notably as
Corporal Newkirk on CBS's *Hogan's Heroes*). Dawson went on to host *Family Feud* from 1976 to 1995 in two different iterations. (Like Shatner and
Star Trek, Dawson and *Family Feud* were spoofed on *Saturday Night Live*,
with Bill Murray impersonating Dawson.)

*   *   *

In late June 1977, Gene Roddenberry announced that Paramount Television would begin working on a new series, *Star Trek: Phase II*, a sequel to
the original NBC series. The plan was to launch the series nationally in 1978
with the original cast returning—minus Leonard Nimoy, who passed on the
project; his memoir, *I Am Not Spock*, had become a bestseller upon its release in early 1976. Paramount set aside $2 million for a television special to
launch the new series and budgeted $500,000 for the twenty-episode season
to follow.

"I can assure the fans the precepts I followed at the beginning of *Star
Trek* will be used for the new production," Roddenberry vowed.[7] Paramount
president Barry Diller said that even if the series wasn't picked up by ABC,

CBS, or NBC, it would launch in syndication since "its syndicated value is so high that it would cover a new production."[8] There was talk in Hollywood that Paramount wanted to start its own television network—with *Star Trek* as its franchise series. It was part of a two-pronged *Star Trek* attack via Paramount; there were also plans for a big-screen *Star Trek* movie, featuring the original cast, on which Roddenberry had been working since 1975. In the summer of 1977, Bill spoke about the proposed television series while promoting both the *William Shatner Live* album and his latest theatrical role opposite Yvette Mimieux in a touring production of *Tricks of the Trade*.

"I might do a two-hour version of *Star Trek*—I'm in negotiations right now," he said, referring to the big-screen movie. "And then later on in the year if they so decide—which I don't see how they would not—I might do the hour [television] version, the renewal, of *Star Trek*."[9]

It would be difficult for Bill to work on the new *Star Trek* television series, should it come to fruition, since he was talking about *Tricks of the Trade* heading to Broadway. "It looks good," he said of the prospect. "It's a two-character play, just me and Yvette Mimieux, about a psychiatrist and his patient."[10] The play was written by Sidney Michaels and directed by Morton Da Costa, who had directed *Auntie Mame*, *The Music Man*, and *No Time for Sergeants* (Andy Griffith's big break) on Broadway. *Tricks of the Trade* did, eventually, make it to Broadway, but not until November 1980—and with George C. Scott and his wife, Trish Van Devere, in the Shatner/Mimieux roles. It closed after one performance.

By the end August 1977, Paramount's plans for *Star Trek: Phase II* had died on the vine, but the studio kept that news quiet for the next several months. Bill must have known the television series was dead since he publicly stated around this time that he was never interested in revisiting the project, which contradicted his earlier enthusiasm. "They've messed around so much over the years," he said. "I don't think the bosses at Paramount really give a damn about *Star Trek* or really understood it in the first place."[11]

Paramount, meanwhile, forged ahead with the big-screen *Star Trek* movie as discussions heated up toward the end of the year. George Lucas's *Star Wars* hit the big screen in the summer of 1977 and was an immediate pop-culture sensation, smashing box-office records with its state-of-the-art special effects and pulse-pounding story line. Steven Spielberg's heavily hyped sci-fi movie *Close Encounters of the Third Kind* was opening in November, and Paramount wanted in on the action. Leonard Nimoy summed it up succinctly: "When *Star Wars* opened to such an enormous, successful audience, I think the people at Paramount decided there's a market for a *Star Trek* movie."

The studio had, in the preceding two years, budgeted $10 million for a *Star Trek* movie[12] and hired director Phil Kaufman (later to direct *The Right Stuff*) for the project. But Paramount rejected Gene Roddenberry's script and also scripts from science fiction heavyweights Ray Bradbury, Harlan Ellison, and Theodore Sturgeon. In one proposed scenario for the movie, Captain Kirk died—which did not please Bill, who heard this news while he was touring with his one-man show. "I was in the middle of nowhere [upstate New York] and I called the producer," he said. "He said: 'We're killing you off in the first third, and I think we'll bring you back to life for the end of the movie. And I said, 'Shit!'"[13]

One major sticking point regarding the *Star Trek* movie continued to be Leonard Nimoy, who was refusing to participate in the project. Following the cancellation of *Star Trek,* Nimoy costarred for two seasons on the CBS series *Mission: Impossible* and wanted to get as far away from Mr. Spock as possible. His mission to escape Spock's death grip on his career took Nimoy to Broadway in 1977, where he starred in the long-running hit *Equus* as Dr. Martin Dysart, the role previously played by Alec McCowan, Anthony Hopkins, Tony Perkins, and Richard Burton.

"Frankly, I got fed up with the entire fiasco," Bill said in late August as Paramount dragged its heels on the *Star Trek* movie. "I don't think Paramount would know good science fiction if it walked up to them and slapped them in the face."[14] The plan, as it stood now, was to adapt Alan Dean Foster's *Star Trek: Phase II* television-pilot script, "In Thy Image," into a big-screen *Star Trek* movie. It sounded promising. Even Bill sounded hopeful about this latest turn of events, but he was also adamant that Nimoy would not be a part of the project. "He has finished playing a part in 'Equus' on Broadway; he has written a book called *I Am Not Spock*, and he definitely refuses to wear pointy ears again," he said. Bill also took a sour grapes snarky potshot at *Star Wars*, which was breaking box-office records around the globe, calling it "a simple-minded cartoon."[15]

In the meantime, Bill turned his attention from fighting Klingons and studio executives to fighting tarantulas in *Kingdom of the Spiders*, a horror movie he shot in Arizona that summer. Bill starred as veterinarian Dr. Robert "Rack" Hansen, who's battling an army of deadly (and angry) tarantulas in the hinterlands. (Some of the spiders in the movie were real tarantulas, others were rubber copies—producers reportedly spent $50,000 on both.) Marcy costarred as Rack's sister-in-law, Terry, and the cast also featured Tiffany Bolling, Natasha Ryan, and Altovise Davis, better known as Mrs. Sammy Davis Jr. *Kingdom of the Spiders* opened in November 1977 and eventually earned $17 million at the box office as one of the decade's biggest independent horror movies.[16] It was also nominated for Best Horror Film by the Academy of Science Fiction (it lost to *The Little Girl Who Lives Down the Lane*, starring future Oscar winner Jodie Foster) and is now considered a cult classic. Marcy's appearance in the movie was one of several acting appearances she made after marrying Bill, including small roles in the television shows *Bronk*, *Barnaby Jones*, and *Police Woman*. Getting Bill's career back on track was the couple's professional priority.

* * *

In the meantime, Bill added a keen interest in karate to his growing list of extracurricular activities (motorcycles, flying, skiing, horses, and his dogs). Several years earlier he met Tom Bleecker, who was working as a scriptwriter for director Blake Edwards along with Cliff Ralke. Cliff's father, Don Ralke, produced Bill's first spoken-word album, *The Transformed Man*, back in 1968.

Bill hired Bleecker and Ralke to write screenplays in which he would star, including one called *The Time of the Tempest* and another movie, *Future Requiem*, in which Bill would play an astronaut who treks into space, becomes possessed by the devil (*The Exorcist* had opened in 1973), and then returns to Earth—where he's ordered by Satan to blow up the world (or something like that). Bill also wanted Tom Bleecker to write a one-man Broadway show for him based on *The Transformed Man*. None of these projects ever came to fruition.

"As a sidelight, Bill was not a big spender in Hollywood, at least with us when we worked for him," Bleecker said. "So, he might have paid us below scale because, at the time, we were not in the Writer's Guild." (Bleecker remembered being paid around $200 a week on retainer from Shatner.) "I liked him a lot," he said. "People say he's an egotist, and he is, but he's an egotist in a nice way. He certainly cares a lot about himself, he has a very strong self-image, but not in a distasteful way. He's got a great sense of humor, he's got a wonderful laugh, and he's a good listener."[17]

Bleecker was also a black belt in the martial arts (Kenpo); he'd trained under Bruce Lee disciple Ed Parker in Los Angeles and was friends with Lee, whose death in July 1973 at the age of thirty-two under mysterious circumstances—followed by the posthumous release of his box-office blockbuster *Enter the Dragon*—heightened worldwide interest in the martial arts.[18] Bill was fascinated by Lee and wanted to learn about his martial arts techniques. When he learned about Bleecker's background in Kenpo, he hired the screenwriter to tutor him in the methodology behind the Japanese martial arts technique.

"I'll tell you a little side story about Bill's sense of humor," Bleecker said.

> When he moved to his home on Berry Drive, it was a big house. It had a gate on the street and a long expanse of lawn . . . and you had to walk up this long staircase to get up to the main house.
>
> The first time I went to that house on Berry, I had not met his dogs. For some reason whenever I was over at the smaller house, the dogs were somewhere else. Bill said, "Just leave your car on the street, there is a small gate there. Just come through the gate and walk up to the main house." So I did, and I got about a third of the way up and all of a sudden these two enormous Dobermans were charging me. Charging right at me. I mean black belt aside . . . these were two large Dobermans, one of them considerably larger, in a full run at me. I thought, these dogs do not look friendly to me. I didn't know the names of the dogs and I figured, knowing Bill, he named one of them Kirk. So as the dogs came up to me, I just looked at one and said "Hey, Kirk!" and thank God the bigger one started wagging his tail and I was safe and sound. I got up to the house and said "Bill! What the hell was that all about?" I don't know if he thought it was funny or if he thought, "Well, what's the big deal?"

In the fall of 1977, Paramount scrapped the *Star Trek* movie even after the original script was rewritten to spare Captain Kirk's life. "We felt, frankly, that it was a little . . . pretentious," studio chief Barry Diller said, adding that the television series was still a go (though it really wasn't). "If you force it as a big 75-millimeter widescreen movie, you go directly against the concept," he told Gene Roddenberry. "If you rip *Star Trek* off, you fail, because the people who like *Star Trek* just don't like it. They love it."[19] Bill was dumbfounded. "It's inexplicable! Inexplicable that the week after *Star Wars* is out, and grossing like crazy" the movie would die, he said.[20] Even though Paramount was no longer planning to launch its new *Star Trek* television series in the fall of 1978, it kept up the charade and Paramount publicists continued to leak plot details about the two-hour pilot to the press. (One tidbit was that the USS *Enterprise* was taken out of dry dock over San Francisco and eventually battles "a mysterious space force.")

Paramount went back to the drawing board and tried to figure out wanted it wanted to do, if anything, with *Star Trek*. As talk of reviving the movie version picked up some steam, Bill kept his nose to the acting grindstone. He appeared in an NBC miniseries production of *Little Women* as Professor Friedrich Bhaer, the German teacher portrayed in the 1933 and 1949 movies by Paul Lukas and Rosanno Brazzi, respectively, and costarred in the television movies *Crash*, *Riel*, and *Disaster on the Coastliner* (with Yvette Mimieux, Raymond Burr, Lloyd Bridges, and E. G. Marshall). He appeared in two episodes of the ABC series *How the West Was Won* (as Captain Harrison) and costarred opposite Colleen Dewhurst in the big-screen Canadian drama *The Third Walker*, shot in Cape Breton. The movie opened and closed quietly but did earn four Canadian Film Award nominations (though none for Bill). "William Shatner and Monique Mercure are fine in smaller roles," noted the *Cinema Canada* critic in an otherwise benign review of the movie.[21]

CHAPTER 9

The Gang's All Here

As the calendar turned to 1978, Paramount finally pulled the trigger on the *Star Trek* movie, making it official in late March by announcing that *Star Trek: The Motion Picture* would soon begin production. The announcement was quite a spectacle, and Paramount proudly held its largest press conference since 1955, when reporters gathered on the lot as Cecille B. DeMille proclaimed that he was making his next opus, *The Ten Commandments*. All the original *Star Trek* cast members were returning for the movie, including Leonard Nimoy—whose battles with Paramount over unpaid *Star Trek* royalties had been quietly resolved. He was back in the fold.

Sixty-four-year-old Robert Wise (*West Side Story, The Sound of Music, The Sand Pebbles*) was hired to direct the $15 million film from a Harold Livingston screenplay, adapted from Alan Dean Foster's story. Wise knew nothing about *Star Trek* or its mythology, but he could count on Gene Roddenberry, brought aboard as the movie's producer, to be looking over his shoulder. There were persistent rumors that Bill and Nimoy would have editorial control over the script, but this, Livingston said, was "totally inaccurate."[1] Paramount targeted a summer 1979 release date for the movie, allowing nearly a year and a half for production and post-production.

While Bill always kept himself in pretty good physical shape, that was growing more difficult. He turned forty-seven in tandem with Paramount's announcement of the new movie, and if Captain Kirk was going to be seen on the big screen, he needed to look good—even if his new uniform was a bit more forgiving than his original skin-tight *Star Trek* ensemble. He went on a crash diet, began jogging daily, and even visited a weight-loss center in

Malibu. "For a week all I did was hike, drink water, and eat carrot sticks; hike, drink water, and eat more carrot sticks," he said. "They didn't have single rooms in this place, and because I insisted on staying by myself, they cleared out a storage closet for me. I put in a cot and slept there."[2] Eventually he met Dr. Ernst Duynder of the American Health Institute, who advised him to give up coffee and sugar, and Bill shed twenty-five pounds. "My body and my health are now substantially different than before," he gushed. "I no longer wake up with my face puffy. I feel better all around."[3]

Filming on *Star Trek: The Motion Picture* movie began in early August 1978 under a cloak of secrecy, lest anything about the film, or its plotline, leak out. (When Stephen Collins, who played Will Decker in the movie, went to audition for the role, he read the script in a small room on the Paramount lot.) George Takei thought Leonard Nimoy had aged considerably in the decade since the series last aired. "And Bill was the center of it all—just as before," he said. "He was laughing, joking, giggling, and reveling in the joy of commencing a project undreamed of by any of us."[4]

Before too long, though, the inevitable production snafus delayed shooting, and filming on *Star Trek: The Motion Picture* did not wrap until January 26, 1979, far behind schedule. The movie's original $15 million budget ballooned to $46 million, with most of that attributed to the film's elaborate special effects, which were farmed out to several different production houses.

Robert Wise was an Oscar-winning director (for *West Side Story* and *The Sound of Music*) and a master technician, but he wasn't a *Star Trek* fan—and there was grousing on the set that he was just going through the motions to collect a paycheck. "He was a very nice person, a master technician, but he didn't have a clue about *Star Trek*," Bill said.[5] The big-screen movie stripped away any trace of humor that intermittently infused the original series (in episodes such as "The Trouble with Tribbles") and played it straight down the line, almost to the point of sheer boredom. "There was always something tongue-in-cheek if not flat-out comedy" in the television series, Nimoy said. "On *Star Trek I* it was forbidden. I mean it was *forbidden*! It was decided that we were doing a very serious motion picture here, we would not do funny stuff."[6] Bill claimed that he and Nimoy "could not stand" the movie as filming continued and that they felt the need to save it. *Star Trek: The Motion Picture* was, they both thought, "just too absurdly serious."[7]

Publicly, the reunited *Star Trek* cast members proclaimed that they were happy to be working together again for the first time in a decade. "I knew it was 1979, but it seemed like 1969 was just yesterday," Bill said. "I felt exhilarated, gratified, nostalgic. At the same time there was a tinge of disbelief and a bit of concern . . . It was difficult, after so many false starts over a number of years, to realize *Star Trek* was really back."[8] DeForest Kelley, reprising his role as Dr. Leonard "Bones" McCoy, described it as "the family . . . just picking up right where it left off," while Walter Koenig, back as Pavel Chekov, painted a word picture of that first day on the set—with Chekov, Uhura (Nichelle Nichols), and Sulu (George Takei) sitting at their consoles as Captain Kirk walked in: "I got such a high, such a rush at that moment that it took all of my self-control not to embrace [Shatner]."[9]

In the movie's ponderous plot, James T. Kirk, now promoted to admiral, is leading the USS *Enterprise* in its mission to stop an alien cloud called V'Ger from destroying the Earth. In addition to the returning cast members, the movie added Collins as Captain Willard Decker—who's been supplanted by Kirk on the *Enterprise* deck (much to Decker's anger)—and a former Miss Universe contestant, actress Persis Khambatta, as Ilia, the ship's Deltan navigator. (Khambatta, who was slated to play the same role in the aborted *Star Trek* television sequel, shaved her head for the role.) Marcy Shatner had a small role as Ilia's assistant, Chief DiFalco. Original *Star Trek* cast members Grace Lee Whitney (Janice Rand) and Gene Roddenberry's wife, Majel Barrett (Christine Chapel), returned in smaller roles.

This big-screen version of James T. Kirk differed drastically from his small-screen predecessor. As written by Harold Livingston, Kirk was humorless and testy while wearing his admiral's uniform (in which he "looked like a dentist," one wag said). There were rumors of on-set tension between Bill and Stephen Collins, including several arguments between the two actors. ("We had some interesting soul-searching conversations about working opposite Mr. Shatner," Walter Koenig said of his chats with Collins.) Some of the decade-old wounds between the *Star Trek* actors were reopened; George Takei recalled an instance where Bill cut Koenig from a scene (and out of the camera frame) after huddling with Wise in an "intensely whispered exchange." Takei continued: "The cuts usually favored Bill. Perhaps Bill had nothing to do with the excisions. But our history-conditioned sensibilities couldn't help suspecting."[10]

Once shooting wrapped on *Star Trek: The Motion Picture*, Roddenberry and Wise spent the rest of the year editing and fine-tuning the movie. Its reliance on special effects and its glacial pacing stripped the film any humanity or compassion, and it possessed none of the zip, panache, or charm (however cheesy) of the original series. The majority of the nation's movie critics were not kind when it opened on December 7, 1979.

"Watching *Star Trek: The Motion Picture* . . . is like attending your high school class's 10th reunion at Caesar's Palace," sniped Vincent Canby in the *New York Times*. "Most of the faces are familiar, but the décor has little relationship to anything you've ever seen before . . . Because most of the drama in such a movie is created in the laboratories, the actors are limited to the exchanges of meaningful glances or staring intently at television monitors, usually in disbelief."[11] *Time* magazine critic Richard Schickel thought the movie's spaceships "take an unconscionable amount of time to get anywhere, and nothing of dramatic or human interest happens along the way" and called the film's dialogue "impenetrable spaceflight jargon."[12] "The deliberate pace that can be perversely hypnotic on TV expands to a large soporific cloud on the giant screen," *Newsweek* noted in its pan of the movie. *New York* magazine: "Here is granitic William Shatner as Captain Jim Kirk, sucking in his gut to appear trim in his outer-space tunic . . . Peering grimly at a quarrelsome subordinate, Shatner holds his expressionless TV-actor's stare for an eternity, and then something goes click in his brain and he begins to *act.*"[13]

Even *Star Trek* writer Harlan Ellison got into the act, writing a review of the movie in *Starlog* magazine. "Shatner dominates as usual. Stuffy when he isn't being arch and coy; hamming and mugging when he isn't being lachrymose . . . The saddening reality is that it is a dull film, a stultifyingly predictable film, a tragically average film."[14]

The lukewarm reviews did not dampen the movie's power at the box office. *Star Trek: The Motion Picture*, enhanced by Jerry Goldsmith's powerful, majestic score, shattered box-office records in its opening weekend, taking in nearly $12 million, and it earned $17 million in its first week and grossed nearly $149 million worldwide when all was said and done. (This in a time when the average price of a movie ticket was $2.50.) It garnered three Oscar nominations, including one for Goldsmith, and convinced Paramount executives there was more life left in the old USS *Enterprise*. Gene Roddenberry, who was keenly aware of the criticism regarding the movie's slow-moving plotline, began working on a sequel.

In the meantime, two hard-core *Star Trek* fans, Sondra Marshak and Myrna Culbreath, were also doing some writing. In 1979, timed to the release of *Star Trek: The Motion Picture*, Grosset & Dunlap published the book *Shatner: Where No Man . . . The Authorized Biography of William Shatner* under its Ace Books imprint. The project was a three-year effort and dated back to at least 1976, when Marshak and Culbreath distributed questionnaires about Shatner to attendees of the 1976 Star Trek America Bicentennial Convention. Bill's face, set against a dark background and staring dreamily upward, was pictured on the book's cover, and Bill was credited as the lead author. He also contributed several personal photographs that were used in the book. *Where No Man . . .* clocked in at nearly three hundred pages, with most of that being Marshak and Culbreath's pseudo-psychological ruminations on Bill's life interspersed with his stream-of-consciousness thoughts, showcased on the written page as one long interview (denoted by quotation marks). In the chapter entitled "Love Story: Part II, The House on the Hill," Marcy joined Bill for an interview that focused on the couple's relationship and how they met and fell in love. (Marcy: "It wasn't that he was a star or actor. I've been surrounded by that all my life, so that was not the immediate thrill. But it was *him* and *he* was the actor.") [15]

Where No Man . . . is a noble effort but a tough slog. What it does offer is Bill Shatner, in his own unvarnished words, talking about his relationships with Leonard Nimoy, Gene Roddenberry, and others. (He never directly addresses the rumors of his infidelities but alludes to his roving eye when talking about his divorce.)

*   *   *

William Shatner's return to the movies in a big-budget, highly publicized motion picture failed to carry over into other areas of his professional life. The next several years found him stuck on the familiar treadmill of television roles, both as a guest star (including one appearance opposite fellow Canadian actor Leslie Nielsen in ABC's short-lived cop-spoof series *Police Squad!*) and as the lead in forgettable television movies (*The Babysitter*, *The Kidnapping of the President*). Sometimes the attention was more than he bargained for; in January 1979, soft-core porn magazine *High Society* published photos of Bill's nude scene with Angie Dickinson from *Big Bad Mama*.

Bill returned to the "straw hat" summer theater circuit, appearing in a national touring production of Ira Levin's *Deathtrap*—"Of course, they had come partly out of curiosity to see Captain Kirk," he said[16]—and in August 1981, he directed and costarred in a Los Angeles production of *Cat on a Hot*

Tin Roof at the Melrose Theater. (Marcy played the role of Maggie.) He returned to Canada for his role in a horror movie, *Visiting Hours*—costarring opposite Lee Grant, Michael Ironside, and Linda Purl—but two of his pet projects around that time never saw the light of day: a Western called *The Red, the White and the Blue* and *Two Weeks with Pay*, "the story of two men who aren't quite able to beat inflation and go off on a vacation in search of gold in a ghost town."[17]

Still, there was always Captain Kirk to fall back on, and in early November 1981 Bill was back on the Paramount lot to begin filming *Star Trek II: The Wrath of Khan*. Unlike its bloated predecessor and its $46 million budget, *The Wrath of Khan* was allotted only $11 million by Paramount. Nicholas Meyer, a 1976 Academy Award nominee for his script adaptation of *The Seven-Per-Cent Solution*, was hired to direct *Star Trek II* from a screenplay by Jack B. Sowards, which was based on a story by Paramount television executive Harve Bennett.

Bennett had screened all of the original seventy-nine *Star Trek* episodes to get ideas for the movie, and he was particularly impressed by the 1967 Season 1 episode "Space Seed," in which a genetically enhanced villain, Khan Noonien Singh (played by Ricardo Montalban), was exiled to an uninhabited planet after trying to take over the USS *Enterprise*.[18] "It was my favorite episode and one that gave me great relief," Bennett said. "At the end of 'Space Seed,' Kirk and Spock exchange a moment, and it's Spock who says, 'Hmmm . . . I wonder if we came back twenty years from tomorrow what we would find.' I jumped up in the projection room and said, 'That's it!'"[19]

Bennett later dispelled rumors circulating at the time that the movie was pegged for television (and would be called *The Omega Factor*). "It was never seriously a television project," he said. "The minute the script began shaping up, it was clear to all that we had something terrific."[20]

Bill described his emotions during the script development process as swinging wildly "from awful lows to exalted highs"[21] but said he was pleased with the finished screenplay: "We had [George Lucas's company] ILM for the effects, so the movie couldn't *look* bad. We also had a very human *Star Trek*-ian script."[22]

This time around, there would be plenty of action aboard the USS *Enterprise*—and, unlike *Star Trek: The Motion Picture*, the core characters would be age appropriate. "The first movie had been shot in an attempt to pretend that no one had aged," Bennett said. "You had the series, and then twenty years later or so, you're doing 'Kirk hasn't gotten any older?' And you do it with makeup and you do it with scrims and soft lighting, but it wasn't real. So, in *Star Trek II* we confronted the problem head-on and we played age—and that worked."[23]

Star Trek II: The Wrath of Khan featured all the *Star Trek* regulars— Leonard Nimoy, James Doohan, George Takei, Nichelle Nichols, Walter Koenig, DeForest Kelley. Future *Cheers* star Kirstie Alley made her big-screen debut as Mr. Spock's protégé, Saavik, a Starfleet commander in training, and veteran actor Paul Winfield played Clark Terrell, captain of the starship *Reliant*. (He's controlled by Khan via an eel that's burrowed into his ear, and he meets an unfortunate end after refusing to kill Kirk.)

The movie's main story line revolves around the two old adversaries, Admiral Kirk and Khan, who find themselves squaring off again in the year 2285. (The sixty-two-year-old Montalban, who was starring in the ABC series *Fantasy Island* as the dapper Mr. Roarke, wore a long rock-star wig and what appears to be a cartoonish, inflated muscle suit. Nicholas Meyer swore, time and again, that Montalban's massive pecs were real, but that's unlikely.)

But the size of Ricardo Montalban's pecs in *Star Trek II: The Wrath of Khan* paled in comparison to the movie's most shocking twist: the death of Spock, who shuffles off this mortal coil after being overexposed to radiation in a bid to restore the crippled warp drive system of the USS *Enterprise*. Spock's final interaction with Kirk, who has to be restrained from rushing in to save his best friend, is intense and riveting—as the two men, separated by thick glass and unable to make physical contact with each other, say goodbye. "I have been, and always shall be, your friend," a gasping Spock says to Kirk, summoning up enough strength to press his hand on the glass in his trademark Vulcan salute and croak out one final line: "Live long . . . and prosper."

Meanwhile, those onscreen emotions paled in comparison to what was unfolding behind the scenes on the set once the cameras were turned off and some of the old tensions between Bill and his costars resurfaced. George Takei, particularly, took umbrage at some of Bill's behavior. When he first read the script for *Star Trek II: The Wrath of Khan*, Takei took a great deal of pride in the fact that Mr. Sulu is promoted to Captain—news that he shares onscreen in a brief scene with Admiral Kirk. It was an important plot point, both to Takei and to his onscreen alter ego's standing in the *Star Trek* canon. "Captain Kirk was Sulu's idol. Sulu patterned his career after him, the same way I, as an actor, watched Bill Shatner as an actor," Takei said. "Sulu was, in many ways, taking his inspiration from Captain Kirk."[24] But when it came time to rehearse the scene, Takei felt that Bill "was breezing through his lines" and, as Admiral Kirk, was not giving Sulu's promotion the respect it deserved. When Takei asked Bill to play the scene with more oomph, he promised he would—but once the cameras rolled he "played it as he had rehearsed it, disinterested, murmuring some trivia about my captaincy, looking straight out into the void. There was no eye contact." Takei described the feeling of "fury" raging within him, particularly after seeing Bill joking around with the crew after the scene was shot. Director Nicholas Meyer assured Takei it would all be fixed in the editing room, but Takei knew better. The scene was cut from the movie.[25]

Star Trek II: The Wrath of Khan finished filming in late January 1982 and premiered five months later. This time, the reviews were mostly enthusiastic, as were *Star Trek* fans, and *The Wrath of Khan* grossed a record $14.3 million in its opening weekend and earned nearly $80 million overall as the year's sixth-highest-grossing movie. Afterward, Harve Bennett, whose story set the framework for *The Wrath of Khan*, was asked to describe Bill Shatner. "A matinee idol, full of himself, but for good reason," he said. "He's good . . . and funny."[26]

"Now this is more like it," *New York Times* critic Janet Maslin wrote in her review of *The Wrath of Khan*. "After the colossal, big-budget bore that was *Star Trek: The Motion Picture*, here comes a sequel that's worth its salt . . . It's everything the first one should have been and wasn't." Pulitzer Prize-winning film critic Roger Ebert liked the movie's special effects but thought they were beside the point: "Fans of the TV series wanted to see their favorite characters again, and *Trek II* understood that desire and acted on it."[27] *Variety's* critic wrote in the publication's unique style that the "final reel is a classic of emotional manipulation: Spock unhesitatingly calculates that he must sacrifice himself to save the *Enterprise* crew."[28]

The movie also impressed the science fiction fan community, winning two Saturn Awards (Bill for his acting, Meyer for his directing) from the Academy of Science Fiction, Fantasy, and Horror Films. The World Science Fiction Society, meanwhile, nominated *The Wrath of Khan* for its Hugo Award (which was claimed by Ridley Scott's *Blade Runner*, starring Harrison Ford and Rutger Hauer). Despite the death of Spock in *The Wrath of Khan*, Paramount was going ahead with plans for a third *Star Trek* movie. (Leonard

Nimoy was making noise about returning to the franchise if he could direct the next film.) "I don't know whether the *Star Trek* series could have gone on without Spock," Bill said. "It certainly would have been different and not as good. The Spock-Kirk interrelationship is really the key to so much for the way the stories are told."[29]

Whether or not Nimoy returned for another *Star Trek* movie was someone else's problem. Bill hoped for the best and, for now, focused on his next project: a new ABC television series called *T. J. Hooker.*

CHAPTER 10

A Series of Adventures

William Shatner celebrated his fifty-first birthday with the launch of *T. J. Hooker*, which premiered on March 13, 1982, as a midseason replacement on ABC. It was seven years since the one-and-done disappointment of *Barbary Coast*, but with television titans Aaron Spelling and Leonard Goldberg launching the series under their Spelling-Goldberg Productions banner, *T. J. Hooker* had a fighting chance to stake a claim in primetime. (Spelling also produced *T. J. Hooker's* Saturday-night ABC stablemates *The Love Boat* and *Fantasy Island*.) Bill had high hopes for his return to a starring series role on television.

The new series was created by Rick Husky, a veteran writer (*Dan August, Mission: Impossible, The Mod Squad*) whose credits included episodes of Spelling-Goldberg productions *The Rookies, S.W.A.T*, and *Charlie's Angels*. "Aaron Spelling and Leonard Goldberg were dissolving their partnership to pursue individual projects on their own and their company had one remaining guaranteed pilot commitment with ABC," Husky said. "Leonard Goldberg phoned me one night to ask if I could come up with a quick pitch for a police series. They had a starting notion about doing a show which would involve the world of young cops, and there was some urgency to come up with a series idea to present to ABC within a few days."[1]

Husky sat down at his typewriter and cooked up a concept he called *The Protectors*, which would feature "a divorced, hard-nosed detective who'd been busted down to a blue-uniform sergeant following a few transgressions."[2] The detective, Thomas Jefferson "T. J." Hooker, was assigned to train young recruits at the Los Angeles County Police Department (LCPD) academy, and Husky's two-hour pilot script included roles for about a half-dozen young recruits. ABC executives read Husky's script for *The Protectors* and ordered a two-hour pilot, with T. J. Hooker as the episode's focal point.

"I had no one specifically in mind when I created the role, other than a prototype of a tough cop based upon some of the dedicated, veteran LAPD cops I'd met during my writing career," Husky said. "There was a casting list which included Bill Shatner, Chad Everett, Bob Conrad, and other available actors of the right age and demeanor [who would be] physically fit enough to believably perform action sequences, which were part of the character's description."[3]

Spelling and Goldberg thought that Bill could be the right actor to play Hooker. Husky met Bill for lunch to discuss the role and was "impressed with his intelligence and instinct" regarding Hooker. "Bill was complimentary about the pilot script and, when we concluded our lunch, wanted to know if I would promise him that I would stay on the series for its duration if it sold." Husky said he would, the men shook hands, and the deal was sealed.

"My managers and I decided that I had been waiting for fine screen opportunities for many years, but what I was being offered was the next level down," Bill said at the time, damning the two *Star Trek* movies with faint praise. "So, since I wasn't making the kind of films I wanted, it seemed like a good idea to take this offer and play a tough, conservative cop—the very antithesis of what people recognize me for—in conjunction with other things. That way I could abruptly break an image and not kill myself doing it."[4]

The executives at ABC were enthusiastic about *The Protectors* but wanted to change its focus to include more of the T. J. Hooker character and less of the ensemble of young police recruits. They asked Husky if he could include more of Hooker "on the street in a patrol car, working as a blue-uniformed cop fighting crime." Husky agreed and gave Hooker a partner (Officer Vince Romano, played by Adrian Zmed in the series), and kept the recruits angle by having Hooker teach classes at the academy. *The Protectors* morphed into *T. J. Hooker*. The tough-as-nails LA cop possessed a *Dirty Harry*-type demeanor—"There's a war going on in the streets and the bad guys are winning. The street-savvy hoods have no fear," he says in the opener—and he has a checkered past: he's a Green Beret who was injured in Vietnam, is divorced, and is always late on his alimony payments. He was, Bill said, "a hot head."

Bill tackled his new role with his characteristic energy, spending a day at the North Hollywood area police station to observe police tactics (including the correct way to search a prisoner—and he was the "prisoner"). Bill planned to do his own stunts, and to whip himself into shape for the role he worked out daily in the gym of his home in the San Fernando Valley and ran three to five miles a day. He talked up *T. J. Hooker* in dozens of interviews— even comparing his new character, only half-jokingly, to Shakespeare's Hamlet: "Action is a very important aspect in all drama—Shakespeare did it with sword fights," he said. "You need some leavening between something that keeps the adrenaline flowing and something that expands the mind."[5]

He kept "the adrenaline flowing" in other ways on the *T. J. Hooker* set. "Shatner was hitting on anything with two legs," wrote actress Claudia Christian, who, in 1984, guest-starred on an episode of *T. J. Hooker*. In her memoir, *Babylon Confidential*, she recounted how Bill invited her to his dressing room to "run lines" and grew amorous as he chowed down on Thai food. "He moved in, and a wave of garlic breath hit me in the face," she wrote, apparently rebuffing his overture.[6] Christian later embellished her recollections of Bill's advances: "I do remember him trying to shove his tongue down my throat in his dressing room after eating Thai food . . . He was a bit of an asshole. He was already wearing the corset back then, so I should have punched him in his stomach."[7]

T. J. Hooker premiered to solid ratings on Saturday, March 13, 1982, with "The Protectors," its ninety-minute pilot episode. "In its own manipulating way, *T. J. Hooker* is a fascinating creation," the *New York Times* noted in its review of the premiere episode. "Sergeant Hooker gets his men, of course, but nothing is more likely to make him very happy as he goes around yearning for the days when the mass was celebrated in Latin and boxers got carried out of the ring instead of quitting because of stomach cramps."[8] Critic Lee Winfrey wasn't as forgiving. "Except for the presence of Shatner, an attractive and likeable star, *T. J. Hooker* looks scarcely different from *Strike Force* or *S.W.A.T.*, another old Spelling-Goldberg crime series," he wrote. "The most emphatic noises on the sound track are those of guns in use and cars in chase."[9]

ABC aired four more episodes that spring and the series continued to pull in good numbers, consistently finishing in the Top 30 primetime shows in terms of viewership. ABC added *T. J. Hooker* to its fall schedule, slotting it to air every Saturday at 8 p.m. as the lead-in to Spelling's *The Love Boat* and *Fantasy Island.*

"When the first episode of the series ran, the ratings were the best ABC had seen on a Saturday night in a long time," recalled series creator Rick Husky. "I called Bill to give him the ratings and to tell him they were good. In fact, the ratings were outstanding. There was a long pause on Bill's end of the phone, so I asked him how he felt about the good news. His answer: 'Vindicated.'"

Most of the *T. J. Hooker* cast remained intact heading into Season 2, with Adrian Zmed, James Darren, and Richard Herd all returning; April Clough, who played officer Vicki Taylor, left the show and was replaced by Heather Locklear's Officer Stacy Sheridan, the daughter of Captain Sheridan (Herd). Locklear was pulling double duty; for the duration of *T. J. Hooker*'s run, she continued in her recurring role as Sammy Jo Dean on *Dynasty*, another of Aaron Spelling's ABC shows. The cast got along well. Adrian Zmed recounted how he and Bill tried to good-naturedly "terrify" each other when the other was behind the wheel of a speeding car.

> We were out on a country road about a mile long, for a shot where three cameras were set up . . . and the director told Bill to quickly come down that mile stretch and stop on the mark we were to get out of the car and chase the bad guy. Now the key word here is the director said "quickly," and Bill thinks that "quickly" is warp speed. I think it was maybe 120 miles per hour when I looked over at and casually said, "Excuse me, are you going to use the brake?" There was about a quarter of a mile left and he glanced over at me and said, "Don't worry, Adrian." I was clutching and white knuckles and everything. Well, he put the brakes on [and] there were clouds of smoke coming out of the back of [the car] and a [skid] patch about a quarter mile long. I can't believe it—the man stopped right on the mark. We got out of the car, took off, the director yelled "Cut!" and he said, "I told you so, Adrian," and I yelled to wardrobe and said, "I need a change of underwear."[10]

On another occasion, while they were filming a *T. J. Hooker* episode in their police car, Zmed and Shatner drove down Sunset Boulevard and decided they would "play around"—by picking up a few prostitutes. "And we put them in the back of the car. We did this whole scene with them, and apparently Aaron Spelling was not happy when he saw that in the dailies," Zmed said. "We weren't allowed to do that anymore. But we did have a lot of fun together."[11]

The stars were aligning for Bill, and ABC's decision to continue with *T. J. Hooker* dovetailed with the success, in June, of *Star Trek: The Wrath of Khan*. Even *Visiting Hours*, the slasher movie he filmed the year before in Canada, opened strongly at the box office in May. Still, Bill was ambivalent about his new series and knew the long days on the set would leave him little time to pursue other acting opportunities—including the third *Star Trek* movie in the planning stages at Paramount.

"It should be fun and entertaining . . . but it's stultifying, debilitating work," he said in June about bearing the load of a weekly series. "It's like Mount Everest—the north slope." He talked about the "flood" of offers that came in after the success of *Star Trek II* and lamented over the fact that his *T. J. Hooker* schedule would prevent him from doing any other outside projects until the following spring—and perhaps beyond. "I really don't want to do a series for five years," he said. "But there is a give and take here. I think that *T. J. Hooker* can remain a successful series, and I think the character can be a viable one—rooted in today . . . I'm hoping the price I have to pay won't be too extreme."[12]

Bill found some time in his busy schedule to film a small role as Commander Buck Murdock in *Airplane II: The Sequel*—which hoped to capitalize on its disaster-movie-parody predecessor *Airplane!*, whose creative brain trust (Jim Abrahams, Jerry Zucker, David Zucker) were not involved in *Airplane II*. It was released in December to scathing reviews and promptly disappeared. Variety weighed in with this assessment: "Among those with nothing much to do are Raymond Burr, Sonny Bono, Chuck Connors, John Dehner, Rip Torn, and Chad Everett. Among those with too much to do is William Shatner."[13]

Bill spent the summer of 1982 shooting *T. J. Hooker* and negotiating his return for the third *Star Trek* movie, which was now scheduled to begin shooting in April 1983. This time around, Harve Bennett, upon whose story *The Wrath of Khan* was based, would write the screenplay. Bill officially signed on for the movie in mid-September, declining to publicly reveal his new *Star Trek* salary—"I don't want to discuss money when there's so much economic disaster in the country," he said—but indicating that he would be handsomely compensated. (As part of his deal to appear in the movie, Para-mount agreed to finance one of his outside projects.)[14]

*   *   *

Bill and Marcy split whatever free time they had together between their house in the San Fernando Valley and a horse-breeding farm Bill purchased in early 1979 in Three Rivers, an unincorporated community nestled in the foothills of the Sierra Nevada mountain range. He'd "fallen in love" with the notion of owning a horse while shooting an episode of *T. J. Hooker* on location at a barn in Los Angeles, but his love affair with all things equestrian was stoked the previous year. In 1978, Bill visited the city of Visalia, about 230 miles northeast of San Francisco, to help raise money for the city's local Shakespeare festival. He met some people who lived in nearby Three Rivers, which they called "heaven on earth"—words which Bill and Marcy remem-bered in 1979 when they returned there as the new owners of a horse farm.

Marcy christened the farm Belle Reve Ranch. (Belle Reve translated to "Sweet Dreams" in French.) The ranch was spread out over eighteen acres, and Bill hired Dalan Smith and his wife Judith, who lived on the property, to run its day-to-day operations. Bill would come to call Dalan "the brains be-hind the operation," and Dalan oversaw the construction of Bill and Marcy's new ranch house, which sat near the end of a long and winding private lane.[15]

The ranch house was open and airy and featured a lot of windows and several decks (one side of the house fronted the river). There, Bill "seemed to feel safe from the prying eyes of the paparazzi or the curiosity seekers," Dalan Smith recalled.[16] Fencing was added, as was an irrigation system and, of course, livestock. Bill bought his first equine, a quarter horse, at an auction in Sacramento when he accidentally raised his hand and bid $2,600 ($1,000 over what he'd budgeted) and was then too embarrassed to admit he'd made a mistake.[17] The gelding, called Dandy Doc Tucker, was welcomed to the ranch. (Bill would sometimes have Dandy Doc transported to Los Angeles so he could ride him there.[18]) Bill's passion for horses, particularly saddlebreds, would eventually lead him to a horse farm in Kentucky after he and Marcy moved on from Belle Reve. "I love physical contact with a horse," he said. "I love to physically put my hands on a horse. I have driven up to the ranch from Los Angeles and back in a day just to see a newborn foal. Seven hours of driving just to see a baby!"[19]

Dalan Smith liked and respected his boss but found it difficult to really get to know him, to learn what made Bill Shatner tick underneath the public facade. Smith thought that Bill had been acting for so long that he "had become so used to putting himself into a role described in detail in writing . . . that he seemed most comfortable when being instructed in that same degree of detail, no matter what he was doing."[20]

Marcy's acting career, meanwhile, was stuck in neutral. She made working on her marriage to Bill her top priority, but she still wanted to act—and after nearly ten years of television and movie appearances she was growing restless. "I never watched TV, but now I'd give my arm for a sitcom," she said shortly before the Season 2 premiere of *T. J. Hooker*.[21] She followed her small role in *Star Trek: The Motion Picture* with an appearance in the 1980 television movie *Dan August: The Trouble with Women* (in which Burt Reynolds reprised his early-'70s television character) and joined her husband in *Airplane II: The Sequel*. But it wasn't enough. "Her career was an extension of mine and that did not make her happy," Bill said later. "She spent a lot of time searching for that elusive balance between being a mother and wife and being a successful actress."[22]

By all accounts Marcy had a warm, loving relationship with stepdaughters Leslie, Lisabeth, and Melanie; any problems in the Shatners' marriage were handled privately—most of the time. A brief item appeared in a syndicated newspaper gossip column in the fall of 1975, noting tersely that "William Shatner and wife, Marcy, reconciled." Marcy and Bill acted together in a Season 2 episode of *T. J. Hooker* called "Blind Justice," with Marcy playing a (blind) witness to a robbery; the episode also featured a cameo from Carl Wilson of the Beach Boys. Marcy returned to *T. J. Hooker* three more times in guest-starring roles over the next few years.

"I think one career has to take a backseat," she said. "We had children to raise from Bill's previous marriage, and he was already an established star. It was my decision that I'd see to our home . . . You are grateful for what you have, and you're ruthless about the four hours that you get on Sunday."[23]

*   *   *

The third *Star Trek* movie, meanwhile, was taking shape, and by the middle of September 1982—as Season 2 of *T. J. Hooker* premiered on ABC—Harve Bennett turned in his first story line for the film, which he titled *Return to Genesis*. The script would change drastically by the time filming began the following summer, but the biggest question for *Star Trek* fans was answered: After months of hemming and hawing and back-and-forth negotiations, Leonard Nimoy agreed to return to the franchise after Paramount gave in to his demand to direct the *Star Trek* movie. He would also reappear as Spock in one form or another. It was up to Bennett to figure out just how Spock would return to the USS *Enterprise* after his death in *The Wrath of Khan* and his somber, stately sendoff as his coffin was jettisoned into outer space, coming to rest in lush vegetation on a nearby planet.

Star Trek III would mark Nimoy's directorial debut on the big screen, but he wasn't a novice behind the camera. In 1973, one year after starring in an episode of Rod Serling's NBC horror anthology series *Night Gallery*, Nimoy directed the series episode "Death on a Barge," starring Lesley Ann Warren. He followed that in 1981 by directing a filmed version of *Vincent*, his one-man stage adaptation of *Van Gogh* in which he played the Dutch artist's younger brother, doomed art dealer Theo Van Gogh. In 1982 Nimoy was, once again, behind the camera, directing an episode of the NBC sci-fi series *The Powers of Matthew Star*. (Harve Bennett was one of the show's executive producers.)

In the late fall of 1982, Bill persuaded Nimoy to appear as a guest star in an episode *of T. J. Hooker*, marking their first joint series television appearance since the final episode of *Star Trek* in 1969. Nimoy agreed to the onscreen reunion, but only if he could direct an episode of *T. J. Hooker*, which turned out to be "The Decoy," which was filmed in late 1982. The episode's plot revolved around a serial killer whose latest victim is a cop. Stacey (Heather Locklear) knew the murdered cop and goes undercover to help nab the killer, Britten (played by George Prendergast)—who's shot by Hooker at the end of the episode.

"The Decoy" aired in late January 1983; earlier that month, Bill and Nimoy began shooting on "Vengeance is Mine," which put Nimoy in front of the camera as Lt. Paul McGuire, a cop and an old friend of Hooker's whose daughter is brutally raped. McGuire, who's unhappy with the lagging investigation, turns to vigilante justice and takes matters into his own hands. He's just about to shoot the suspected rapist when—gasp!—he's talked down by his old pal T. J. Hooker. "I did cross the line, Hooker," McGuire says in the closing jailhouse scene. "Thank God you were there to stop me."[24]

In early February 1983, around the time that "Vengeance is Mine" was airing on ABC, word broke in the press about Bill's involvement with former Green Beret Lt. Col. James "Bo" Gritz. The forty-four-year-old Gritz, a veteran of the Vietnam War, believed that up to 120 American POWs were still being held in a cave in Laos, seven years after the fall of Saigon.

In late November of 1982, Gritz organized a $45,000, nineteen-man mission (four Americans, including Gritz, and fifteen Laotian guerillas) to search for and rescue the men in what he dubbed "Operation Lazarus." The men were armed with Uzi submachine guns, but the mission was scrapped three days in when Gritz and his men were ambushed by local security forces and driven across the Mekong River into Thailand. Two Laotians were killed and an American, Dominic Zappone, was wounded and taken prisoner. Gritz reportedly paid $17,500 for Zappone's safe return. US intelligence officials confirmed Gritz's account but said they warned him ahead of time not to proceed with the covert operation.

Then, in February, Gritz told the *Los Angeles Times* that he would return to Laos for another rescue mission, this time with a sixteen-man unit of former Green Berets. To get to Laos he had to go through Thailand, and officials in Bangkok threatened to arrest Gritz and charge him with illegal entry and possession of illegal weapons if he was caught. Both charges carried lengthy prison sentences. Gritz was interviewed about the threats from the Thai authorities and said his rescue mission was financed with contributions from private citizens—including William Shatner and Clint Eastwood.

Bill and Gritz had met on the set of *T. J. Hooker.* Bill claimed that he paid Gritz $10,000 for the rights to make a movie about his life—a plausible explanation—and said he was unaware that any of that money was being used by Gritz to fund his rescue mission. "I didn't finance an undercover operation, just the life story of a man with whom I became enthralled," Bill said. "What he was going to do with the money was none of my business." Shatner did admit that Gritz told him he was "contemplating" launching a search-and-rescue mission for missing American POWs. "I have an ongoing story development deal at Paramount to buy stories I find interesting," Bill said. "The man is a fascinating man."[25]

Clint Eastwood, who allegedly gave Gritz $30,000 for the rights to a movie (subject matter unknown), never commented publicly on the situation. Both Bill and Eastwood were criticized in the press by family members of the missing POWs. "It was irresponsible," said Ann Griffiths, executive director of the National League of Families. "This kind of activity is not helpful. The US government has a better capability of pulling something like this off."[26]

Bill did come to a quieter rescue that summer when a huge fire gutted parts of the Paramount Studios set in Hollywood during the filming of *Star Trek III*. He was dubbed "a real-life hero" in press accounts when he reportedly grabbed a fire hose and sprayed the sound stage with water, helping to save the expensive set from a fiery destruction. (It depicted a Vulcan planet with "rocks" made from highly toxic polyurethane.)

The blaze broke out behind a tattoo shop façade on a back lot known as "New York Street," which dated back to 1927 and was used for dozens of movies—including *The Bells of St. Mary*, *Breakfast at Tiffany's*, and *The Godfather*. The fire threatened to spread to Stage 15, where *Star Trek III* was filming and which also housed the sets for the television shows *Happy Days, Cheers*, and *Family Ties*. "We had a hose on the stage that was starting to burn," Bill recounted. "We came within about 30 seconds of losing the set."[27] That was the version fed to the media; there were reports that Bill was driven to the set, where he posed with a fire hose, only to be driven away shortly thereafter.[28] "Shatner was there on the news and helped put it out," recalled *Star Trek III* producer Ralph Winter. "It wasn't staged, but Bill was not helping with the garden hose."[29]

On May 19, 1983, Bill was immortalized with a bronze star on the Hollywood Walk of Fame for his contributions to the television and movie industries. His star, cemented into the sidewalk near Mann's Chinese Theater on Hollywood Boulevard, cost $3,000 and was paid for by a group calling itself the William Shatner Fellowship, a group of over one thousand Shatner fans. Over one hundred of Bill's fans turned out for his Walk of Fame induction ceremony and watched as Leonard Nimoy gave a speech on his friend's behalf. Seventeen years later, in 2000, Bill was honored in his native Canada with a star on Canada's Walk of Fame with a red granite plaque located in Toronto's theater district.

(Leonard Nimoy received his star on the Hollywood Walk of Fame in 1985, followed by Gene Roddenberry that same year, George Takei in 1986, DeForest Kelley in 1991, and Nichelle Nichols in 1992.)

The third *Star Trek* movie, now called *Star Trek III: The Search for Spock*, began filming in August 1983 while Bill was on hiatus from *T. J.*

Hooker. The movie was budgeted at $18 million, and all the principal *Star Trek* players returned, as did Merritt Butrick as Dr. David Marcus, the physicist son of Kirk and old flame Carol Marcus (played by Bibi Besch), who was introduced in *The Wrath of Khan.* (David was killed off in *The Search for Spock*; Butrick, who appeared in a Season 1 episode of *Star Trek: The Next Generation*, died in March 1989 at the age of twenty-nine from toxoplasmosis complicated by AIDS.)

Principal shooting on *The Search for Spock* was completed in a tidy forty-nine days, despite the fire on the Paramount lot. In the movie, a bruised and bloodied Admiral Kirk fought Klingon baddie Kruge (Christopher Lloyd) but triumphed in the end. He found Spock, who was brought back to life and initially suffered from amnesia but finally recognized Kirk ("Jim . . . Your name is Jim") and the others—just in time for the fourth *Star Trek* movie, which was already in the planning stages.

There was some initial tension on the set of *Star Trek III*, most notably between Bill and Leonard Nimoy, who, in addition to directing his onscreen colleagues for the first time, had to worry about everything else connected to a big-budget movie production. This was different than Nimoy directing Bill in an episode of *T. J. Hooker*, and there was much more at stake. And then there were the egos involved; Shatner/Kirk the star was having trouble taking orders from Nimoy/Spock, his onscreen subordinate. Nimoy did not suffer fools gladly; he was intense and laser focused on the task at hand, and after pushing hard to win the directing job, now his ass was on the line. "I simply took it as fact that I had their best interests at heart," Nimoy said of his *Star Trek* colleagues while claiming that he was unaware, when shooting on the movie began, of their innate competitive streaks after years of working together. "There were apprehensions at the beginning," said George Takei (Sulu). "When you're working as an actor, you're always fighting for your place in the sun. Now he's the big boss . . . The one you used to be competing with is now in charge."[30]

The competition was particularly intense for Bill, who would be criticized by Takei, Nichelle Nichols, and James Doohan (in their personal memoirs) for his dominating nature and (in their eyes) his machinations to get more screen time. And Bill had trouble, at least initially, with taking orders from Nimoy, now top dog on the set.

"Whenever we were to deal with management, we'd plan it out together," Bill said about his relationship with Nimoy. "Now, suddenly, my 'brother' was saying, 'Well, you should do this, and I think you should do that.' There was an awkward period of time for me, although I don't think for Leonard, when I felt more alone in anything I might have objected to. From my point of view, it was more awkward in the beginning than with either of the other two directors. But that slowly erased itself."[31]

Star Trek III wrapped filming on October 20, 1983, on Bill and Marcy's tenth wedding anniversary. It didn't take long for Bill to swap Admiral Kirk's duds for his blue uniform as Thomas Jefferson Hooker. The series was performing well for ABC at 8 p.m. on Saturdays, leading into *The Love Boat* and *Fantasy Island*, and Bill didn't ease up on his frenetic work schedule. In the spring of 1984, after *T. J. Hooker* finished production on Season 3, he flew off to Vancouver to shoot the NBC movie *Secrets of a Married Man* in which he played Chris Jordan, an errant husband whose life takes a sordid turn. Michelle Phillips played his wronged wife, and Cybill Shepherd played a prostitute whose pimp creates trouble for Jordan as he tries to repair his marriage. "Gratuitous can hardly begin to describe the entire exercise," sniped one critic about *Secrets of a Married Man* when it aired in September.[32] Bill might have flinched at the movie's title since he was keeping some secrets of his own.

Star Trek III: The Search for Spock premiered on June 1, 1984, to mixed reviews. Most critics thought it was a bit of a letdown from the action-packed *Wrath of Khan* and was, at times, sluggish. Janet Maslin, reviewing the movie in the *New York Times*, noted the cast's "gung-ho spirit" and praised the "earnestness" of Nimoy's directing even while noting: "The *Star Trek* saga remains a television series at heart . . . It isn't even necessary to sit through the film to know what its closing words will be. They are, of course: 'And the adventure continues.'"[33] The movie grossed over $16 million in its opening weekend against stiff competition, including *Ghostbusters*, *Indiana Jones and the Temple of Doom*, and *Top Secret!*, and went on to earn a solid $87 million worldwide.

"This is a good but not great *Star Trek* movie, a sort of compromise between the first two," Roger Ebert wrote in the *Chicago Sun-Times*. "It has some of the philosophizing and some of the space opera, and there is an extended special-effects scene on the exploding planet Genesis that's the latest word in fistfights on the crumbling edges of fiery volcanoes."[34] The *New Yorker* found it "tolerable but yawny," and Bill received no hometown discount from the *Toronto Globe and Mail*, which dubbed it "The Search for Schlock: a mission that renders the eyelids heavy."[35]

Bill played coy in the press about another *Star Trek* movie—"the box office will give us the answer to that," he said[36]—but it was a foregone conclusion, and he was already playing hardball with Paramount to return as Admiral Kirk. He wanted $2 million and 10 percent of the profits—reasonable demands for a movie franchise that, to date, had grossed over $320 million. Paramount had other ideas. It was contractually committed to paying Bill and Leonard Nimoy the same salary, and Nimoy was signed to direct the next *Star Trek* movie—and was, in fact, already working on a treatment with Harve Bennett. "I wanted more money," Bill said. "They didn't want to pay me."[37] Paramount eventually caved to his demands, and in February 1985, Bill announced that he would return for *Star Trek IV*, which would not begin filming for another year.

*   *   *

ABC, meanwhile, was having trouble with its prime-time schedule. The network finished the 1985–86 television season in last place for the first time in a decade. In May, it cleaned house and cancelled a slew of shows, including *T. J. Hooker*. The series, airing on Saturday night, had lost a chunk of viewership the past few seasons, and there was no good reason to keep it on the schedule. It was also a casualty of ABC's network-wide executive shuffle.

"The ABC executives who initially ordered the series, and who were very happy with our ratings for several years, were replaced," said *T. J. Hooker* creator Rick Husky. "A new regime came in, and they wanted to put their stamp on the ABC schedule. Our ratings had eased off somewhat, but we were still winning the time slot most nights. However, the new geniuses decided they wanted to change the Saturday-night lineup with new shows."[38] In addition to *T. J. Hooker*, ABC also axed four other series produced by Aaron Spelling: *Matt Houston*, *Finder of Lost Loves*, *MacGruder & Loud*, and *Glitter*. *T. J. Hooker* was replaced on the network's fall schedule with *Hollywood Beat*, another Spelling-produced cop drama headlined by Jack Scalia and ex-NFL star John Matuszak, but it was cancelled after two months.

But Thomas Jefferson Hooker wasn't finished nabbing the bad guys just yet. CBS was looking to establish a presence in the late-night hours and decided to grab ABC's castoff and to resurrect *T. J. Hooker* as part of its new late-night crime-oriented programming block. It featured a rotating roster of one-hour shows that aired on alternating nights to compete against *The Tonight Show* on NBC and *Nightline* on ABC. "Bill Shatner and I met with [the CBS] execs and decided we could make that work," Husky said. CBS also acquired the rights to rerun ABC's old *T. J. Hooker* episodes.

The series' new life on CBS brought its episode count to ninety-one, enabling Columbia Pictures Television, which owned the show, to sell *T. J. Hooker* into the lucrative syndication market. There were some cosmetic changes as the series changed networks; the seventeen CBS episodes and a two-hour *T. J. Hooker* movie, *Blood Sport*, were shot on a limited budget. The series' locale moved from Los Angeles to Chicago, and the role of recurring cast member Hugh Farrington (who played Lt. Det. Pete O'Brien, confined to a wheelchair) was significantly beefed up. Adrian Zmed left the series after three seasons, but Heather Locklear and James Darren returned for the CBS run. To cut costs, action sequences from past episodes were reused in the show's revamped iteration.

Bill directed ten episodes of *T. J. Hooker* that season, including "Shootout," in which a twenty-six-year-old Mexican-born actress named Vira Montes had a small role as a teller in the bank where Hooker, Corrigan (Darren), and Stacy (Locklear) respond to an armed robbery. Montes would play a much bigger role in Bill's life soon enough.

*   *   *

T. J. Hooker was cancelled by CBS in late 1985 after one season on its new network. There was talk that the series might be salvaged if the *T. J. Hooker* prime-time movie, *Blood Sport*—which found Hooker and his sidekicks protecting the lives of a US senator and his wife—struck a ratings nerve when it aired at 9 p.m. in late May 1986. It didn't. "There's [*sic*] certain actors who are chameleons and who just vanish into a part," said Stan Berkowitz, the story editor for *T. J. Hooker*'s final season. "But there are others who are movie stars or TV stars, and Shatner is certainly one of them. When people turn on the TV, they want to see *William Shatner*, which is unfortunate in one way, because he has much more range in him than people know. But you did not see that range on *T. J. Hooker*. He had the kind of charisma like a John Wayne or James Garner, both of whom play the same guy doing different things. Steve McQueen was always Steve McQueen, right?"[39]

Bill looked back on *T. J. Hooker* with a bit of whimsy—and with an oblique criticism of the constraints of prime-time television. "It could have been a wonderful show," he said. "It was a terrific show and I loved doing it—I ran up and down the streets of LA for five years and had a great time—

but because it's TV it couldn't fulfill the original premise . . . an older cop . . . before the Miranda Rights concepts now having to read everything that applied to it and having to be there when he knew the bad guy needed a poke in the eye."[40]

The timing of *T. J. Hooker*'s small-screen exit was fortuitous vis-à-vis Bill's big-screen ambitions. With *T. J. Hooker* out of the way, he could focus on *Star Trek IV: The Voyage Home*. The movie, budgeted at $21 million, started shooting in late February 1986 with Leonard Nimoy once again in the director's chair (and appearing onscreen as the resurrected Spock).

Star Trek IV boasted all the usual suspects—Bill, Nimoy, DeForest Kelley, Nichelle Nichols, George Takei, Walter Koenig, and James Doohan—plus *Star Trek* newcomer Catherine Hicks as biologist Dr. Gillian Taylor and veteran actress Jane Wyatt (who appeared in the 1967 *Star Trek* episode "Return to Babel"). "I just felt it was time to lighten up and have some fun," Nimoy said, a none-too-subtle indication of the tone the movie would adopt.[41] The screenplay was credited to five writers (including Harve Bennett) and had a little bit of everything: slapstick humor, wisecracks, an eco-friendly message, and lots of "fish-out-of-water" situations that harkened back to the more whimsical episodes of the original series. "There is a texture to the best *Star Trek* hours that verges on tongue-in-cheek, but isn't," Bill said. "It's as though the characters within the play have a great deal of joy about themselves, a joy of living."[42]

(Comedian Eddie Murphy, who was a big *Star Trek* fan, was penciled in to play a college English professor in *Star Trek IV* but decided to work on another movie, *The Golden Child*, a box-office failure. "I thought it would be better for my career," he said. "In retrospect, I think I might have been better off doing *Star Trek IV*.")[43]

The movie opens in 2286 and finds the aging *Star Trek* crew departing the planet Vulcan to face the consequences of their actions in *Star Trek III* (including the destruction of the USS *Enterprise*: Kirk now commands the *Bounty*, the rechristened Klingon Bird of Prey ship captured in *Star Trek III*). But their trip back home takes a detour when the *Bounty*, under Admiral Kirk's command, travels back in time to 1986 San Francisco in search of humpback whales. Spock believes the whales' signature way of communicating can short-circuit an alien signal in the twenty-third century that's blocking the sun and threatening to destroy the Earth.

Nimoy shot *Star Trek IV* in fifty-three days and the movie was targeted for a fall release. Plans for *Star Trek V*, this time with Bill directing his first big-screen movie, were set into motion. "I think of myself as a filmmaker. I've been in it all my life and I know many aspects of the business," Bill said when news broke about his directorial debut. "And who would know more about *Star Trek* than I, or Leonard Nimoy? So from every point of view, there's nobody they could hire who is better qualified for the job."[44]

Star Trek IV: The Voyage Home opened in November 1986 over Thanksgiving weekend and earned nearly $40 million in its first five days, $14 million more than *Star Trek III* earned in the same time frame. In conjunction with the movie's release, Pocket Books published a tie-in novel (written by Vonda N. McIntyre) that spent eight weeks on the *New York Times* bestsellers list; the movie eventually grossed $133 million worldwide against a budget of $21 million—netting Paramount a healthy profit and keeping the franchise humming along.

Reviews of the movie aligned with its positive public reception; even *New York Times* critic Janet Maslin, calling its premise "demented," praised *Star Trek IV* for ensuring the franchise would continue. It knocked Paul Hogan's popular *Crocodile Dundee* from its top perch at the box office, and there was even talk that *Star Trek IV* would be shown in the Soviet Union—a first for a *Star Trek* movie. (It was screened in Moscow the following June.)

Newsweek magazine put *Star Trek IV* on the cover of its December 22nd issue. "The Enduring Power of *Star Trek*" the cover headline blared next to a photograph of Leonard Nimoy as Spock. Inside, the magazine devoted several pages to "*Star Trek*'s Nine Lives" and wrote extensively about the new movie, including a sidebar with separate biographical snippets of DeForest Kelley, George Takei, James Doohan, Walter Koenig, and Nichelle Nichols. (It included information about Nichols's new cabaret album, *Uhura Sings*.) "We're after a larger audience now," Bill told the magazine. "We're after people who haven't seen *Star Trek*—and we're learning what the ingredients are. The interplay of the characters is an important aspect."[45]

Star Trek passed yet another pop-culture milestone on December 20 when Bill hosted NBC's popular late-night series *Saturday Night Live*—the first *Star Trek* cast member to achieve the honor. The timing couldn't be better (and was not coincidental). *Star Trek IV* was going great guns at the box office and was expected to continue its charge with the Christmas holiday approaching. *Saturday Night Live*'s sketch-comedy format underscored

Bill's willingness to tackle self-deprecating comedy and to poke fun at him-self—two traits not usually associated with his public image of egocentric self-reverence. (At the age of fifty-five, though, he still refused to poke fun at his much-maligned choice of toupees or even admit to wearing a hairpiece. There was only so far he would go.)

Bill, looking fit and trim in a stylish zip-up sweater—topped off by a head of healthy dark hair—was met with raucous applause when he walked onto the *Saturday Night Live* stage to deliver the show's traditional opening monologue. He faithfully promoted *Star Trek IV* and then segued into the worldwide popularity of the television series—citing the *Star Trek* phenom-enon and "the Trekkies, Trekkettes, and Trekkers" who, he hoped, "have a sense of humor." The short monologue then cut to a six-minute sketch mocking hard-core *Star Trek* fans gathered at a Holiday Inn in Rye, New York, for a *Star Trek* convention.

Most of the fans are wearing *Star Trek* garb (including an "I Grok Spock" T-shirt and Spock ears); all of them are stereotypically nerdy and slavishly devoted to the series. They're in awe of Bill Shatner, who's come to speak to them ("Captain James Tiberius Kirk!") and answer arcane questions about the series. After a few minutes Bill loses his cool and lashes out at the crowd: "Get a life, will you people! I mean, for crying out loud, it's just a TV show! Look at the way you're dressed!" He scolds his audience for turning their devotion to *Star Trek* "into a colossal waste of time" and tells them to "move out of your parents' basements and get your own apartments and grow the hell up!" The sketch, cowritten by Jon Vitti and Robert Smigel, is often cited as one of the best in *SNL*'s storied history. Bill loved the "Get a life!" line so much he used it for the title of his 1999 book (cowritten by Chris Kreski) in which he grappled with Captain Kirk's legacy and ruminated on the ups and downs of *Star Trek* conventions. "In a very strange way that sketch allowed me to erase some of the distance I'd kept from the Trekkies," he said.[46]

During his appearance on *Saturday Night Live*, Bill also poked fun at himself by spoofing *T. J. Hooker*. In the sketch, T. J. clings for hours on end to the hood of a speeding car driven by the bad guys, all the while bantering with Vince and Stacy (played by Dana Carvey and Victoria Jackson) and even reading the perps' license plate with his foot. He reappeared as Captain Kirk in a second *Star Trek* sketch: it's *Star Trek V*, and the ship has been bought by the Marriott Corporation and turned into a *Star Trek*-themed restaurant that the health inspector, Khan (Dana Carvey), tries to shut down.

Khan's plan is stymied when Kirk bribes his assistant with a few bucks—but he vows to get his revenge.

The *Star Trek V* reference was no coincidence. Right before hosting *Saturday Night Live*, Bill stated publicly, and forcefully, that he would direct the movie—and that he was looking for a screenwriter to flesh out his story. "I've pre-tested my story idea to Paramount and they got excited," he said, "but there is still a lot to be done."[47] A spokesman for Gene Roddenberry said Bill was jumping the gun. "So far as we know, Paramount has not even approached us with a proposal for Shatner to direct," the spokesman said. Shatner's agent countered with a definitive statement: "I have a contract in my hands from Paramount which guarantees him director's control on the next *Star Trek* project." Paramount had no comment and Harve Bennett backed Shatner—but pointed out that Roddenberry did, indeed, have final say over who would write and direct the movie. It was superfluous at best, since Roddenberry hadn't exercised that same option over the last three *Star Trek* movies. He was busy working on *Star Trek: The Next Generation*, which, he hoped, would be his television sequel to *Star Trek*.[48]

CHAPTER 11

Fitted for New Suits

Bill and Marcy sold the ranch in Three Rivers in 1985 and bought a 360-acre horse farm in Versailles, Kentucky, from acclaimed horse trainer Donna Moore. That same year they also changed their address in Los Angeles, moving from their ranch house in the city's Hillcrest section to a bigger place on Berry Drive in Studio City. The mountaintop house had a panoramic view of the city. They also bought a beach house in Malibu.

They kept the Belle Reve name for the new farm in Kentucky (it was officially known as Belle Reve Farm), and Donna Moore stayed on to manage the place and to oversee breeding its award-winning line of American saddlebreds and quarter horses—including a world champion stallion, Sultan's Great Day, which was put out to stud at Belle Reve.

(That wasn't the end of the story for Sultan's Great Day. Several years later, Bill was sued by acclaimed Kentucky horsewoman Linda Johnson over breeding rights to the stallion. Bill won the suit in 1990, with a judge ruling that he hadn't agreed to a lifetime breeding agreement with Johnson. Bill testified that he bought Sultan's Great Day from Johnson and her business partner for $300,000, acknowledging that he allowed Johnson to mate her mares with the stallion from 1984 to 1988—but that he had never agreed to a lifetime breeding commitment.)[1]

The new horse farm paid immediate dividends. In November 1986, just before *Star Trek IV* hit the nation's theaters, Bill—"wearing a maroon jacket, navy plaid, and a nervous grin"—rode his American saddlebred, Kentucky Dream, to a blue ribbon at the National Horse Show at Madison Square Garden in New York City. (Bill claimed he changed the horse's name from

Sinatra because it just didn't sound right.) He "kept his hands held high and his face impassive," even when the crowd recognized him and started cheering every time the judge looked in his direction. "I knew there were 10,000 pairs of eyes staring, but my focus was on the horse the way an actor's focus stays on his role," he said.[2]

His focus was also on other, more pleasurable, pursuits—including his romance with onetime *T. J. Hooker* guest star Vira Montes, which reared its head in a very public way as Bill turned fifty-six in March of 1987. The show-business gossip mill shifted into high gear when word broke that that Marcy had "stormed out" of Bill's birthday party in Hollywood, angry over the alleged Montes affair and over allegations that Bill claimed Vira was a relative when they were spotted in public.

Marcy's reported outburst was a rare public display of friction between the Shatners. That same month, journalist Vernon Scott, who covered the Hollywood beat for United Press International, wrote a glowing article about Marcy and her starring role in *Vivien*, a play about the life of actress Vivien Leigh that was being staged at the Melrose Theatre in Los Angeles and was adapted from a ten-minute film, also called *Vivien*, that Marcy wrote, produced, and starred in four years earlier.

Marcy was a longtime admirer of Leigh, the two-time Oscar winner (*Gone with the Wind*, *A Streetcar Named Desire*), dating back to her days as a drama student at USC. She never met Leigh, who died in 1967, but avidly researched her life and her career. "I own a beautiful white ball gown that Vivien wore onstage in 1955 for the play Lady of the Camellias," she told Scott. "I read thirteen biographies about Vivien and more than fifty lengthy articles about her from all over the world. A lot of the dialogue for the play was inspired by interviews she gave after [Laurence] Olivier left her." Scott ended the article with a quote from Marcy about Bill's support for the project. "Bill has been very supportive and encouraging about my devotion to this play," she said. "I've done more than fifty plays, but this is the greatest experience of my life."[3]

There was more trouble four months later, in July, when Bill was spotted walking on Sixth Avenue in New York City outside Radio City Music Hall with a woman who was not Marcy but was identified in press reports as "his enticing brunette companion." (Bill was in town to fill in on CBS's morning show for a few days.) Mike Ferguson, a photographer for Globe Photos, attempted to snap a picture of Bill and his companion, and when Bill accosted him, Ferguson asked Bill why he was trying to grab his camera. "I just want my privacy," he replied. As Bill's companion slunk into the background, trying to avoid what became a very public scene, Bill handed Ferguson twenty dollars for the negatives (after Ferguson threatened to call the cops). Bill's agent, Carmen Lavia, told the *New York Post* that, as far as he knew, Bill and Marcy had been living together the past four months: "I haven't heard different from either one." Ferguson later identified Bill's companion as Vira Montes.[4]

*　　*　　*

Bill spent most of the winter, spring, and summer of 1988 preparing for the rigors of directing and starring in *Star Trek V*, which was scheduled to begin filming in the fall with a reported budget of $30 million. Somehow, he found time in his crammed schedule to costar with Susan Blakely in a forgettable ABC television movie called *Broken Angel*, playing a father searching for his errant, rebellious daughter (Erika Eleniak) in the seedy underbelly of teenage suburbia. "If mannequins could walk, talk, write, and direct, they would put out a better movie than this," sniffed *People* magazine. The *Los Angeles Times* was more succinct: "Shatner woefully overacts."[5] [6] In April, he spent half an hour with Koko, the famous sixteen-year-old "talking" gorilla who understood roughly two thousand words of spoken English and six hundred signs. "We touched hands and we touched minds," he said in his best Captain Kirk voice, invoking a bit of Spock-ian *Star Trek* imagery.[7] "I got right in front of her and said, 'Koko,' and looked into her deep brown eyes. I said, 'I love you, Koko,' and she put her hand out and grabbed me by the balls."[8]

Earlier that year, Bill's youngest daughter, Melanie, appeared in a television ad for Oldsmobile ("My father drove a Starship so it's only natural I fly around in something space age"), with Bill materializing in the car's front seat—all in the name of helping to sell "the new generation of Olds." Melanie was pursuing an acting career; she appeared briefly (and uncredited) as a jogger in *Star Trek IV* and reappeared in *Star Trek V*, this time as the captain's yeoman, after auditioning for another part. "My dad called and said I didn't get the part," she said, "but there was another small role . . . if I wanted it, and I said of course."[9]

Bill's contract to direct *Star Trek V* included the proviso that he also develop the story with *Star Trek* veteran Harve Bennett. It proved to be a problematic process in a "too many cooks" kind of way. Bill insisted on his vision for the story and Bennett had big reservations about the plotline Bill cooked up. "Bill would come in and present a concept and he thought he was discovering the wheel," Bennett said.[10] It was not a recipe for success. The movie's executive producer, Ralph Winter, put it bluntly: "*Star Trek V* almost killed the franchise."[11]

There were others who felt that Bill wasn't ready to direct a big-screen movie—that his outsized ego and alpha-dog personality were not well suited to interacting on such a close and personal level with his *Star Trek* castmates. But it was that very Shatner-type doggedness and determination that spurred him along. No one ever accused Bill Shatner of lacking in self-confidence; he was sure that his vision was the right way to go, and he tried to mold *Star Trek V* as closely to that vision as possible.

"My one idea was, 'Star Trek' goes in search of God and instead of finding God they find the devil," Bill said. "During the finding of the devil the three main characters are at each other's throats for various reasons. The devil grabs McCoy and takes him into hell and Spock and Kirk . . . join forces, go back down to the River Styx and rescue McCoy and bring him out."[12] Gene Roddenberry hated the idea. The concept of God, he told Bill, meant different things to different people. "Gene did come down strongly against the story and set up circumstances that were negative and unfortunate," Bill said. "There's nothing wrong with a good story about the search for the meaning of life."[13] Paramount agreed with Roddenberry, and the story arc was changed. "After the success of *Star Trek IV*, they wanted to make sure that we retained as much humor and fun as possible, because they felt that was one of the reasons for the big success of that film," noted *Star Trek V* screenwriter David Loughery. "They just wanted a balance between the darker elements and some of the lighter stuff."[14]

Filming on the movie, now called *Star Trek V: The Final Frontier*, began in October 1988. The pressure on Bill was intense—not only was he directing his first big-screen movie, but he was answering to studio executives questioning his ability, both technically and financially (to stay within the movie's budget). Bill's intensely competitive nature posed another self-imposed challenge: could he equal, or maybe even surpass, Leonard Nimoy's success directing *Star Trek III* and *Star Trek IV*? And, if so, would it open other doors for him? Nimoy followed his two *Star Trek* stints behind the camera by directing two successful big-screen movies, *Three Men and a Baby* (in 1987) and *The Good Mother* (1988).

Bill, meanwhile, was also facing competition from another corner: the *Star Trek* franchise itself.

Gene Roddenberry's long-talked-about *Star Trek* follow-up, *Star Trek: The Next Generation*, had finally premiered in late September 1987, over eighteen years since the final episode of *Star Trek* aired on NBC. The syndicated television series, starring Patrick Stewart as USS *Enterprise-D* Captain Jean-Luc Picard, was set in the year 2364, ninety-nine years after the original *Star Trek* began its five-year mission "to boldly go where no man has gone before."

Nearly 27 million viewers watched the new show's two-hour pilot, which aired on over fifty stations nationwide in prime time. Reviews were mixed; the *New York Times* thought that "the *Enterprise* and its new crew simply fail to take flight,"[15] while the *San Diego Tribune* critic enthused that "it has captured much of the original magic."[16] Fans ignored the critics and embraced the new series. *The Next Generation* garnered solid ratings in its first season, averaging around 9 million viewers per episode, and was renewed for a second season scheduled to air in conjunction with the premiere of *Star Trek V*. The heat was on Bill to keep the *Star Trek* faithful interested in the big-screen movies, which now had new competition in the form of *The Next Generation*.

Filming on *Star Trek V: The Final Frontier* was completed in late December 1988. The shoot was not an easy one for Bill, who worked extremely long hours and oversaw almost every aspect of the production—including on-location shooting in Yosemite National Park for a scene in which Kirk scales a mountain. Notwithstanding Nimoy and, to a lesser extent, DeForest Kelley, Bill wasn't particularly close to his *Star Trek* castmates. There was the usual friction with supporting players James Doohan, Walter Koenig, and Nichelle Nichols—and, to a lesser extent, with Nimoy and Kelley. James Doohan recalled seeing Nimoy and Kelley "snickering" to each other about Shatner, "waiting for him to make some new mistake."[17]

Still, Bill insisted that he had fun directing *Star Trek V*. "This was the first time that I had my hands on so much money," he said. "It was quite an experience just from that point of view . . . On the other hand, I made a vow not to take it too seriously. And I did enjoy the whole thing tremendously."[18]

"He's argumentative and has a very, very healthy ego, and an ego fueled by watching his costar reap the benefits of directing the previous two movies," the movie's publicist, Eddie Egan, said of Bill. "Unfortunately, I just think he wasn't as collaborative as Leonard is by nature."[19] Bill admitted how difficult it was for him to direct his *Star Trek* cohorts: "I suppose it's like having a child who has a characteristic you wish he wouldn't have, and you don't know what to say . . . Some of the cast have characteristics you wish they wouldn't do and, politically, it's hard for another actor to say, 'You'd do so much better if you wouldn't do such-and-such.' But as a director, it's your duty."[20] He also talked about the difficulties of directing himself, calling it a "dangerous proposition" that he was unsure about heading into the project. "You know, a lawyer who conducts his own defense has a fool for a client," he told a reporter. "I think the same thing can apply to a director who is acting in his own picture. He has an actor of dubious qualifications."[21]

Personality conflicts were one thing; interactions between actors, however much they might detest each other, could be faked onscreen. (They're actors, after all.) The consensus by those working on *Star Trek V* was that it suffered from a weak plotline, and not bad chemistry among the cast—and *that* was more difficult to overcome. "It failed because of the story concept," Koenig said. "I don't think it was well thought out. We had the same problem on *Star Trek: The Motion Picture*." "All we needed, and all of us say this, was a good script," said Doohan. "Unfortunately, we didn't have one in *V*."[22]

The movie opens with Kirk, Spock, and Dr. McCoy camping at Yosemite National Park. As the plot lurches forward, the *Enterprise* and Spock's half-brother, Sybok (Laurence Luckinbill), breach a barrier to land at Sha Ka Ree—the planet where creation began. Kirk, Spock, McCoy, and Sybok beam down to the planet's surface. An entity Sybok believes is God (it isn't) attacks Kirk; Sybok sacrifices his life in order to save the others, and the entity is destroyed by a Klingon ship pursuing the *Enterprise*. The crews of the *Enterprise* and the Klingon ship reach a détente—and Kirk, McCoy, and Spock resume their camping trip in Yosemite.

The happy ending of *Star Trek V: The Final Frontier* did not carry over into the film's post-production process, which was plagued by delays and snafus regarding the movie's special effects. "We ran out of money for the ending," Bill said. "We had a lot of technical problems, but there are wonderful moments in *Star Trek V* that I'm very proud of."[23] The movie was still undergoing revisions in April 1989 before it was finally deemed ready for its premiere.

That didn't go well, either.

Star Trek V had the misfortune of opening on June 9 against a backdrop of big-budget sequels, including *Ghostbusters II* and *Indiana Jones and the Last Crusade*. Initially the signs were positive; the movie grossed over $17 million in its first week with a publicity blitz that included a tie-in computer game, a novelization (which spent four weeks on the bestsellers list), a *Star Trek* clothing line, and even a *Star Trek* marshmallow dispenser courtesy of Kraft. By its second week in release, *Star Trek V* was fading fast, and in the end, the film tallied only $63 million worldwide. Paramount reaped a profit of $30 million, but it was not the windfall the studio expected.

Bill's directorial debut was met, at turns, by eviscerating criticism and a modicum of praise. The *Washington Post* dubbed *Star Trek V* "a shambles, a space plodessy, a snoozola of astronomic proportions," and wrote that "the story is uneventful, the effects warmed over from *Star Wars*."[24] "Of all the *Star Trek* movies, this is the worst," sniped *Chicago Sun-Times* critic Roger Ebert. "*Star Trek V* is pretty much of a mess—a movie that betrays all the signs of having gone into production at a point where the script doctoring should have begun in earnest. There is no clear line from the beginning of the movie to the end, not much danger, no characters to really care about, little suspense, uninteresting or incomprehensible villains, and a great deal of small talk and pointless dead ends."[25]

Other critics were more forgiving. *USA Today*: "Though [Shatner] doesn't exactly parallel-park *Star Trek V* . . . into a meteor, the journey is (at best) an amiably lazy Sunday drive." The *Los Angeles Times*: "*Star Trek V: The Final Frontier* is as much a spiritual odyssey as a space adventure . . . It has high adventure, nifty special effects, and much good humor, but it also has a wonderful resonance to it." The *Boston Globe*: "There are times when *Star Trek V* seems padded and low-impact, but there are things to like, too."[26]

In July, one month after the movie's release, Pocket Books published *Captain's Log: William Shatner's Personal Account of the Making of Star Trek V: The Final Frontier*. The book was cowritten by Bill and his daughter Lisabeth and chronicles Bill's first-person account of the movie's production. ("As told by Lisabeth Shatner," the book noted on its cover.)

Captain's Log wasn't the only literary effort Bill undertook as the decade was drawing to a close. Perhaps emboldened by his involvement with the *Star Trek V* story—and considering himself steeped in the science-fiction tradition (and, by extension, its community of fans)—he signed a deal with Putnam to "write" a series of sci-fi novels called *TekWar* on which he collaborated with prolific author Ron Goulart, who was well versed in the fiction and non-fiction genres.

Goulart was uncredited on the book jackets, which listed Bill as the sole author. But Bill was very complimentary of him when discussing the *TekWar* books and their working relationship—which was conducted mostly over the telephone by tossing ideas back and forth. He also thanked Goulart profusely in the original book's introduction: "Ron Goulart, a wonderful writer, showed me the way out and showed me the way in to completing the novel."

The protagonist of *TekWar* was a futuristic detective named Jake Cardigan, who Bill said he based on T. J. Hooker. The first book was set in the twenty-second century, and "tek" refers to the illegal, mind-altering drug, in the form of a microchip, that Cardigan is accused of dealing. (He was framed, of course.) Cardigan is sentenced to a fifteen-year prison sentence aboard an orbiting prison. He's released four years later and vows to hunt down the tek drug lords responsible for dealing the evil drug. "In my book, computer software is the drug," he said in describing the first *TekWar* novel. "People use software to alter moods. I let my imagination run wild. I had talked to policemen for almost five years during the [*T. J. Hooker*] TV series. I found their lives interesting and strange and vital. They live on the edge with anxiety and tension—where the action is."[27]

TekWar was published in October 1989, and the reviews were mixed. *People* magazine panned the book: "Shatner tries to disguise language and narrative weaknesses under a blizzard of futuristic details and a pell-mell plot. It's a nice try, but *Tek War* is undone by superficial characters and stilted dialogue. Even devout Trekkies won't care to become tekkies."[28] Other critics were kinder: "While it's unlikely that Shatner's prose will ever rival Isaac Asimov's for density of plot . . . Shatner has nonetheless delivered a witty, no-nonsense rollicking adventure. If Trekkies fork over their cash for *TekWar*, it will be assured a place on the bestsellers list. Strangely enough, it deserves one."[29] *Publisher's Weekly*: "While the writing is awkward in spots, the pace is unrelenting."[30]

The Shatner-Goulart partnership proved to be a fruitful one as *TekWar* hit the bestsellers list and would spawn nine further books in the series that were published through the late 1990s. There were other *TekWar* spinoffs, both literary (an Epics Comics/Marvel comic book series called *Tek World*, set fifty years in the future) and electronic (a video game, "William Shatner's TekWar"). Bill wasn't shy about his desire to translate the *TekWar* franchise onto the big screen, and he would eventually achieve his goal of getting it onto film—though not in the medium he envisioned—when his *TekWar* television series premiered in 1994. "Shatner's a good storyteller, and he has a very good sense of how to reach a large audience," Goulart said. "That's always helpful. All the suggestions he has made are toward making this thing work."[31]

*   *   *

Television, meanwhile, continued to be the one constant in Bill Shatner's life. He was fifty-eight now and a millionaire, thanks mostly to the *Star Trek* movies and his frenetic work schedule, which never slowed down. His marriage to Marcy, which had peaked years earlier, seemed to be mostly valleys now, but they remained a couple, at least publicly, and continued to breed horses on their Belle Reve Farm in Kentucky. There were reports that Marcy, tired of Bill's roving eye, walked out on him in the spring of 1989, only to return several months later when he promised to change his ways.

Bill expected to direct the next *Star Trek* movie, which was projected to start filming sometime in 1990. There were rumors that *Star Trek VI* would be the final movie using characters from the original television series. If Bill wasn't working on his next *TekWar* novel or materializing at *Star Trek* conventions—signing autographs, posing for pictures (for a fee), and engaging fans in the requisite question-and-answer sessions—he was acting on the small screen. His projects around that time included *Voice of the Planet*, a ten-hour, $3.5 million Turner Broadcasting miniseries, based on the Michael Tobias novel, in which Bill costarred (with the voice of Faye Dunaway) as a university professor who heads for the Himalayas and encounters the spirit of the Earth. The miniseries was two years in the making and included twelve months of shooting in eighteen countries; Bill shot his scenes before beginning work on *Star Trek V*. "I chose William Shatner because I admire his great acting ability," Tobias said. "Will brings a life and sensitivity that is unique to the character."

In early 1989 Bill was hired to host three CBS specials spotlighting the real-life experiences of paramedics, police, firefighters, and other emergency responders. Network president Kim LeMasters ordered the specials after hearing an episode of *The Osgood Files*, a CBS Radio program hosted by Charles Osgood, which featured a frantic 911 emergency call made by a nine-year-old girl whose father was being attacked by an intruder, who was gunned down by the girl's older brother. NBC was already airing its popular series *Unsolved Mysteries*, with host Robert Stack, which focused on true crime and the paranormal. But first responders? That was an untapped television genre.

Enter *Rescue 911*.

LeMasters initially suggested that Leonard Nimoy host the new series, and executive producer Arnold Shapiro countered with Bill Shatner. "[LeMasters] said, 'Oh, that's an interesting idea. Explore it,'" Shapiro recalled. "The reason I'd said that was because I'd worked with Shatner twice before. I'd done two years of a special called the *Science Fiction Film Awards*, which was a syndicated two-hour special. The first one aired in 1978 and was hosted by William Shatner and Karen Black, and the second one, we figured since Shatner did such a good job, he could just handle it himself, and that's what we did."

In 1987, Shapiro hired Bill to narrate a CBS special called *Top Flight* to celebrate the fortieth anniversary of the US Air Force. "The thing about Bill is he can do narration," Shapiro said. "And on-camera, he is good. So, CBS business affairs reached out to Shatner's representatives and a deal was made" for him to host the *Rescue 911* specials.[32]

The specials were scheduled to air in April and May of 1989, and Bill promoted them enthusiastically in newspaper interviews, telling the *New York Post* that he'd experienced his own 911 emergency several years earlier, while driving in Philadelphia, when he witnessed a man threatening a woman with a knife. He said he called 911 and police soon arrived at the scene. "It has two things going for it," he said of *Rescue 911*. "It rips your head off with excitement. You hear the real telephone calls, see the news footage, and watch the harrowing things that are happening in front of you. And it serves a purpose by showing what a 911 call does . . . it's useful information."[33]

The first *Rescue 911* special aired on April 18, 1989, highlighting, among other first-responder heroics, the rescue of children stranded in a bus crash and a babysitter tossing eight babies out of a window during a raging fire. The special won its time slot and was followed three weeks later by the second special. That, too, won its time slot in total viewership. CBS smelled a winner. "They told us that it was likely that we were going to get a series and to hold the third special to be an episode of the series, which is what happened," Shapiro said.

In May, the network announced that *Rescue 911*, with host William Shatner, would return in the fall as a regular prime-time series. Bill was in a sound booth doing a voice-over for the special when the news broke. "We got the news that we had been picked up for more episodes and he was thrilled," recalled *Rescue 911* director Nancy Platt Jacoby. "I mean, he jumped out of his seat. It was like a first-time actor getting a pickup. I mean, it was such a surprise to me. We were all thrilled."[34]

Bill's *Rescue 911* shooting schedule was flexible and could accommodate his other projects; he filmed his on-camera appearances every other Sunday at a 911 call facility in Huntington Beach, thirty-five miles from downtown Los Angeles, which also housed a fire department and ambulances. Filming was often interrupted by real 911 calls and would resume only after the situations were handled. "I can't tell you how many times Bill would be in the midst of a perfect take and the phone would ring," Shapiro said. Bill recorded his voice-over narration for *Rescue 911* every Friday at a sound studio in Hollywood.

"He was the face of the show," Shapiro said. "In that era of so-called 'reality television,' you pretty much needed a host. In a period of one year, *Rescue 911* came on the air, *Cops* came on the air. There was *Unsolved Mysteries* at NBC, *America's Funniest Home Videos* on ABC, *America's Most Wanted* on Fox."[35]

"One day, we were filming in the dispatch center when a woman called and said her husband had shot himself," Bill recalled. "He was still alive. You're standing there, once removed from the tragedy, as the dispatcher calmly tries to help the woman on the other end whose life has been shattered."[36]

As it turned out, Bill could have used the help of *Rescue 911* in his personal life, too.

In late January 1990, Vira Montes—who met Bill back in 1984 and who had appeared in an episode of *T. J. Hooker*—sued him for palimony. She claimed they had a years-long affair and that Marcy eventually learned about their trysts and threatened to kick Bill out of the house if he didn't end the relationship, perhaps alluding to the incident in 1987 when Marcy stormed out of Bill's fifty-sixth birthday party. Montes hired pit bull attorney Marvin Mitchelson to handle her palimony case. Mitchell pioneered the palimony precedent ("marriage with no rings attached," he quipped) when he sued actor Lee Marvin on behalf of Marvin's former live-in girlfriend, Michelle Triola, in what became a landmark legal case.

Mitchelson's link to Bill actually dated back to 1970, when Gloria Shatner hired him to defend her as she fought for a percentage of Bill's residuals from *Star Trek*. (She won the case.) "I'm sure the charge has no validity," Shatner's agent, Carmen Lavia, told the press about the Montes palimony case. "The phrase 'palimony' makes no sense. Palimony assumes you're living with someone. It's hard to live with someone when you're living with someone else."

Bill was on vacation (with Marcy and his three daughters) when the news broke but released a statement to the press without mentioning Vira's name. "It's a shame this had to happen," he said. "The case she presents is ridiculous. She was a friend whom I tried to help. Someone obviously got to her and convinced her that she could possibly make a killing by suing me."[37]

In her $6 million palimony suit, Montes claimed that she met Bill when she was a twenty-two-year-old medical assistant and that he promised to maintain a high standard of living for her for "the rest of her life," that he promised to marry her, and that he talked with her about having a child together.[38] She claimed that her affair with Bill included a jaunt to Vancouver for their "unofficial honeymoon" and that, in 1986, he bought her a house in the San Fernando Valley and visited there frequently. Bill was terrific in bed, she said, despite his wearing a toupee and a corset: "We would make mad love, then he would race back to his home in time for dinner," she said. "I heard he had lots of women, and the only thing I insisted was that I should be the only one apart from Marcy."[39] She also claimed that Bill promised to buy her a car, horseback riding lessons, an Arabian horse given to Bill by Wayne Newton, and another horse for her eight-year-old son.

The case was quietly settled out of court for an undisclosed amount—as was another palimony case, this one for $2 million, that was brought against Bill in late 1989 by Eva-Marie Friedrick, who was hired by Marcy in 1986 as an associate producer and personal assistant. Friedrick claimed she and Bill embarked on a two-year affair in the same time frame he was allegedly bedding Vira Montes.

In court papers filed in late December 1989, Friedrick sued Bill for breach of contract, fraud, negligent infliction of emotional distress, violation of state labor laws, and negligence—charges he called "totally unfounded." Friedrick claimed that Bill "promised her that she wouldn't be stuck behind a desk and she'd learn to become a producer," that they had an "intimate relationship," and that Bill abruptly ended the affair after she was seriously injured in a car accident in October 1988. She was fired a month later, she claimed. [40] The case was featured on the syndicated television newsmagazine *Inside Edition*, which breathlessly reported on Bill's "showdown with a human Klingon—a woman, determined to cling on to what she insists is rightly hers."[41] Bill declined to comment.

British network Thames Television chose this embarrassing, tabloid-y time in Bill's life to feature him as its surprise guest on *This Is Your Life*, its long-running biographical series adapted from the original NBC version, which premiered on television in 1952 with host Ralph Edwards. (*This Is Your Life* debuted on the BBC in 1955 with host Eamonn Andrews.) Bill was popular in the United Kingdom, and the BBC had been airing *Star Trek* since 1969, repeating the series off and on throughout the 1970s and '80s and generating a big fan base almost as devoted as their American cousins. *T. J. Hooker* was also a big draw in England, premiering on ITV in 1983 and airing regionally on Friday and Saturday nights.

Bill's episode of *This Is Your Life*, which aired on December 27, 1989, was shot at Universal Studios in Florida. In order for the show to succeed, it needed an element of surprise, and the show's unofficial "rule" called for an episode to be cancelled if the intended subject was tipped off beforehand. Bill, who was dressed in a suit and tie and was standing on a replica of the deck of the USS *Enterprise*, thought he was going to be interviewed about *Star Trek* before a live audience. *This Is Your Life* host Michael Aspel ambushed the honoree, who appeared genuinely shocked, throwing his head back and laughing. "You're kidding!" Bill said. "Oh, my Lord, I have seen this show in the United States, you know the idea that you stole. I've seen it and I can't believe it!"

Bill and Aspel were then "beamed" via cheesy special effects onto an adjoining sound stage furnished with several rows of chairs, including several empty seats to be filled by the surprise guests. Smiling *Star Trek V* producer Harve Bennett was there, though he didn't say a word but was identified and shown on camera. Following a montage of Captain Kirk locking lips on *Star*

Trek with a bevy of women—somewhat awkward, considering Bill's recent palimony cases—the rest of the half-hour show unfolded. Aspel introduced Bill's daughters—Leslie, Lisabeth, and Melanie—and Marcy (who recounted how they met on the set of *The Andersonville Trial* and how she fell "madly in crush with him"). Bill's longtime friend Hilliard Jason was there, recalling their days as counselors at Camp B'nai Brith—where "as our one talented member of the staff," Bill created a character called "The Mad Professor," which he was called upon to perform time and again—including right then and there. (He gamely gave it a whirl.)

Bill's costar from *A Shot in the Dark*, Julie Harris, appeared on the episode via videotape ("Let's do it again, let's go back to Broadway!"), and following a brief clip of Bill and Spencer Tracy from *Judgment at Nuremberg*, Leonard Nimoy came out on the stage, regaling everyone with the long-in-the-tooth *Star Trek*-era bicycle story ("He's a terrible person! He took it upon himself to torture me with this bicycle!") but getting a lot of laughs nonetheless. *T. J. Hooker* costars Adrian Zmed and Richard Herd were there in person and each said a few words (Zmed telling a funny story about Shatner's "warp speed" driving while filming a particular scene), while another *T. J. Hooker* alum, Heather Locklear, appeared via videotape. ("I learned so much from you. You were always such fun to work with. You always had a great sense of humor.") Bill's love of horses was addressed by trainer Donna Moore, who appeared on tape from the Shatners' horse farm in Kentucky with Bill's pride and joy, stallion Sultan's Great Day, and said a few (scripted) words. The episode closed with a brief appearance from Bill's son-in-law, Gordon Walker (Leslie's husband), holding Bill's grandson, twenty-month-old Grant.

* * *

Bill turned sixty in March 1991 and, in April, shooting began on *Star Trek VI: The Undiscovered Country*.

The original NBC television series was turning twenty-five that year, and Paramount's original plan was to celebrate the milestone with a prequel movie, overseen by Harve Bennett, called *Star Trek: The Academy Years*—recounting how Kirk, Spock, and McCoy first met at Starfleet Academy. Bill and Leonard Nimoy (but not DeForest Kelley) would appear at the beginning and end of the film for contextual purposes. *Star Trek* fans gave the idea a big thumbs-down, as did the original cast members (why miss out on another paycheck?), and the plan was abandoned. Bennett quit in a huff. "I wasn't too clued in on the politics of what was happening," Bill said, somewhat disingenuously. "I heard about the prequel and was considering my options, but it was never approved, and we didn't know whether or not there would be another *Star Trek* until the last second."[42]

With the twenty-fifth anniversary quickly approaching, and the prequel movie idea scrapped, Paramount had to act quickly. The studio tapped Leonard Nimoy to be the movie's executive producer. Bill expected to direct *Star Trek VI*, hoping to redeem himself after flopping behind the camera with *Star Trek V*, but Nimoy bypassed him in favor of *Star Trek II: The Wrath of Khan* director Nicholas Meyer. "Let's face it, nobody wanted to have anything to do with anybody who had anything to do with *V*, except as necessary," noted *Star Trek VI* cowriter Denny Martin Flinn. "I don't think *Star Trek V* was entirely Shatner's fault by any means . . . but no one was happy with it."[43] Bill was disappointed but took the high road, claiming he felt "a sense of tremendous relief" at not having to direct the movie under severe time constraints and with a frugal budget and Paramount executives breathing down his neck.[44]

The *Star Trek VI* script, written by Meyer and Flinn, was based on a story by Nimoy, Lawrence Konner, and Mark Rosenthal and was completed in October 1990—one year after the fall of the Berlin Wall. It transposed that historic event onto the context of the *Star Trek* universe: a détente between the Federation (the United States) and the Klingons (Russia). The *Star Trek* gang returned for their big-screen swan song—Bill, Nimoy, DeForest Kelley, Nichelle Nichols, James Doohan, George Takei, and Walter Koenig. Future *Sex and the City* star Kim Cattrall joined the *Enterprise* as Vulcan helmsperson Valeris; David Warner, Christopher Plummer (Shatner's old pal from their Stratford Festival days), and Rosanna DeSoto played Klingons Gorkon, Chang, and Azetbur. Future star Christian Slater, best known at the time for his role in the big-screen dark comedy *Heathers*, had a small role as a young ensign (perhaps due to the persuasive powers of his mother, a Hollywood casting director).

The Undiscovered Country opens with the explosion of the Klingon moon Praxis, which destroys the Klingons' ozone layer and forces them to sue for peace with the Federation. The *Enterprise*, captained by a resentful Kirk (whose son, David, was killed by Klingons), is sent to escort Klingon Chancellor Gorkon to Earth. Kirk and McCoy are wrongfully accused of assassinating Gorkon and are arrested by General Chang. They're found guilty and sentenced to life imprisonment on the frozen asteroid Rura Penthe. (Bill and DeForest Kelley shot their Rura Penthe scenes on a soundstage, with a real Alaskan glacier used for establishing shots.)

Through a series of events that includes their encounter with a shapeshifter, Martia (played by the fashion model Iman), Kirk and McCoy are eventually beamed back aboard the *Enterprise* by Spock, who's captaining the ship in Kirk's absence. Gorkon's real assassins (including—gasp!—Valeris) are found, peace talks between the Federation and the Klingons are saved (Chang is killed trying to sabotage the summit), and Kirk proclaims that the *Enterprise* has flown its last mission.

The old on-set problems between Bill and his *Star Trek* family occasionally flared up during filming of *The Undiscovered Country*. Bill, George Takei later wrote, held up the shooting of a scene because he disagreed with the way director Nicholas Meyer wanted to film it, only because Kirk was not the scene's intended focal point: "Bill had changed over the years. He had hurt people and seemed ignorant of the pain he had inflicted. He had denigrated his colleagues and blithely giggled about it. He had taken without feeling. And in so doing, he had diminished himself . . . The vibrant young actor radiating star energy whom I met back in 1965 had reduced himself to the sad, stubborn, oblivious butt of derisive jokes."[45]

Bill enjoyed reconnecting on the set with Christopher Plummer, who, he recalled, was a part of the "in" group when they were both at Stratford. "He was flamboyant and would hoist a few with the guys, and I was on the outside looking in at all these people," Bill said, "so I now had an opportunity to examine who this man was, and it was wonderful."[46]

Gene Roddenberry flew off into the eternal sunset when he died at the age of seventy on October 24, 1991, six weeks before the official *Star Trek VI* premiere. (He was well enough to attend a screening of the movie in early October.) The creator of *Star Trek* lived a hard, fast life and had been in declining health since suffering a stroke in 1989. Bill, for reasons of his own, did not attend Roddenberry's memorial service, which was held on November 1 at the Hall of Liberty in Los Angeles. "He was the only one who was not there," George Takei said. "As always."[47] Takei was there along with Leonard Nimoy and Nichelle Nichols (who sang two songs dedicated to Roddenberry, one of them Paul McCartney's "Yesterday"). James Doohan paid his respects, and *Star Trek: The Next Generation* stars Patrick Stewart and Whoopi Goldberg joined Isaac Asimov and several others in sharing their memories of Gene during the memorial service. Bill, writing in later years about his relationship with Roddenberry, described it as "lousy: rather formal, cool, and strained." But he regretted that Gene died "before [he] ever *really* got to know him."[48]

Paramount put on a full-court press to promote both *Star Trek VI* and the television show's twenty-fifth anniversary. In November, Leonard Nimoy appeared as Spock in a two-part episode of *Star Trek: The Next Generation* to ramp up interest in *Star Trek VI*. (He was reportedly paid $1 million for his cameo.) The episodes averaged over 25 million viewers, huge numbers for the series. Paramount planned marathon screenings of all the previous *Star Trek* movies. On December 5, one day before the official premiere of *Star Trek VI*, Bill, Nimoy, and the other *Star Trek* regulars participated in that vaunted Hollywood tradition of signing their names into the concrete on Hollywood Boulevard in front of Grauman's Chinese Theatre.

All the promotion paid off. *Star Trek VI: The Undiscovered Country* opened on December 6 and grossed over $18 million in its opening weekend, setting a new record for a film series as the weekend's top-grossing movie. When all was said and done, the movie earned nearly $75 million at the box office (in North America) and grossed nearly $97 million worldwide. It was nominated for two Academy Awards (sound effects editing and makeup) and was the first *Star Trek* movie to win a Saturn Award as the year's best science fiction film. The reviews, most of which were quick to point out the cast's advancing ages, were overwhelmingly positive.

The *New York Times*: "There are no signs of waning energy here, not even in an *Enterprise* crew that looks ever more ready for intergalactic rocking chairs."[49]

USA Today: "*Star Trek VI* more than upholds the tradition, making it a satisfying send-off for a mighty ship of foils."[50]

Variety: "Weighed down by a midsection even flabbier than the long-in-the-tooth cast, director Nicholas Meyer still delivers enough of what Trek auds hunger for to justify the trek to the local multiplex."[51]

The *Hollywood Reporter*: "The film has a conviction and pulp-adventure integrity that cannot be underestimated . . . Not the best of the series, but a suitable farewell."[52]

But Bill wasn't quite ready to throw in the *Star Trek* towel just yet, even though the lucrative movie franchise was receding into his rearview mirror.

CHAPTER 12

The End of a Chapter

In June 1992, with the sheen of *Star Trek VI* fading, Bill signed a contract with HarperCollins to write a book about his experiences working on the original series. The deal was reportedly worth just under $1 million and was sealed after a bidding war that also involved Simon & Schuster and Putnam. Bill was paired with author Chris Kreski, who'd cowritten the memoirs of actor Barry Williams, a.k.a. Greg Brady on the early '70s ABC sitcom *The Brady Bunch*. That book, published by HarperCollins and called *Growing Up Brady*, sold over two hundred thousand copies in its first six weeks.

The Brady Bunch, which ended its five-season run on ABC nearly twenty years earlier, had a kitschy quality and, like *Star Trek*, enjoyed a syndicated resurgence after its mediocre network run. But it had nothing approaching the fan worship of *Star Trek,* and no big-screen movies with the original cast—though it did spawn several television reunion films; a variety show, *The Brady Bunch Hour*; and several big-screen spoofs. If Barry Williams could sell hundreds of thousands of books, HarperCollins figured, imagine what William Shatner could do?

The Shatner-Kreski book, *Star Trek Memories*, was published in 1993 and clocked in at over three hundred pages. In its pages, Bill walked readers through his experiences of shooting *Star Trek* at Desilu Studios and becoming involved in the series, and he shared memories of his favorite episodes, mixing in behind-the-scenes tidbits and anecdotes and breaking down each of the show's three seasons on NBC. The final chapter, entitled "Captain's Epilogue," included Bill's feelings about Gene Roddenberry and their relationship.

Bill took his literary pursuit one step further in the book, interviewing most of his *Star Trek* costars. James Doohan refused Bill's invitation, hinting at the long-simmering distaste that most of Bill's costars held for him through the run of both the television series and the big-screen *Star Trek* movies. In the coming years, that bile would spill out onto the pages of the memoirs written by Nichelle Nichols, George Takei, Doohan, and Walter Koenig, all cashing in their *Star Trek* chits. "I was never rude, I was never angry at anybody, I loved them all," Bill said in his own defense in *Star Trek Memories*. "They can't be angry at me because I loved them. So how can you be angry at somebody who loves you? You can be annoyed, you can be a little jealous—whatever the things are, I have no animosity."[1]

(Leonard Nimoy's two *Star Trek*-related books—*I Am Not Spock*, published in 1975, and its follow up, *I Am Spock*, published twenty years later—focused mostly on his Vulcan alter ego. DeForest Kelley, by all accounts a humble, gentle man, never wrote his memoirs and never publicly criticized Bill. His biography, *From Sawdust to Stardust*, was published in 2005, six years after he died at the age of seventy-nine.)

The book's "Captain's Epilogue" chapter also included Bill's recollections of spending most of a day in February 1993 interviewing Nichelle Nichols and "laughing, flirting and catching up with each other." Bill wrote that, as their chat was ending, Nichols said to him: "Wait a minute. I'm not finished yet. I have to tell you why I despise you." Bill thought she was kidding at first, but the look on her face indicated otherwise. He quoted her at length as she told him: "You can be very difficult to work with, and really inconsiderate of other actors who need to be considered! . . . You may not realize it, but there are times when you get totally involved in yourself, and you're unkind."

He asked Nichols to explain herself, and she recounted how "this went on, on the set, from day one to this day," citing one specific example in which Bill pulled a *Star Trek* director aside during a scene that included her character, Lt. Uhura, telling him: "Look, Uhura doesn't NEED to say that! It's extraneous." Bill noted in the book how "a couple of other cast mates have publicly been rather cool to me" and how, shortly after his interview with Nichols, he learned that she and spoken to Koenig, Takei, and Doohan, who all agreed to confront Bill when it was their turn to be interviewed for *Star Trek Memories*. (This was before Doohan decided not to participate in the project.)[2] Leonard Nimoy came to his friend's defense. "What can you say, Bill is a power on the set," he said. "He was very powerful and aggressive, not necessarily in a way that was intended to damage or to injure, but because of what he felt he had to offer and what he thought was appropriate in a given moment."[3]

Next on Bill's interview list for the book was George Takei, who decided to shy away from confronting Bill—who described him in the book as "wonderful" with a "pleasant demeanor" during their long talk. Takei would have more to say soon enough. Walter Koenig, in *his* chat with Shatner, expressed sentiments similar to those of Nichols, though he and Bill apparently spent more time talking about *Star Trek* and Gene Roddenberry than about any personal conflicts. Doohan cancelled his meeting with Bill, refused to return his calls, and then "flatly refused" to speak to him. He was, he said, convinced that Bill would not use anything he said, particularly if it was negative. Bill's response? "Certainly, this makes me angry, but for the most part it just makes me sad."[4]

Doohan got his revenge three years later with the publication of his memoir, *Beam Me Up, Scotty*. He kept it brief but concise. "I have to admit, I just don't like the man," he wrote of Bill. "And, as has been well-documented elsewhere, he didn't exactly have a knack for generating good feelings about him. It's a shame that he wasn't secure enough in himself or his status to refrain from practicing that sort of behavior."[5]

Star Trek Memories was released in December 1993 and generated generally positive reviews. *Publisher's Weekly* called it "candid, captivating . . . packed with stellar anecdotes and backstage lore," while the *New York Times* praised the book: "Sprinkled throughout this memoir are wonderful bits of gossip" that "even non-Trekkers will find engaging."[6] *Kirkus Reviews* thought that "there's enough here to satiate the most avid Trekker, delivered with pop and pizazz," while *People* magazine called *Star Trek Memories* "a breezy, entertaining memoir." The hardcover book hit the bestsellers list and remained there through 1994, when HarperCollins published a paperback edition.

*   *   *

As the calendar turned to 1994, Bill kept up his frenzied work schedule, plowing ahead with movies, television shows, and books—almost as if he was trying to keep the personal wolves at bay. The year ahead would prove to be a difficult one for the sixty-three-year old actor, who faced the breakup of his marriage, scathing assessments from several of his *Star Trek* costars, and legal problems. There was some positive news—his return to the big screen as Captain Kirk, the television series premiere of *TekWar*—but overall, 1994 was best viewed for Shatner in his rearview mirror.

The year began inauspiciously. In February, Bill and Marcy announced their plans to divorce after twenty-plus years of marriage. The writing was on the wall; to anyone who knew the couple's rocky history, it couldn't have been a surprise. Bill's roving eye was legendary, and he'd settled two palimony suits brought against him. Marcy reportedly threw him out of the house several times; it seemed only a matter of time before their marriage irreparably imploded.

Bill and Marcy issued a public statement calling their divorce "amicable" and admitted that they had been separated for several months. "Life took us apart and it was time to move on," Marcy said diplomatically. "We both share the highest regard for one another and our loved ones."[7]

"I hadn't learned anything from the failure of my first marriage," Bill wrote in his memoir *Up Till Now*. "Marcy and I had a very passionate relationship; when we were in love, we were really in love, but when I got angry . . ."[8] Their divorce, finalized in 1996, cost Bill around $8 million.[9] He also forked over their luxury condo in Vail, Colorado, and their time-share homes in Mexico and Indonesia. There was one unusual clause in their divorce agreement: each year, Bill was to provide Marcy, who continued to breed horses, with fresh samples of semen from one of his prized stallions. (Frozen sperm wouldn't cut the mustard.) That proviso would, like one of Bill's stallions, rear its head further down the road.

The year 1994 also saw the publication of Nichelle Nichols's book, *Beyond Uhura: Star Trek and Other Memories*, and George Takei's memoir, *To the Stars*. Both painted unflattering portraits of Bill, and both were unsparing in their antipathy toward their former costar.

In her book, Nichols skewered Bill as a self-absorbed, arrogant jerk who pushed for Kirk's famous interracial kiss with Uhura (on the "Plato's Stepchildren" episode of *Star Trek*) only after learning that, in the original script, it was Spock who locked lips with Uhura. Bill, she wrote, thought he "could generate a lot of publicity" from the historic kiss (the first of its kind on national television) and demanded that the script be changed. Elsewhere in *Beyond Uhura*, Nichols wrote: "[Bill] began to make it plain to anyone on the set that he was the Big Picture and the rest of us were no more important than the props. Anything that didn't focus on him threatened his turf, and he never failed to make his displeasure known." She described him as feeling threatened by male costars during the run of *Star Trek* (particularly by Ricardo Montalban in the "Space Seed" episode), and she contradicted several scenarios mentioned by Bill in *Star Trek Memories*, including the details of their one-on-one interview in early 1993.[10]

George Takei's book, *To the Stars*, was also published in 1994. Takei, for the most part, painted Bill in an unflattering light. He had nothing but nice words for Bill and costar John Cassavetes when they appeared together on "Wind Fever," an April 1966 episode of NBC's *Chrysler Theater*. Bill, he wrote, "was crafting a fascinating portrait of an idealist with a dark underside" and was a "cracking-good" actor. He also praised Bill as "brilliant" in the Season 1 *Star Trek* episode "The Naked Time," writing that "given the constraints of television, Bill's performance . . . was an amazing display of virtuosity." That tone darkened in Takei's retelling of working with Bill on the *Star Trek* movies, including their reunion on *Star Trek: The Motion Picture*, when Takei and the other cast members suspected Bill of masterminding rewrites that magically cut their lines of dialogue from the script. Or maybe they were just imagining a worst-case scenario. "Bill's almost ingrained behavior troubled and puzzled me," he wrote. "He was the star of the picture. Why was he so insecure about any of us even getting a brief chance to shine? None of us were threats to his position."[11]

Takei recalled an incident during the filming of *Star Trek III: The Search for Spock* when, during a lull in his filming schedule, he took a stroll around the Paramount lot. He was returning to the soundstage when he encountered an irate James Doohan, who was "in a flying rage" when he suspected Bill of changing a camera angle to ensure that Doohan's Scotty was out of the camera frame. "It's that bastard!" Doohan sputtered to Takei. "I'll never let him do that to me again! I mean it!" Takei chalked it up to Bill's "self-absorption" and "deep-seated insecurity."[12]

Bill didn't fare much better in Walter Koenig's memoir, *Warped Factors* (1998), in which Koenig portrayed Bill as a smug, egotistical camera hog. Koenig described an instance during the filming of *Star Trek II: The Wrath of Khan* when, during a setup for a scene in which Kirk is surrounded by several characters, including Chekov, Bill asked him to move and move . . . until he was virtually out of the camera frame. But he was honest and self-analytical in never having criticized Bill to his face. "We have complained about him to each other and in interviews and at conventions and in books," Koenig wrote, "but no one ever looked him in the eye and said, 'Cut the shit, Shatner!' And because we haven't, I'm not sure we can be quite so self-righteous about feeling dishonored."[13]

Koenig did, however, write that his relationship with Bill improved while they were shooting *Star Trek Generations*, most likely because Bill was a small cog in a bigger picture. "Not carrying all the baggage did wonders for his sense of proportion. He was much more a regular guy than I had seen him be before." The bad feelings, though, never quite vanished completely. In 2016 I sent an e-mail to Koenig, requesting an interview for this book. His response? "Unless you will have several photos in your book showing Mr. Shatner having sex with a horse, I must politely decline."

The *Star Trek*-related memoirs from Nichols and Takei were perfectly timed; although their big-screen careers aboard the USS *Enterprise* were over, *Star Trek* and its crew remained a big part of the zeitgeist. The second *Star Trek* television series, *Star Trek: Deep Space Nine*, premiered in syndication in 1993, which allowed its predecessor, *Star Trek: The Next Generation*, to gracefully bow out of production the following year in order to transition to the big screen with *Star Trek Generations* (also referred to as *Star Trek: Generations*). That movie featured Bill, James Doohan, and Walter Koenig in smaller supporting roles opposite the *Next Generation* cast, headed by Patrick Stewart as Captain Jean-Luc Picard. "Bill had a bit of a brutal reputation that precedes him, particularly in his relationship with his colleagues and I was uneasy about that," Stewart recalled. "But when we finally sat down together it was perfect, because it gave us the opportunity to really talk. We didn't talk about our careers. We certainly didn't talk about *Star Trek*. We talked about very personal things and it was the foundation to help us work so well together when the movie began. He became a good friend."[14]

It also marked the end of Captain James T. Kirk, who dies at the end of the movie. "They said, 'We're going to make movies with that cast and we're not going to use you guys anymore, because you guys are getting older and top-heavy with salaries," Bill recalled. "[They said], 'We're going to make a transitional movie. You can come and die, or not. I decided to die. The pay was good."

Star Trek Generations was directed by David Carson from a screenplay by Brannon Braga and Ronald D. Moore. (Doohan and Koenig were hired after Leonard Nimoy and DeForest Kelley declined offers to appear in the film: "I guess this is called working one's way down the food chain," Koenig wrote.[15]) Its plot, in a nutshell, featured Captain Kirk, who was presumed dead earlier in the film, returning to team with Captain Picard to prevent the mad scientist Soran (Malcolm McDowell) from blowing up the planet Veridian IV. They accomplish their mission, but Kirk dies during a fight with Soran when the shaky metal bridge he's clambering on collapses and falls down a steep cliff, pinning him underneath its twisted metal. Kirk's death scene was filmed in Nevada's Valley of First State Park on June 3, 1994. In the scene, Captain Picard finds Kirk pinned underneath the twisted metal, blood running out of his mouth. "Did we do it?" the dying Kirk asks Picard. "Did we make a difference?" Assured that he did, Kirk signs off with his final words: "It was . . . fun," he says, a slight smile on his face. Then, sensing his last breath, a look of wonderment crosses his face as whispers his final words: "Oh my."

Picard then buries Kirk underneath a pile of stones in a plain grave atop a hilltop, placing Kirk's Starfleet insignia atop the grave to mark his final resting place.[16] "We all got emotional when we shot Captain Kirk's death scene," Stewart said. "We were saying goodbye to a legendary, iconic, fictional character of television—and, in a sense, too, we were saying goodbye to a great part of Bill Shatner."[17]

"I thought about dying, my death, and this beloved character who's going to be put to rest," Shatner recalled of the scene. "How do I play it? You know there's got to be a moment, you're alive, and you're going to die, now you're alive and now you're going to die. There has to be a moment when we all, at the moment of death, we say, 'Holy cats, I'm dying!' And you're dead."[18]

The critics were not pleased when *Star Trek Generations* opened on November 18, 1994, though most of the criticism was leveled at the movie's script (and not at Bill or Patrick Stewart). The *New York Times* wrote: "[It's] predictably flabby and impenetrable in places, but it has enough pomp, spectacle, and high-tech small talk to keep the franchise afloat . . . Mr. Shatner can't match Mr. Stewart's thespian manner and Shakespearean intonations. But he's the one with the twinkle in his eye and the pampered, cosseted look of a star beloved by a gazillion fans."[19] "Picard meets Kirk, Stewart meets Shatner, baldy meets the super-rug," noted the *Washington Post*. "Toupee or not toupee? By the end, there's no question that Kirk is the captain of captains . . . Stewart's captain is thoughtful, a bit hesitant. Shatner's goes as boldly as a photon torpedo."[20] *Entertainment Weekly* wrote that Bill "ambles through his relatively brief on-screen time like the winningest of retired football coaches."[21][22]

Roger Ebert, who was never a fan of the *Star Trek* franchise, thought the movie was "undone by its narcissism," while *Los Angeles Times* critic Kenneth Turan thought that *Star Trek Generations* felt "more like engaging in some kind of recurring religious ritual than taking part in the conventional moviegoing experience." He sniped that "Stewart makes Shatner look like a graduate of the Klingon Academy of Dramatic Arts."[23]

It didn't matter, really, what anyone thought of the movie. *Star Trek* was here to stay, and its impact even began to spill over into academia. In the Washington State city of Olympia, Evergreen State College was offering a course on the *Star Trek* television series and its movies and required students who signed up for the class to take it for two full semesters. The course included a science professor analyzing early episodes of *Star Trek*; students searched for hidden elements in the movies and then wrote a script for an imaginary *Star Trek* episode.[24]

There was also news for Bill on the *TekWar* front, both in the publishing world and on television.

The book series, still being written by Bill and Ron Goulart, continued to hum along. The fourth book, *Tek Power*, was published in 1994. Two years earlier, Marvel Comics published the first *TekWorld* comic book. Bill also extended his literary reach by teaming with author Michael Tobias, with whom he'd worked on *Voice of the Planet*, on a sci-fi-tinged historical novel called *Believe*. Published by Putnam in June 1992, it paired escape artist Harry Houdini with *Sherlock Holmes* author Sir Arthur Conan Doyle and was based on an actual contest that was sponsored by *Scientific American* magazine in 1923 and revolved around the age-old question: is there life after death? *Believe* didn't make much of an impact upon its publication, but it reared its head two years later, in 1994, when Bill was sued in Bucks County Court in Pennsylvania by Ralph Miller, the owner of the Bucks County Playhouse, for more than $150,000, for reneging on a promise to costar with Leonard Nimoy in a stage production based on *Believe* at the Playhouse.

Miller claimed that he struck up a friendship with Bill in the spring of 1972, when Bill and Marcy were starring in a production of *Love Letters* at the Bucks County Playhouse. In June, Bill and Miller went tubing on the Delaware River, and Bill said he wanted to stage a play based on *Believe* called *Harry and Arthur*, in which he and Nimoy would costar. According to Miller, the deal was sealed in a limousine while Bill was doing a round of interviews in New York City. *Harry and Arthur* would be staged the following spring, with Bill and Nimoy each being paid $4,000 a week provided the show amassed over $50,000 in ticket sales. There was a proviso: *Harry and Arthur* would be pushed to later in 1993 if Bill's obligations to another *Star Trek* movie or to his new series, *TekWar*, interfered. Bill announced his plans for *Harry and Arthur* at a *Star Trek* convention in Philadelphia in July and on the cable-television sports network ESPN, according to Miller. The premiere was postponed twice and was rescheduled a third time; Miller wanted to recoup the money he claimed was spent on promoting the show and selling tickets.

Bill's agent, Carmen Lavia, said that Bill never announced the production and that a date was never set, though Bill "had all good intentions" of staging the play, but that when he was contacted by the Playhouse in March 1993 to arrange rehearsal dates, he said he couldn't make it—though the Playhouse printed new brochures announcing that *Harry and Arthur* would run December 8–16. According to Miller's lawsuit, Bill called him in August to tell him he couldn't do *Harry and Arthur* because of his filming schedule on *TekWar* and followed up with a letter:

> It was my intention to do the play, *Harry and Arthur*, sometime in the 1993 season with Leonard Nimoy also starring in it. Surprise. Leonard is directing a major motion picture. Surprise. *TekWar* sells to television. Worst surprise of all, I don't get to do *Harry and Arthur* at the Bucks County Playhouse. Let me tell you another fantasy of mine. I would love to think that both Leonard's and my schedule will open up in the next year so that we can do the play at Bucks County Playhouse . . . I hope this explains the comings and goings of your advertising to some extent and let the audience know that I apologize for the inconveniences that may have occurred for them and you. I will be there.

Harry and Arthur never made it to the stage; it is unclear what became of Miller's lawsuit.[25]

Rescue 911 kicked off its fourth season on CBS in September 1992, with Bill hosting the series every Tuesday night at eight o'clock, introducing its reenactments and providing voice-over narration. Since its premiere in 1989, over one hundred people had written into *Rescue 911*, claiming it saved their lives. "It shows people in a good light, in a positive light," Bill said. "It shows that ordinary people are capable of such total unselfishness."[26] "I think it kept him on network television," said *Rescue 911* executive producer Arnold Shapiro. "We were on Tuesday at 8 p.m. on CBS and we never moved. I mean, that's like Milton Berle's record. He was on Tuesday at 8, too, but on NBC. Sometimes CBS would call and say, 'Somebody didn't deliver, we need another episode of *Rescue* next week.'

"Maybe in Season 3 we had one hundred stories with two sources of verification that the show had been responsible for somebody being alive. So, we decided to do a '100 Lives Saved' special as an episode," he said. "I think we did maybe four or five stories that we re-created; the rest we showed the photograph of the person with their name and age. It was everything from toddlers to senior citizens. You couldn't help but get teary when you watched the montage of photographs. We kiddingly said it was the only show on CBS that was saving lives—but that was a fact."[27]

* * *

Bill had always intended *TekWar* to transition from the written word to the screen (big or small), and he continued to push the idea in the five years since the first *TekWar* book's publication. The studio chiefs in Hollywood felt the project would be too expensive, but Bill persisted and, through his Lemli Productions company, signed a deal with Canadian production company Atlantis Films to turn *TekWar* into a television series. (Atlantis Films president Seaton McLean bought a copy of *TekWar* in a bookstore and saw its potential.) Writer Stephen Roloff was hired to develop the project, which eventually morphed into four two-hour television movies, budgeted at $4.5 million each, to be produced in conjunction with Universal Studios. Universal planned to air the movies under its "Action Pack" umbrella of twenty-four action-adventure movies scheduled to air throughout the year—including movies from *Animal House* director John Landis and Hal Needham. The deal was finalized in early 1993 and the two-hour pilot was scheduled to shoot in Toronto in May, with Bill directing. He considered taking the role of *TekWar* protagonist Jake Cardigan. While he was in good shape at the age of sixty-two, he thought better of the idea and hired forty-year-old television actor Greg Evigan, best-known as the costar of the NBC sitcom *My Two Dads* (opposite Paul Reiser), to play Jake. Bill was also an executive producer and would appear occasionally as Jake's boss, Walter Bascom. Warren Zevon composed the theme music.

"I had a great time working with Bill," Evigan said. "We became what I consider good friends. I had a humorous audition, which was a great way to start off because he has so much respect for other actors. I mean, I'm sure there are reports that don't say that, but from my point of view he had great respect for me.

"When I came into the room [to audition] he just went on about how much he loved my work and the funny thing was, he said, 'I don't want you to read. I just want to tell you how happy I am that you are here and that I love your work.' We talked for a little while and then he said, 'OK, let's read.' By the time I got home my agent was all over my answering machine telling me I got the part."[28]

The first of the four syndicated movies, *TekWar*, featuring guest star Barry Morse (best-known to television audiences as Lt. Gerard from the classic 1960s ABC series *The Fugitive*), adhered closely to the first book's plotline. (It was set fifty years in the future, in the year 2044, mostly for budgetary reasons to keep the special effects manageable.) *TekWar* premiered in the United States in mid-January 1994, about a week before airing on CTV in Canada, a pattern that would be repeated with each movie.

The show-business bible *Variety* gave the movie an enthusiastic review: "Viewers expecting a strong *Star Trek* influence, based on the involvement of exec producer/director/creator Shatner . . . will be surprised to find *TekWar* owes more to *T. J. Hooker* than to *Star Trek* . . . The story may be a little too clever—the complicated plot will challenge viewers of all ages—but there's plenty of imagination involving characterizations and compelling conflicts to keep viewers interested."[29] The *Los Angeles Times*, however, wasn't as enthralled—"No one will confuse William Shatner's *TekWar* with serious science-fiction"—while *Entertainment Weekly* ripped it as "your average cop show in a post-20th-century setting . . . Intended to be hard-boiled, the dialogue in *TekWar* is instead just pitiful."[30]

Ratings for the *TekWar* premiere were strong in Canada, and in the United States it boosted viewership significantly on local stations nationwide. The movie's inaugural telecast spiked viewership by 350 percent from the previous November on San Francisco's KOFY, while WPIX (Ch. 11) in New York City scored the biggest *TekWar* ratings in the country. St. Louis and Miami also reported sizable increases in viewership—129 percent and 225 percent, respectively—over the previous November.[31]

Bill visited NBC's *The Tonight Show* in June and revealed that *TekWar* would air as a television series on cable's USA Network, with Greg Evigan reprising his role as Jake Cardigan. In August, USA announced that the series would premiere in January 1995, with Bill executive-producing and returning as Walter Bascom. USA also bought the rights to the four two-hour *TekWar* movies airing in syndication.

The *TekWar* series premiered on January 7, 1995, to record viewership on USA Network, earning a 3.4 rating as the most-watched premiere episode in basic-cable history. *Variety* hated the opener, calling Evigan "David Hasselhoff without the charisma" and ripping the show's "humorless script" and the "problematic pastiche" of its production design while calling Bill "cool, calm and all-knowing" and "the coolest thing on screen." Viewership eventually tailed off, and in June, USA cancelled the series after airing fourteen episodes. In January 1996, the four remaining episodes were moved to USA's cable sister network, Sci-Fi Channel, while it aired on CTV in Canada, completing its run in February.

CHAPTER 13

Nerine

Bill's divorce from Marcy didn't have much of an impact on his romantic life. "I've never been good at being alone," he wrote in *Up Till Now*. "I've had a lot of casual relationships: one-night stands, two-week stands, six-month layabouts . . . But almost always I've lived with the hope of a long-term relationship."

He was in Toronto in 1993 directing "Secret Place," an episode of the syndicated television series *Kung Fu: The Legend Continues*, when he met Nerine Kidd, a thirty-four-year-old model and actress who was in the city visiting friends. Bill recalled meeting Nerine in a hotel bar, how he was "struck instantly by her beauty and this marvelous sort of fuck-you attitude" and her "strawberry-blond hair and freckled pale Irish skin . . . and a spectacular figure." The attraction was mutual and soon blossomed into a full-blown romance, which they no longer needed to hide from the public once Bill divorced Marcy.[1]

Nerine was born in 1959, the second oldest of five children, and grew up in Roslindale, a heavily Irish and Italian neighborhood in South Boston. She spent summers with her family in their vacation cottage near a lake in Sandown, New Hampshire, and, from the get-go, displayed a gregarious personality which was described by family members as "bold, almost fearless." Nerine grew into a willowy, striking blonde and aspired to become a model and actress. She also had moxie; when she was in high school, she contacted Boston's famous department store, Filene's, after seeing one of its commercials on television. "She called them up and said, 'I've seen the girls you use as models. I think I'm better, if you want to give me a try,'" her father remembered. "Apparently, they liked her."[2]

She also brought a handful of modeling photos to Boston modeling agent Janet Chute, who remembered her "cute little nose" and Nerine's Boston accent, "as thick as chowder." Nerine asked Chute if she wanted to see her modeling "pitchers" and charmed her with her outgoing, wisecracking personality and her model-ready good looks. Chute agreed to take her on as a client, and within a year of graduating high school—and losing her Boston accent—Nerine moved to New York City and soon found work on various photo shoots and through runway-modeling jobs. "She was a typical girl from a working-class family who knew nothing about this business," Chute said. "But she was also spirited. And in a business where there's a lot of deadheads, she really stood out."[3]

Nerine's modeling career also took her to Europe, where her circle of exotic friends included model Suzanne Gregard, who was married for a brief time (in 1986) to Dodi Fayed, killed eleven years later with Princess Diana and their limo driver while being chased by paparazzi in Paris. In 1987, Nerine starred in a television commercial for Brut cologne ("For every man who wears Brut, there's a woman who loves what he smells like") and, three years later, landed a small role as Rose Schwartz in the 1990 movie *Artificial Paradise*. The biopic of Hollywood director Fritz Lang was shot in Yugoslavia (in Slovenian) and was screened at the 1990 Cannes Film Festival.

Nerine had a penchant for dating older men—one boyfriend designed yachts, another beau raced cars—and for alcohol. She was also very generous, and once flew her sister from Boston to New York by helicopter. "She was like a windup doll that never wound down," her brother Warren remembered. "Family was her source. Nerine always took care of us. She was the one who held us together. That was Nerine's way. She made all of us feel special."[4] Bill later alluded to Nerine having spent some time in rehab prior to their relationship, apparently for a cocaine addiction.

Bill and Nerine continued their long-distance romance for a while until she eventually moved into his beach house in Malibu. "I had met the girl of my dreams," Bill wrote later. "I fell in love with her and believed she was everything I'd spent my life looking for in a woman. She had the beauty and brains and a joy for living that I had rarely seen before."[5]

Bill turned sixty-five on March 22, 1996, but this "senior citizen" showed no signs of slowing down in his professional life. With his advancing age, though, came some health issues.

In the late 1980s, while he was walking on the beach in Malibu with Marcy, Bill thought that the ocean sounded louder than usual. He asked Marcy if she noticed anything amiss about the roar of the waves. She didn't. From that point onward Bill noticed a dull ringing in his left ear, which never fully dissipated. "At first the hissing noise was sufficiently low, so I could kind of forget it," he said. "What caused it? I really don't know."[6] Leonard Nimoy told Bill that he, too, suffered from a constant ringing in his (right) ear, which he thought was caused when they filmed a scene for the 1967 *Star Trek* episode "Arena," in which Bill and Leonard were standing near a prop explosion on the set. The dull roaring sound in his ear, Bill said, sounded "like a radio left on, but just the static. And you can't turn it off."[7]

He was eventually diagnosed with tinnitus, a disorder of unknown origin that causes a buzzing, clicking, hissing, or ringing in the ears and afflicts untold sufferers. (Estimates range from 12 to 40 million people worldwide.) The ringing in his ear, Bill claimed, drove him to the point of considering suicide. "It can be frightening, and my terror came from two things: One is the sound itself. The other is that it is going to get worse, and you're never going to be able to sleep or concentrate again. I began to think, 'What are the ways to take my life? How does one kill oneself?' I went so far as to start making plans."[8]

His heavy workload offered a bit of relief—he could concentrate on learning his lines and focus on a given project—but his tinnitus grew progressively worse. Bill tried various remedies to ward off the hissing—herbs, eardrops, earplugs, masking devices, and recordings of soothing sounds, including Japanese music. But nothing seemed to work, and he was at his wit's end. He paid a visit to Dr. Howard House, founder of the House Ear Institute in Los Angeles. Of the visit, he said: "We had had tears rolling out of our eyes because he too suffered from tinnitus. Our tears were tears of loss, because we realized that we would never hear a silent night again or hear the crickets alone. They would always be mitigated by this 'wrenching' sound." Bill went "hysterically around to anyone I thought could help" and was fitted with a hearing aid, but he was convinced the feedback from the device would make his tinnitus worse, and he threw it away.[9]

Bill's son-in-law also suffered from tinnitus, and in 1996, he recommended that Bill go to see Dr. Douglas Mattox and Dr. Pawel Jastreboff at the University of Maryland Medical Center. Mattox and Jastreboff invented a device that resembled a hearing aid; once placed in the damaged ear(s), it emitted a white noise that helped reduce the chronic ringing. They claimed an 80 percent success rate with their invention, including their most famous patient, William Shatner, who became a convert and helped to publicize the doctors' efforts. "There's something comforting about it, like hearing rain on the roof or traffic in the background but not listening to it," he said of the curative white noise. "My anxiety has left me. My ability to deal with the noise I'm hearing is more or less 80 percent there. I've got tinnitus, but it doesn't affect me in my general life." He was so impressed that he offered to help raise money for the American Tinnitus Association, the University of Maryland, and Dr. Jastreboff.[10]

*   *   *

As Bill's romance with Nerine charged full-steam ahead, he began to notice, with some alarm, that she was drinking heavily, and that the alcohol altered her demeanor and attitude. But he brushed it off and was unwilling, at that point, to admit to himself that Nerine was exhibiting the classic signs of an alcoholic: "I thought she just had a mean streak," he wrote. "I didn't like it, but because I loved her, I accepted it: nobody is perfect." A reformed heavy smoker—he'd gone cold turkey during the second season of *Star Trek*—Bill knew how difficult it was to break an addiction. But he had stuck to his guns; surely it couldn't be that difficult for Nerine to curb her drinking.[11]

It was.

Bill proposed to Nerine, and they targeted the fall of 1997 for a wedding date. But the impending nuptials did little to stanch Nerine's drinking. Earlier that year she was arrested for drunk driving after picking up Bill's daughter at a spa in Palm Springs, stopping at gas stations during the ride back home to down shots of alcohol in the ladies' rooms. Nerine's driving grew erratic, and she was pulled over by a patrolman after exiting the freeway. "What kind of insanity, what kind of mental illness, allows someone to do that?" Bill wondered. "To drive drunk with a young person in the car?" Nerine swore to Bill that she would never again drive drunk—and was then arrested a second time for driving while intoxicated right before their wedding, forcing Bill to postpone the nuptials for a week.[12] He believed that

Nerine could overcome her demons—he *wanted* to believe that—but he wasn't diving into their marriage wearing blinders. Or maybe he was. Shortly before their wedding, Bill, Nerine, and several other couples were invited to a dinner party thrown by Leonard Nimoy and his wife, Susan. Leonard was himself a recovering alcoholic who had battled the bottle since the original run of *Star Trek*. As the evening progressed, he began to notice that Nerine was acting "erratic in her behavior" and called Bill the very next day, asking him if he realized his bride-to-be was an alcoholic. Bill told Leonard that he was aware of her problem, but that he loved Nerine and was going to go through with the marriage. "You're in for a rough ride, then," Leonard told him. Bill ignored that pearl of hard-fought wisdom.

Bill and Nerine were married on November 15, 1997, in a black-tie ceremony in Pasadena several weeks after Nerine's second arrest for drunk driving. Bill was sixty-six; she was thirty-eight. Several members of Nerine's immediate family were invited, including her brother, Warren, and her sister, Jeanine. Leonard Nimoy served as the best man. Bill tried to keep the wedding as under-the-radar as possible, but the tabloids were alerted, causing a circus-type atmosphere. "We changed locations, did all that stuff, and we thought we should have just hired the guy from the tabloids to take our picture," Nerine joked. "We thought this guy did a better job than the person we hired."[13]

Bill wrote a heartfelt poem for the ceremony, reading it aloud to Nerine—pledging his love and allegiance "to you, Nerine, my queen." He placed the ring on her finger. "When it is dark and there is trouble, you need but wave that bauble and there will be light," he said to his bride.[14]

Nerine, in turn, pledged her "sobriety" to him. "I married against the advice of my family and friends, against my own good sense," Bill wrote later. "But I thought it might be the only chance we had."[15] They partied the night away, and Nerine didn't touch a drop of alcohol. By the next morning, she was drunk; later, Bill found little bottles of vodka that she had hidden around the house. Shortly thereafter, as her drinking continued unabated, Bill installed an electronic device in Nerine's car that made it impossible for her to start the engine with alcohol on her breath.

Leonard Nimoy tried to help Nerine when he could, talking to her about her addiction and accompanying her to meetings of Alcoholics Anonymous, where he sat next to her for support. But Nerine couldn't shake her demons; she checked into rehab facilities three times, including one visit to the Betty

Ford Clinic in Rancho Mirage, California, founded by the former First Lady. Her third trip to rehab was cut short within days when she was kicked out of the facility for drinking. Bill, at his wit's end, threatened to divorce her, "but the monster had her in its grip and would not let go."[16] They separated for a short time, but Nerine begged Bill to take her back and swore she would get sober. She followed one of her stays in rehab by returning home sober—and then getting drunk the very next day. She nearly drank herself to death several times, once registering a blood-alcohol reading of 3.9 (0.08 was considered legally drunk) and spending four days in a Santa Monica hospital—then getting drunk one day after Bill brought her home. On another occasion she disappeared—and Bill, who was frantic, got a phone call three days later from a "flophouse" in downtown Los Angeles. The person on the other end told him there was a woman there calling herself "Mrs. Shatner." It was Nerine.[17]

Bill filed for divorce on October 21, 1998, asking the judge not to award alimony to Nerine. She never responded to the lawsuit, and they reconciled shortly thereafter. Bill did not pursue the divorce, though he did not have it dismissed.[18]

Through it all Bill continued his frenetic work pace, barely stopping long enough to catch his breath. He returned to the *Star Trek* orbit by lending his voice (as Captain Kirk) to the video games *Star Trek: Starfleet Academy* and *Star Trek: Generations*, and in 1998, he flew to New Zealand with Nerine to star as "The Storyteller" in *A Twist in the Tale*, a television series for and about kids that ran for fifteen episodes in New Zealand. Nerine appeared in one episode of the series entitled "A Ghost of Our Own." They accompanied the show's producer on a chartered plane to Kaikoura, a town on the east coast of the South Island of New Zealand, to observe the region's marine life—where they were "overwhelmed" by witnessing a sperm whale surfacing from the ocean, causing a look of "sheer wonder and joy" in their eyes.[19]

That same year, Bill spoofed himself in a big-screen romantic comedy, *Free Enterprise*, starring Eric McCormack (later to find fame as Will Truman on NBC's *Will & Grace*) and Rafer Weigel and written by *Star Trek* gurus Mark Altman and Robert Meyer Burnett (with music provided by Scott Spock). The movie concluded with Bill rapping out lines from *Julius Caesar* in a musical number called "No Tears for Caesar." (In the movie, "Bill" wants to be taken seriously as an actor and is working on a one-man musical version of *Julius Caesar*.)

A decade earlier, in an interview with *Playboy* magazine, Bill said he believed he would never slow down as long as he could "keep upping the limit of what I think I'm capable of doing." He tested that theory in early 1999 when he guest-starred in a Season 3 episode of *3rd Rock from the Sun*, an NBC sitcom about four extraterrestrials (played by John Lithgow, French Stewart, Kristen Johnston, and Joseph Gordon-Levitt) sent on a mission to study earthlings in Ohio, where they identify themselves as the all-American Solomon family.

Bill played The Big Giant Head, the leader of the Solomons' mission and "Ruler of the Galaxy" who pays them a raucous visit in a two-part episode. He reprised the role in three more episodes the following season, and a later plotline revealed that The Big Giant head was, in actuality, Dick Solomon's (Lithgow) father. The role garnered Bill his first Emmy nomination in 1999, but he lost to Mel Brooks, who snared the award for his role as Uncle Phil on NBC's *Mad About You.*

∗   ∗   ∗

In 1997, a forty-two-year-old, Cornell-educated inventor/entrepreneur named Jay S. Walker founded a company called Priceline, a service that offered consumers discounted rates on airline tickets, car rentals, hotel rooms, and vacation packages—telling its customers to "Name Your Own Price" in order to get the best available deals. It was a brilliant marketing ploy, and the following year, with the fledgling Internet in its infancy and revolutionizing the digital economy, Priceline.com was launched, making the service available to anyone able to log on to the worldwide web.

Walker, seizing on the opportunity to reach millions of consumers, planned a Priceline.com media blitz in the form of $15 million radio advertising campaign. He needed an official spokesman for the radio ads. "We were going to be the largest radio advertiser in America, we wanted a radio voice," he said. "I approached what I thought was the best radio voice in the world: Bill Cosby." The comedian took a hard pass—or, rather, his representatives did (all while demanding a huge salary). "He said, 'Absolutely not. We're not talking to you.'" Walker considered actor James Earl Jones before turning to his third choice: William Shatner.[20]

Priceline's marketing whiz, Jord Poster, had a personal connection to Bill—his ex-wife was Marcy's college roommate—and he arranged a ten-minute meeting between Bill and Jay Walker in the bar of the St. Regis

Hotel in Manhattan. "I said, 'Look, I'm gonna build a giant company, you need to hear what I'm gonna do,'" Walker said he told Bill. "We met for ten minutes [and] when it was an hour later he says, 'Okay, I'm in, how much are you gonna pay me?' I said, 'I have no money, I'm paying you in stock.'" Bill agreed to record a series of radio spots, which became famous for his tagline dubbing Priceline.com's deals as "Big, *really* big." He agreed to take the bulk of his $500,000 fee in Priceline stock ,which amounted to 100,000 shares—by the following year, the shares were worth about $7.5 million. Walker wrote the copy for the radio ads.[21]

The ads proved to be a hit, but Bill was hesitant when, in 1999, Walker wanted to expand the company's radio marketing campaign to television.[22]

"He was on his horse farm, and Jord went down to the farm [in 1999]. He literally had to get Bill Shatner off the horse because he was pretty much retired and done," Walker said. "His career was pretty much finished at the time. So, Bill Shatner's whole second career is because of Jord Poster. In those days of the Internet, there was nobody who hired celebrity brands, and there was nobody who did advertising on radio and television for Internet brands, for e-commerce brands. There was nobody doing that."[23]

In Walker's retelling of the story, Bill then sent a representative in a limousine to the Priceline headquarters in Norwalk, Connecticut, to check things out before he would agree to appear in the TV ads. "The giant stretch limousine pulls up and the guy opens the door, and a little dog gets handed out of the stretch limousine. This little lap dog," Walker said. "Jord takes the lapdog, and then this woman's leg comes out of the limousine, and this incredibly tall, beautiful bombshell steps out of the limousine. No Shatner, just her. And she says, 'Bill Shatner has sent me here to do due diligence on what you guys are doing.'" Jord Poster walked the unidentified woman through the Priceline headquarters and back out to the limousine. "She said, 'I will tell Bill everything here is just as I expected.'"[24]

Bill still needed to be convinced. "Jord basically persuaded Shatner to do television for very little money because he convinced Shatner that this would be good for the Shatner brand, and by the way, it was great for the Shatner brand," Walker said.

Bill's Priceline.com television ads, in which he played "The Priceline Negotiator," began airing in 1999. In the ensuing years he starred in dozens of ads, all underscored with comic earnestness, including one ad in which he smashed a guitar and ad-libbed, "If saving money is wrong, I don't want to be right," which became the slogan for the entire ad campaign. Was Bill lampooning his own celebrity? He never quite answered the question. "The line between the sincerity of a true performance and the farcical irony, however you might characterize what it is I'm doing, is so fine that you don't know when you treat it," he told Connie Chung in a 2002 interview on CNN to publicize his new VH1 series, *One-Hit Wonders*. "You don't know where it is. But somewhere in that area is an ironic look at that."[25]

He reaped millions of dollars from his association with Priceline, mostly in stock options, and sold off around half of his company stock in early 1999 for an estimated $3 million. He also lost around $9 million in September 2000 when the company's stock collapsed, dropping 53 percent in one week alone. (At one point in 2000, Priceline stock was selling for $104.25 a share; that dropped to $5.56 in October 2000; in November, it dropped to $4.28.)[26] Walker, by comparison, lost an estimated $410 million and left Priceline later that year.[27]

The ads kept Bill in the public eye and triggered a slew of dot-com ads featuring celebrities, with everyone from supermodel Cindy Crawford (Estyle.inc.com) to *Sister Act* star and Oscars host Whoopi Goldberg getting into the game. "I pay homage to William Shatner because he made it viable to go to folks like me," Goldberg said. "It was an opportunity to make a little dough . . . It doesn't make you feel bad [that] you didn't have a huge opening weekend."[28]

*   *   *

Nerine turned forty on July 13, 1999. Her third trip to rehab in August (the instance when she was asked to leave because she was drunk) would be her final push to get better. Bill felt completely helpless and hopeless regarding his wife's addiction, and after picking her up from rehab, he once again floated the idea of a divorce. He called the director of the rehab facility and "begged" her to take Nerine back and she said that she would, provided that Nerine could stay sober for one day. Bill then called a friend of his in New York City, a psychiatrist specializing in addiction, who suggested that staging an intervention could save Nerine from her personal demons. Bill called some friends and planned the intervention for Tuesday, August 10. He would take Nerine back to rehab the next day hoping for a better resolution this time around.

Bill spent most of August 9 in Orange County, visiting with two of his daughters, but he made certain to check in with Nerine at regular intervals to make sure she was okay. By 8:30 that night he was back on the road, heading for home in Studio City, when his daughter Melanie called. She was alarmed that Nerine was not answering her cell phone and told Bill to call the couple's landline. He tried the home phone several times. There was no answer.

Bill finally arrived home around 9:30 p.m. to a quiet house. He found their three beloved Doberman Pinschers, who were usually attached to either Bill or Nerine, in the kitchen. There was no sign of Nerine. Bill walked around the house and called out for his wife several times, assuming she was out when she didn't answer him. He checked the garage. All the cars were there. Where could she be? The phone rang: it was Nerine's sponsor from Alcoholics Anonymous. "'I don't know where she is,'" Bill recalled telling the sponsor. She asked Bill if he'd checked their backyard pool. Nerine liked to drink a cocktail of Gatorade and vodka before taking a dip. Bill put Nerine's AA sponsor on hold and walked into the dark backyard. He saw something floating in the deep end of the pool—and he knew, instinctively, that it was Nerine. "It had to be a shadow. It couldn't be my wife. I took several steps backward to try to avoid the horror in front of me," he wrote. Nerine was lying naked, face down in the pool.

Bill staggered back to the phone and told Nerine's sponsor his wife was floating in the pool. She told him to call for help—life imitating life in Bill's personal nightmarish version of *Rescue 911*. He dialed 911 and screamed to the operator—"Oh my God! My poor wife is at the bottom of the pool!"—then ran into the backyard. He dove into the pool and dragged Nerine's body out of the water. "I had enough breath for one deep dive," he wrote. "One of her arms was floating above her and I grabbed her by that arm and lifted her, pulling her toward the shallow end," screaming "What have you done?!" as he struggled to lift her out of the pool. Bill noticed that Nerine's skin was blue, and that her hair was still curled. He also noticed the news helicopter already circling above like a mechanized vulture, its local television station alerted to the unfolding tragedy at William Shatner's house by monitoring the area's 911 calls.[29] While Bill tried frantically to revive Nerine, a female neighbor redialed 911. "We kept the lines open through the neighbor and we gave her first-aid instruction to relay to [Shatner]," an LA City Fire Department spokesman said later.[30]

Within minutes paramedics arrived at the Shatner home on Berry Drive. But there was nothing they could do. Nerine was dead. Once her body was removed, Bill spoke briefly to the flock of press assembled outside the house's wrought-iron gate. "My beautiful wife is dead," he said quietly. "She meant everything to me. Her laughter, her tears, and her joy will remain with me the rest of my life." He felt his composure about to slip and quickly went back into the house. Sobbing, he called Nerine's parents, June and Warren, to tell them the horrible news. He emerged briefly the next day to embrace friends on his driveway who'd come to console him. "I appreciate your concern," he said to a reporter. It was only five years since the double-murders of Nicole Brown Simpson and Ronald Goldman, and the acquittal of O. J. Simpson following his sensational 1995 trial. Bill was keenly aware that there were some people who suspected that Nerine's death was not an accident or suicide—that it was a case of another celebrity getting away with murder. "A day after I'd made my statement about loving her forever someone sent a note to the police, 'Anybody who is innocent doesn't stop and pick up a newspaper,'" Bill wrote. He was never seriously considered a suspect.[31]

The LAPD eventually ruled that the cause of Nerine's death was an accidental drowning with no foul play suspected. "Subsequent investigation revealed Mrs. Shatner was home alone for a short period of time and accidentally drowned while swimming in the family pool," said LAPD Det. Mike Coffey.[32] "Nothing was apparent through the physical exam at the scene."[33]

One of Nerine's unidentified relatives thought that the way in which she died was "kind of odd . . . I mean, Nerine grew up in a lake. She waterskied, and she was an excellent swimmer. It's just odd that she would die in a pool."[34] An autopsy was scheduled. "I had called her the night before and I couldn't understand a word she said," recalled her lawyer, Peter Knecht. "She didn't appear to be in good health."[35] Even Bill's first wife, Gloria, weighed in. "She liked to tipple a little," she said of Nerine. "That was the fault that did her in, I think." She was also asked about Nerine's recent stints in rehab. "I don't know the details, but it didn't work out," she said.[36]

Nerine's agent at LA Talent told the *Los Angeles Times* that Nerine was a strong swimmer who regularly swam laps in the pool. "That's why it's so strange what happened," she said. "Nerine was in great shape. She was the kind of person, if anything was really important to anybody, she was always there. She was like a comet, very bright, vivacious, the biggest heart you could come across."[37] It was yet one more devastating loss for Nerine's family: one of her brothers, who was hit by a car in 1994, was still in a convalescent home; in 1995, another brother, Robert, died in his thirties of a brain aneurysm.[38]

The results of Nerine's autopsy were released in mid-October, showing that she'd been drinking heavily that night and taking sleeping pills. She had a blood alcohol level of 0.27—over three times the legal limit for driving—and doctors found bruises on her face and two cracked neck vertebrae, indicating that she dove into the pool, banged her head on the bottom, and lost consciousness. "The totality of the whole investigation indicates an accident," said LAPD Det. Mike Coffey. "Drinking was definitely a problem for her. Everyone knew she was an alcoholic. She just couldn't beat her problem." He added that Bill was, officially, never considered a suspect, but that he'd provided a time-stamped restaurant check proving that he was in San Clemente with his daughter at the time of Nerine's death.[39]

Bill spent the following weeks grieving. He sat Shiva, the Jewish tradition of mourning, and established the Nerine Shatner Memorial Fund to help those suffering from alcoholism and drug dependency. He heard that the *National Enquirer* was going to publish a "Did he do it?" story and, in an effort to short-circuit any more lurid speculation, gave the tabloid an exclusive account of what happened that night, donating his $250,000 fee to Nerine's memorial fund. It was a noble gesture; still, Bill said that some of Nerine's friends never forgave him for talking about her alcoholism so publicly in a tabloid notorious for its blaring headlines and sensational stories. Bill made sure that proceeds from the Nerine Shatner Memorial Fund were used to finance the Nerine Shatner Friendly House, a twenty-four-bed haven for women with addictions located in Los Angeles on South Normandie Avenue. It opened in 2001 and continues to help women to this day.

He leaned on family and friends for support, including Leonard Nimoy, who "enveloped me in his arms as his brother, and we cried together."[40] While Bill was still mourning Nerine, he had an idea: why not turn this experience into a big-screen movie? He planned to direct and produce *The Shiva Club*, whose plot would revolve around two young showbiz hopefuls who turn up at the home of a famous Jewish comic (perhaps Bill's role) grieving the loss of his wife. "During the process of sitting Shiva, the concept occurred to me: Grief can be funny," he told the *Hollywood Reporter* in 2000. The project remains in limbo two decades later.

Captain Kirk locks lips with Uhura (Nichelle Nichols) on the 1968 *Star Trek* episode "Plato's Stepchildren"—TV's first interracial kiss. (*CBS Photo Archive/©CBS/Getty Images*)

Bill and his first wife, Gloria, mid-1960s. They met a decade earlier on the set of *Dreams*, a TV play Bill wrote for the CBC. (*ZUMA Press, Inc./Alamy Stock Photo*)

Family time: Bill and Gloria with daughters Lisabeth (left), Leslie and Mela-nie (in Bill's lap) during the late-'60s run of *Star Trek*. (*ZUMA Press, Inc./Alamy Stock Photo*)

The cast of *Big Bad Mama*: Bill, Angie Dickinson, Susan Sennett, Tom Sker-ritt and Robbie Lee. Bill and Skerritt came to blows during the shoot. (*NEW WORLD/Ronald Grant Archive/Alamy Stock Photo*)

Bill and his second wife, Marcy, on their wedding day in Los Angeles (October 1973). They stayed together for over two decades. (*Bettmann/Getty Images*)

The cast of *T.J. Hooker*, 1982: Bill (from left), Heather Locklear, James Darren and Adrian Zmed. The series ran for five seasons on ABC and (later) CBS. (*ABC Photo Archives/©ABC/Getty Images*)

'*Toon in*: Bill provided Captain Kirk's voice for *Star Trek: The Animated Series*, which ran for two seasons in the mid-1970s and featured most of the original *Star Trek* cast. It would be another fifteen years until they reunited on the big screen. (*CBS Photo Archive/©CBS/Getty Images*)

Guess who? Jeff Cable (Bill, left) goes undercover with Cash Conover (Doug McClure) on *Barbary Coast,* which lasted one season (1975-76) on ABC. (*ABC Photo Archives/©ABC/Getty Images*)

Bill tries his hand at comedy opposite Jonathan Winters and Robin Williams on a 1978 episode of *Mork & Mindy*. (*AF Archive/Alamy Stock Photo*)

Bill and Marcy in happier times at the L.A. premiere of *The China Syndrome* (1979). (*Ron Galella/Getty Images*)

Captain Kirk meets his end after battling evil Tolian Soran (Malcolm McDowell) in 1994's *Star Trek: Generations*. Kirk's final words: "Oh, my!" (*Moviestore Collection Ltd/Alamy Stock Photo*)

Bill and Nerine in 1996. They married the following year. (*Jeff Kravitz/ Getty Images*)

Bill speaks to the press following Nerine's death (August 10, 1999). (*Associated Press*)

Denny Crane and Alan Shore share a moment (and a customary cigar) in *Boston Legal.* Bill and James Spader's on-screen chemistry was undeniable. (*Craig Sjodin/©ABC/Getty Images*)

A triumphant Bill holds his Emmy Award after winning for *Boston Legal* (2005). (*Mathew Imaging/Getty Images*)

Bill with his "brother," Leonard Nimoy, in later years. They were not speaking at the time of Nimoy's death and Bill was criticized for not attending his funeral. (*Photofest*)

As grumpy Ed Goodson on the short-lived *$#*! My Dad Says* (2011), the first sitcom to be adapted from a Twitter feed. (*CBS Photo Archive/©CBS/ Getty Images*)

Bill was eighty when he was awarded an honorary degree by his alma mater, McGill University. (*Canadian Press (Photostream)/Associated Press*)

In 2012, Bill returned to Broadway for the fourth time, this time as the headliner, in *Shatner's World: We Just Live In It.* *(Walter McBride/Getty Images)*

Bill with his fourth wife, Elizabeth. They've been married for nearly twenty years. (*Paul Archuleta/Getty Images*)

Rocket man: Showing his playful side with an onstage visit with frequent musical collaborator Brad Paisley at the 2015 CMA Awards in Nashville. (*Taylor Hill/Getty Images*)

CHAPTER 14

Date with an Emmy

Slowly, Bill returned to work.

Miss Congeniality, released in December 2000, featured Bill in a comedic supporting role as a vain beauty pageant host opposite stars Sandra Bullock, Michael Caine, Benjamin Bratt, and Candice Bergen, his future costar on *Boston Legal*. The fluffy comedy about an FBI agent (Bullock) who goes undercover at a beauty pageant marked Bill's first mainstream movie appearance in nearly a decade (since *Star Trek VI* in 1991) and generated mostly positive reviews. ("There are scores of boob jobs and chin implants among the contestants, but none has had as much work done as Shatner," noted one critic.)[1] The *Boston Herald* claimed: "[Bill is] dead-on as the unflappable but clueless pageant host who keeps singing no matter what is happening around him. Given the declining value of Priceline.com stock, it's good to know that Shatner continues to have other opportunities to mock himself."[2] The movie did well enough at the box office to inspire a 2005 sequel, *Miss Congeniality 2: Armed & Fabulous*, in which Bill reprised his role as emcee Stan Fields.

He lent his voice to the character of "Mayor Phlegmming" for *Osmosis Jones*—a big-screen comedy mixing animation and live action that also featured Bill Murray, Chris Rock, Laurence Fishburne, Molly Shannon, and *Frasier* star David Hyde Pierce. It bombed at the box office and was quickly relegated to the home video market. In 2001, he appeared in an episode of *Seinfeld* costar Jason Alexander's short-lived ABC sitcom *Bob Patterson*.

In the meantime, he'd fallen in love again.

In the wake of Nerine's death, Bill was inundated with letters from fans and people concerned about his plight. Most of the letters offered advice, sympathy, and words of comfort for the grieving widower. Some of the letters from women included their pictures, hoping Bill might take a further interest in them. He claimed to have read all the letters—but one stood out from the rest.

It was from Elizabeth Martin, a onetime high school homecoming queen from Indiana who owned a saddlebred farm in Montecito with her husband, Mike, and was acquainted with Bill through their mutual connections in the horse world. She was born Elizabeth Joyce Anderson in December 1958 and was riding horses by the age of five. By the age of eight, Elizabeth owned her first horse, and six years later, she was teaching horseback riding and judging competitions with the Indiana Arabian Club. She attended Purdue University, where she studied equine and animal science, and then transferred to Butler University in Indianapolis, studying telecommunications.[3]

Elizabeth eventually became a professional horse trainer and, in 1983, married Mike Martin, who died from bone cancer in August 1997—nearly two years to the day before Nerine's death. When Elizabeth heard the news about Nerine's death, she reached out to Bill, writing him a letter and telling him that she knew what he was going through. "Since then I've been through all the stages of grief," she wrote. "I know what it is. If there is anything I can do to help you get through this period, I'd be delighted." Bill wanted to call Elizabeth to thank her for her letter, and got her number from his business manager, who owned a horse Elizabeth had trained. They spoke on the phone every day for months, but Elizabeth's busy schedule precluded them from meeting each other in person.[4]

"She was a trainer for thirty years and we had met at horse shows," Bill said. "We spent a long time talking to each other and gradually we fell in love. There's temporal love and physical love, which is also very important— it's central, critical, the chemistry."[5] They finally met each other in person on the pier in Santa Barbara and dined at a restaurant Elizabeth had frequented with Mike. She wasn't familiar with *Star Trek*—she'd never watched a complete episode, according to Bill—and he invited her to join him on a two-week nature photography trip to the South Pole. When Elizabeth turned down his offer, Bill cancelled his plans for the trip, not wanting to spend any significant amount of time away from her.

Bill continued to pursue Elizabeth, and shortly thereafter invited her to join him for a long weekend in New York City (separate rooms, of course). She accepted the invitation, then accompanied him on a three-hour car ride to Albany, where Bill was participating in a charity event. The romance took off from there. They shared their first kiss, Bill wrote in typically dramatic fashion, in a field "covered with fresh snow just glistening in the moonlight."[6]

He proposed six months later.

They planned to get married in Indianapolis, on the farm owned by Elizabeth's father, and took out a marriage license at the Boone County Courthouse in February 2001, eighteen months after Nerine's death. (He wore leather, she wore fur—they paid $62 for the marriage license, which required them to get married within sixty days.) The timing was right: not only would they be married in Elizabeth's home state, but Bill was slated to host the Miss USA Pageant at the Genesis Convention Center in Gary, Indiana, on March 2. (The pageant was televised on CBS.) Bill could thank his *Miss Congeniality* role as smarmy pageant emcee Stan Fields for the Miss USA gig.

Bill would be turning seventy in March following his fourth marriage. Elizabeth was forty-two. "I think one thing that both Bill and I have learned is nobody really ever knows what's going to happen, so if I let the fear of an age difference get in the way of my having this experience of this phenomenal, interesting man, then that's just fear-based living," Elizabeth said. "And I chose not to do that."[7] They married in a small ceremony on February 13, 2001, after moving the wedding to the home of Elizabeth's sister, Gayle Anderson, in Lebanon—about fifty miles from Indianapolis—once word leaked to the media about their taking out a marriage license. (They were "remarried" in Los Angeles the following year when they discovered that their 2001 nuptials were illegal; since they'd moved the wedding to another county, their Indiana marriage license was invalid.)

Bill also started work on his next movie project, *Groom Lake*. He wrote, directed, starred in, and partly financed this low-budget science fiction tale, which he called "a memorial" to the Shatners' late spouses, Mike and Nerine. (He claimed his California ranch was inhabited by the spirits of Native Americans and "the spirits of Nerine and Mike" and said, "It's a magical place and there's where my grief exists as well."[8])

The *Groom Lake* narrative unfolded in Area 51, the remote US Air Force facility in Nevada mythologized in pop culture for supposedly harboring extraterrestrials (and where scientists conducted extraterrestrial autopsies). The film was shot in Bisbee, Arizona, on a shoestring budget, and Bill was bedeviled by problems with the movie's spendthrift producer, in one instance losing his personal credit card when he ordered pizza for the movie's extras.[9]

Bill played Air Force commander Gossner, who's conducting highly classified experiments on an extraterrestrial at Groom Lake, near Area 51. A dying young woman and her husband (played by Amy Acker and Dan Gauthier), who are searching for evidence of life after death (so they can be reunited), kidnap Gossner's alien test subject. He seeks vengeance. "It just didn't tie together smoothly," Bill recalled, though he praised *Groom Lake's* "fine performances by some very good actors" and figured he eventually broke even on the production vis-à-vis tax write-offs.[10]

The movie came and went without a ripple, but it did have one added bonus when Bill was approached by executives at cable's Sci-Fi Channel to come up with more ideas. He eventually pitched a movie called *Alien Fire*, which he planned to direct on a $1.5 million budget, but other commitments precluded his involvement. In 2002, after a hiatus from Priceline.com, he resumed his role as the company's spokesman in a series of radio and television ads, touting its Priceline Super Computer "that toils day and night to find airline tickets, hotel rooms, and other travel products at discounts." Priceline.com sweetened the deal for Bill's fans with a collectible William Shatner bobblehead doll, free to anyone making a travel purchase on the company's website. The new ad campaign eventually crossed the Atlantic to the United Kingdom in a series of radio ads. "William Shatner is as much a fixture in UK households as he is in the US," Priceline.com's chief marketing officer noted.[11]

*   *   *

Their love of horses had, in a roundabout way, brought Bill and Elizabeth together, and equine-related activities (breeding horses, horse shows, charitable foundations) continued to play a leading role in their lives. Elizabeth was very much involved in the Hollywood Charity Horse Show, which Bill founded in 1990 after watching an exhibition called *Ahead with Horses*, in which children with severe disabilities went through a series of exercises riding on the backs of horses.

The celebrity-driven Hollywood Charity Horse Show was sponsored by Priceline.com and Wells Fargo and continues to be staged to this day in Burbank, raising funds for Los Angeles-area charitable organizations that support children with special needs and US military veterans. The Shatners' philanthropic pursuits would lead them, in 2010, to start the All Glory Project. Spearheaded by Elizabeth, who was inspired by a program called Central

Kentucky Riding for Hope, the All Glory Project (named after one of the Shatners' standardbred horses) offers injured war vets the chance to improve their balance, strength, and flexibility—and emotional well-being—while working with and riding horses.[12]

Bill and Elizabeth's philanthropic pursuits vis-à-vis the horse world expanded internationally, to Israel, where they partnered with the Jewish National Fund for the William and Elizabeth Shatner/Jewish National Fund Therapeutic Riding Consortium Endowment to help raise $10 million for the thirty therapeutic riding programs located throughout Israel, including the Red Mountain Riding Center at Kibbutz Grofit in the Negev desert. "We want all kids—Jews, Bedouins, Israeli-Arabs, Jordanian, Palestinian, and Egyptian—to benefit from these therapeutic horseback riding centers," Bill said, recalling how he learned a phrase in Hebrew while in Israel: "Sussim osim nissim," which translates to "horses make miracles."[13]

Bill's love of horses reared an uglier head in his life in late April 2003, when Marcy took her ex-husband to court for allegedly breaching a clause from their 1995 divorce agreement. The unorthodox clause required Bill to provide Marcy with fresh horse semen samples each year from three of his prize stallions. Marcy claimed that the March 2003 sample arrived frozen— and not in the "fresh cooled format" agreed upon in their divorce agreement. "Mr. Shatner's offer to provide semen from the three stallions in question in frozen form is unacceptable to Ms. Lafferty," the suit stated. "Potential buyers of the breeding privileges do not want the semen in frozen format."

Marcy made no financial claim for damages; according to a report in the *Lexington Herald-Leader*, she claimed the offspring of her horse Espere and Bill's horse, Sultan's Great Day, could have yielded as much as $165,000 had the "fresh cooled" semen been used (instead of the frozen semen). The details of the case were fodder for snarky headlines (E! News: "The trouble with Shatner's semen"). Bill's attorney argued for the suit to be dismissed, claiming the divorce settlement didn't contain any restrictions on the form in which the semen was to be delivered. Bill, he said, was never personally served with the lawsuit, which was dismissed by joint agreement in June. Settlements details were not disclosed.

Save for *Groom Lake*, the bulk of Bill's onscreen work in the new millennium found him in comedic roles (*3rd Rock from the Sun, Osmosis Jones, Bob Patterson, Airplane II, Miss Congeniality*, and its sequel, *Miss Congeniality 2*) and acting in other mediums. In 2003, Bill—heavily stubbled (and heavy) and wearing a tight black T-shirt—parodied *American Idol* judge Simon Cowell in a reality-show-spoofing video for "Celebrity," a song by country music star Brad Paisley. (Actors Jim Belushi and Jason Alexander also appeared in the video.) Bill starred in humorous television commercials for Crest toothpaste and, in the United Kingdom, in a series of light commercials for Kellogg's All-Bran (in which he interacted with couples). He reteamed with *Star Trek* costar Leonard Nimoy for a few Priceline.com commercials, with the jokey premise that Nimoy is replacing Bill as the company's spokesman, but a reluctant Bill just won't let it go.

His comic appearances did not go unnoticed—particularly by television series writer/creator David E. Kelley, whose quirky CBS comedy, *Picket Fences*, amassed fourteen Emmy Awards during its four-season run (1992–96). In 1997, Kelley launched two competing ensemble legal shows, both based in Boston but airing on different networks: *The Practice*, on ABC, premiered in March; it was followed, in September, by *Ally McBeal* on Fox.

Both series were successful and garnered multiple Emmy Awards. By the time *Ally McBeal* called it quits in 2002, *The Practice* was teetering on the verge of extinction after ABC moved it to Monday nights (from its longtime Sunday-night perch). "It was a terrible blow for us," Kelley said. "Our ratings struggled, and it quickly became clear [that], okay, we were not going to survive on Monday nights. We were an aging show, creatively, at this time, as well . . . We had run our course with a lot of our storytelling." It looked as though the series would be cancelled.[14]

In May 2003, just days before ABC announced its fall schedule to advertisers, Kelley got a call from the network's chairman, Lloyd Braun, asking if he would be willing to bring *The Practice* back for one more season—at half the price. "I had about five minutes to think about it," Kelley said. "It wasn't the worst thing to sort of shake up the show. The idea was that we come back for one more year and one more year only."

ABC fired seven of the show's eleven regular cast members—including stars Dylan McDermott, Lara Flynn Boyle, Lisa Gay Hamilton, Chyler Leigh, Marla Sokoloff, and Kelli Williams—and brought in James Spader to play the show's new protagonist, the brilliant, ethically-challenged lawyer Alan Shore. "The show caught on creatively again," Kelley said.

In February 2004, with *The Practice* having reclaimed a bit of its creative and ratings mojo, word broke that Bill would guest-star in a semi-comedic role as a quirky, egotistical, eccentric attorney. (Bill wasn't the first big name hired by Kelley for *The Practice* that season. Sharon Stone guest-starred on a three-episode arc as a brilliant, schizophrenic litigator named Sheila Carlisle, who hired Alan Shore to defend her in a wrongful termination suit.)[15]

"Apparently David Kelley wanted me for the role," Bill said. "And so, on one fateful morning, we met for breakfast . . . he described this role he was writing that would go, I think, six shows in *The Practice*. I didn't want to do another series; doing a series is debilitating in every way, for your health, your relationships . . . but you're making money, so that weighs in the balance." Bill figured his role would be supporting in nature, with a finite ending, something impressive to add to his fifty-plus-year acting resume.[16]

Seventy-three-year-old William Shatner signed on to appear in four of the season's final six episodes as Denny Crane, the pompous head of Crane, Pool & Schmidt. Denny is hiding a secret: he's battling Alzheimer's disease and repeats his own name ("Denny Crane . . . Denny Crane") in what appears to be a personality quirk but is, in actuality, his way of remembering who he is. In the universe of *The Practice*, Crane, Pool & Schmidt butts heads with Young, Frutt & Berlutti. Actor Vince Colosimo was also added to the cast as Denny Crane's junior partner, Matthew Billings. Kelley had the option of bringing both actors back for additional episodes.

Bill made his first appearance on *The Practice* on March 21, 2004, in an episode entitled "War of the Roses," in which James Spader's Alan Shore, who's about to be fired, sabotages his firm's computers and hires rivals Crane, Poole & Schmidt to sue for wrongful termination. Crane's habit of repeating his name in the third person—"You want Denny Crane to talk. When Denny Crane talks, E. F. Hutton listens"; "I'm Denny Crane, dammit!"—endeared him to viewers and critics alike.

"Something magical happened that I've only seen happen in a play, where the author sees what's happening . . . and starts to write and create more because it has audience appeal," Bill said. "And that's what started happening with Denny Crane—Kelley began to create more, and I began to get the idea of how to play the guy. And so, there was this symbiotic relationship between David Kelley and myself."[17] In an effort to avoid alienating longtime viewers of *The Practice*, Kelley took "small steps" to incorporate Denny Crane's firm into the series' story line.

Kelley's faith in Bill paid off: In September 2004, nearly forty years after the premiere of *Star Trek*, Bill won his first Emmy Award, beating out Bob Newhart (*ER*), Matthew Perry (*The West Wing*), James Earl Jones (*Ever-*

wood), and Martin Landau (*Without a Trace*) as Outstanding Guest Actor in a Drama Series. "I was exultant," he said of the Emmy win. "It was the first time [winning an Emmy] after a lifetime of making a living at it and it was just extraordinary. I was delighted."[18] His costar, James Spader, won an Emmy as Outstanding Lead Actor in a Drama Series.

"I'm always suspicious of icons [like Shatner], because sometimes they're not always able to laugh at themselves," Kelley said. "We definitely have to be willing to laugh at [Denny Crane] and with his character and sometimes we're not going to know the difference. And when Denny speaks, we won't always know what he's talking about. From Day One [Shatner] came in and inhabited his character and started walking around saying, 'Denny Crane, Denny Crane.'"

By that time, *The Practice* had morphed into its spinoff series, *Boston Legal*, which premiered on ABC in September 2004. The dramatic and comedic foundation of *Boston Legal* was built on the weirdly symbiotic relationship between Alan Shore and Denny Crane and the world of their law firm, Crane, Poole & Schmidt. (Candice Bergen played founding partner Shirley Schmidt.) Rhona Mitra and Lake Bell returned for *Boston Legal*, reprising their roles as Tara Wilson and Sally Heep from *The Practice*.

Bill had some trepidation in accepting a role as a series regular and was well aware that the grueling schedule would keep him on the set for long hours and away from Elizabeth. "I'd been married two or three years before and my promise was that we would explore the world and each other and friends and I had to renege on that promise to my wife that I would slow down," he said. "In fact, what happened was that I sped up."

Perhaps, but *Boston Legal* and Denny Crane would usher in another remarkable chapter in Bill's career. "[Shatner] and James Spader *were* the show," said Stephen McPherson, who replaced Lloyd Braun and Susan Lyne as President of ABC Entertainment in April 2004. "It was about those two, and it wouldn't have been *Boston Legal* without them, and I don't say that lightly. In this case, the casting of those two guys was absolutely critical to the show, and I think their chemistry is what made it so successful."[19]

Bill described Denny Crane as a cross between the blustery Big Giant Head from *3rd Rock from the Sun* and some of his more dramatic roles. "[Denny resided] somewhere in this marginal area," he said. "I found that all the notes that I can play as an actor were there for me and I was playing chords of harmonics that were only me. I'm sure there are many other actors who could play the role better, or worse, but not the way I played it—because it was uniquely me."

He credited David E. Kelley, whom he rarely saw throughout the entire run of *Boston Legal*, with creating a unique character, a prism through which Bill could refract the many different facets of his own personality. Denny, Bill said, was a man "who vacillated between the arrogance of his talents and the humiliation of his failing memory and his ability to think things through and losing it." Bill had personal experience with the ravages of Alzheimer's after watching Elizabeth's father struggle with the disease. The family bought her father a tape recorder so he could record some of his memories daily but, after a week, the recordings descended into nonlinear, disjointed thoughts. "I remembered looking at him and thinking, 'What can be more frightening than to be conscious of the insanity of your brain rotting?'" Bill said. "And that's the approach I took [for Denny]—the fear, the absolute terror."[20]

Sometimes, Bill was just lucky and instinctive. He recalled a scene between Denny and Alan, early in their relationship, in which Alan asks Denny if he's gay. Bill had no idea how Denny was supposed to respond to the question and asked one of the show's executive producers for guidance. His reply? "I don't know, why don't you just do nothing?" "So, I probably did nothing," Bill recalled. "Now, having had the benefit of playing the character [for so long], I would have thought of something to do. Or maybe 'nothing' was the right way, so that's funny in itself. In any case that sort of thing happened all the time."[21]

Kelley, who wrote most of the *Boston Legal* episodes (a monumental task), frequently had Denny breaking the so-called "fourth wall" of reality, as if he was speaking directly to the audience with lines like "Cue the music!" or "Fade to black!" Denny eventually explained to Alan that he used those lines because he felt that his own life was like a live television show in which he played the starring role. "The character used to say his name all the time and so it occurred to me he would say [his] name like feeling somebody out," Shatner said. "I once likened it to a lizard sticking his tongue out, darting it out. Smell that air. 'Denny Crane. Denny Crane.' Every time he said it, it would be a query, a different reason, like saying hello with a different nuance every time you say hello. Kelley wrote a lengthy scene in which all I said was my name, but I said it innumerable times, so I searched for different ways to say it . . . and that evolved and so I didn't know enough to change anything."

Bill said he based Denny, in part, on a friend from Kentucky he knew through horse circles: "A phenomenal character who became a friend of mine over the years . . . he was a wild guy, especially in his youth... he was into drinking, drugs, women . . . losing and winning millions of dollars. He'd be up and down . . . he was vivid and laughs and has got a big voice. Somewhere in there are some antecedents of Denny Crane."[22]

Television viewers warmed to the oddly endearing relationship between Denny Crane and Alan Shore, and before too long *Boston Legal* even had its own cultural calling card, ending each episode with Denny and Alan smoking cigars on their office balcony and ruminating about life. "What we didn't know was that the chemistry [between Shatner and Spader] was going to be so special," said *Boston Legal* executive producer Bill D'Elia, who joined *The Practice* in the spring of 2004 and worked with Bill and James Spader to hone their characters for the spinoff. "Nobody knew. David [Kelley] didn't know. I didn't know. We discovered it along the way and the two actors could not have been more different. Bill is very spontaneous and likes to make stuff up. James is very specific and very organized and likes to rehearse. Bill doesn't like to rehearse, but for whatever reason we had Abbott and Costello. We had this chemistry that was evident right from the start, and I can tell you that because of that, the balcony scenes became a staple of the show."[23]

D'Elia and Bill got off to a rocky start. Early in their collaboration, they had a serious disagreement about how Bill should play a scene. D'Elia told the crew to take a break while he and Bill repaired to the star's dressing room for a heated discussion. "We stood, almost toe to toe," D'Elia recalled. "He had his point of view, I had mine, and I was trying to convince him that all I was trying to do was help him discover this character, and that I thought he was going in the wrong direction. He argued vehemently that he was right, because he's always right. It's another great attribute of his, actually."

The scene was shot the way D'Elia wanted. "That scene in his dressing room was pivotal to us understanding each other and his understanding that I was there to help him, and my understanding of what was driving him," D'Elia said. "And I think that was the critical moment that he and I began a real working relationship and a real friendship."

The *Boston Legal* balcony scenes featuring Denny Crane and Alan Shore, which became the show's trademark, were, in fact, a happy accident. The original *Boston Legal* pilot, directed by D'Elia, had a different ending, which

David E. Kelley thought was "too funny, too silly" and not true to the show's thematic context. "It wasn't the two guys on the balcony . . . So, we tinkered with that some more and I shot some additional scenes that David wrote, and we went back and forth with this to try to find exactly what the tone of the show might be," D'Elia said. "David wrote the very first balcony scene as a result of those changes. It was originally designed so that Denny Crane should have a balcony because he's the most important character—to himself and to the firm. So, I wanted him to have this big balcony out off of his office and that's why we built it." The initial thought was to use the balcony only occasionally. On the day that the first balcony scene was scheduled to be filmed, D'Elia, who was on the sound stage by himself, took two chairs that were facing Denny's office, turned them around, and asked Bill and Spader to sit in the chairs while the scene was being shot. The moment was born.

"It resonated with the audience, so it became a standard thing," Bill said of the balcony scenes. "It became a mainstay of the relationship between the two characters, and what started to happen was a genuine feeling of affection that turned to love between two men. That love that [David E.] Kelley began to explore between two heterosexual men became an element of the show—how to have two guys who really love each other and be sexually attracted to women."[24] "The very first scene, something just seemed to work right," Spader recalled. "It worked right for the two of us working together and it worked right for the two characters."[25]

"We just caught lightning in a bottle," D'Elia said. "Now, the two actors discovered the same thing that we'd discovered and so they had a real working relationship that they both respected. Those two guys were never going to be buddies off-screen, but they were friends, if you know what I mean. Just the way we are all friends during the course of a production. You hang out and you like people, but [Shatner and Spader] were so different in their personalities—and that's why it worked."[26]

The premiere episode of *Boston Legal*, "Head Cases," aired on October 3, 2004, and snared over 13 million viewers. Reviews were mixed. *Variety* thought: "[It] suffers from the pervasive feeling of been here, seen this . . . Kelley's fertile mind still disgorges occasional gems, but for the most part here, he's delivered more rhinestones than diamonds."[27] The *New York Times*, in an article headlined "Old-Time Sexism Suffuses New Season," criticized the show's characterization of women as "bustier-busting sidekicks . . . which dilutes the funny and iconoclastic James Spader by pairing him with William Shatner, who plays an even more eccentric, licentious law partner."[28]

Other critics disagreed.

"Shatner, for one, is having a ball playing his technicolor blowhard: In one scene, he eloquently dares an angry client to kill him," noted *Entertainment Weekly*. "Sure, he could just tell the guy that his gun is a useless starter pistol, but then he'd miss out on some prime humbuggery. Having the self-referential Shatner play a man who's become a crafty spoof of himself is another of *Boston's* meta-amusements."[29] The *Los Angeles Times*: "Here are at least two reasons to watch *Boston Legal* . . . and their names, in alphabetical order, are William Shatner and James Spader. They are not the only reasons—there are some other interesting players on board . . . But Shatner and Spader, as lawyers with elastic ethics—unconventional methods, shall we say—are the twin islands upon which the show has been built, and all else flows around them or against them."[30]

The show's strong opening numbers continued throughout that first season, with *Boston Legal* averaging 13 million viewers a week. The one-two punch of Denny Crane and Alan Shore also resonated with Bill's and James Spader's industry peers, who nominated them for Emmy Awards. On September 18, 2005, Bill won his second Emmy as Denny Crane, this time for Outstanding Supporting Actor in a Drama Series, beating out Naveen Andrews (*Lost*), Alan Alda (*The West Wing*), Terry O'Quinn (*Lost*), and Oliver Platt (*Huff*). Bill looked a bit surprised as the CBS television cameras captured the moment: wearing a black suit jacket, white shirt, silver tie, and big white carnation in his lapel, he hugged Elizabeth in the audience at the Shrine Auditorium in Los Angeles before walking up to the stage to accept his award from actress Kyra Sedgwick, joking in his acceptance speech about his lack of interaction with series creator David E. Kelley.

"The other day I saw David Kelley and said, 'Hi, David.' That was the longest conversation I've had with him in two years of doing this show," he said to much laughter in the audience. "If he had given me a chance, I would've said, 'David, I admire and respect your great talents." He also singled out James Spader, the show's cast, and "my wife Elizabeth." Spader, too, took home an Emmy that night for Outstanding Lead Actor in a Drama Series. "Although he never saw *Boston Legal,* I think he might have liked it," he said of his late father. "He wouldn't have known what the hell to make of my character but," he said, pointing to Shatner, "I think Bill would have made him laugh."

Bill and Spader's onscreen chemistry were a big part of the show's success; so, too, were the parade of guest stars who appeared on *Boston Legal* throughout its run, including Betty White, who recurred on the series sixteen times as Alan's childhood neighbor, Catherine Piper. "William Shatner is one of the most brilliant actors you could possibly ask for and also one of the brightest minds off camera," she said. "I was a big Trekkie. I loved *Star Trek* and Captain Kirk was my hero. But Bill Shatner is something altogether different [on *Boston Legal*] and he's playing such a complex role . . . this egotistical, wonderful lawyer . . . who's losing it, just a little bit, and everybody knows it. It's like a blowing curtain; sometimes he loses it at the wrong times . . . but less and less the other characters on the show are beginning not to trust [Denny]. They know that he's in a little bit of trouble.

"This makes a wonderful week in, week out thing," she said. "Every once in a while, you see this little shadow come in, something bad is happening there, and that's when the writing gets exciting and all of the sudden you see somebody about to put that on the page and then Bill execute it. It's just wonderful."[31]

Bill and Spader did not socialize off-camera and would not keep in touch with each other once the series ended, but Bill got a kick out of his costar and continued to praise him in public. "I love him, he's a great guy, and we became—I don't know how you define friends, really, but by many definitions we're great friends," he said. "I laughed for days." He recounted one instance where Spader regaled Bill off-camera about the fragrance of his Hawaiian plumerias (the flowers used by some cultures to make leis), and their effect on him in his new house. "He said, 'You know, I got stoned the other day. And I got into the plant.' And then he looked around to see if anybody was looking, and he inhaled the fragrance—this is acting—well, he did it like he must've done after he had taken a couple of hits," Bill said. "I started laughing. It was . . . the best acting I've ever seen."[32]

"I'll tell you one little story showing the difference between James and Bill," said *Boston Legal* executive producer Bill D'Elia.

> I was directing [an episode], this was during the course of the season . . . it was a scene between Bill and Candice Bergen and as he

was getting ready to go on, Bill was doubled over in pain. I went over to him and said, "Are you okay?" and he said, "My back is really bothering me, but let's keep going." He was insistent. I said, "Action!" he straightened up, he went in, did the scene, I said, "Cut!" and he doubled over in pain. We did two or three takes. He went to the hospital the next day and passed a kidney stone. He was back at work the next day. James came in and pulled the crew together and he said, "I just want everybody here to know, that if what happened to Bill last night happens to me, I'm out six months." And that is really the difference between the two guys.

Bill's work ethic also impressed his *Boston Legal* costar Rene Auberjonois, who played lawyer Paul Lewiston, and who and called Bill's friendship "one of the great gifts" of acting in the series. "There would be hours when we would be sitting in our directors' chairs in the dark and we would just talk, talk, talk," he said. "I just adored him. I love the guy. He's a character and he's got a reputation. He's . . . *Shatner*. But he's genuine and he's interested in other people. In real life he's right there. He's really interested, and he loved my artwork. He always reminds me, he says, 'You know, in the bathroom in my office is a whole wall of your drawings.'"[33]

*   *   *

Bill's back-to-back Emmy victories and the success of *Boston Legal* underscored his remarkable career resurrection. Thanks in no small part to his Priceline.com ads, he was now in demand as a pitchman, appearing in a series of regional television commercials for attorneys (in Connecticut, Missouri, Oklahoma, and Maine). And, in 2004, feeling emboldened by his professional resurgence, he ventured back into the recording studio to cut his first album since mangling the songs of Bob Dylan and the Beatles on *The Transformed Man* in 1968.

This time around he enlisted the help of singer/songwriter/producer Ben Folds for *Has Been*, a spoken-word/indie rock mashup released by the Shout! Factory label in October to dovetail with the premiere of *Boston Legal*. (Shout! Factory was run by brothers Richard and Garson Foos and Bob Emmer, who'd reissued parts of *The Transformed Man* as a comedy album.)

Has Been was recorded over a two-week period in Nashville and was, at turns, introspective and autobiographical. Tracks on the album included "What Have You Done?"—a spoken-word ode to Nerine and her tragic death, which continued to haunt Bill. "The death of my wife was a cataclysmic event in my life," he said around that time. "And that kind of thing, that suddenness and that shock, of that kind of death . . . I have never lost my sense of grief with Nerine, never gotten over the sadness of a life that left us, the waste that it was because she was so bright and beautiful."[34]

He dedicated another track, "Ideal Woman," to Elizabeth. "I'm trying to distill moments of my life, so I can enlighten my loved ones," he told one interviewer. "This album was made for the people I love so that they can remember what it was I was feeling, thinking." In addition to Ben Folds, who produced and arranged the album, *Has Been* included appearances from Joe Jackson, Aimee Mann, Lemon Jelly, punk icon Henry Rollins, guitarist Adrian Belew, and country music star Brad Paisley, who wrote a song entitled "Real" specifically for Bill.

Novelist Nick Hornby (*High Fidelity*, *About a Boy*) contributed the song "That's Me Trying," about a father trying to mend his relationship with his adult daughter (Bill's nod to Leslie, Melanie, and Lisabeth?). Folds, for his part, had been a Bill Shatner fan since buying *The Transformed Man* at a yard sale as a kid and getting "a little Shakespeare burned into my head, and hearing that next to Bob Dylan, that's pretty interesting." He said he "locked onto" Bill's voice and his timing on *The Transformed Man* and appreciated that album's "method behind the madness."[35]

Has Been was not the first collaboration between Bill and Folds. Bill appeared on Folds's 1998 album, *Fear of Pop, Volume 1*—performing two spoken-word pieces—and Folds returned the favor by costarring alongside Bill in a Priceline.com commercial. "I recognize Bill as being a brother in working-class entertainment," he said about their collaborations. "You do your job, you do it with integrity, and you don't worry about the reviews and what the cool kids think."[36] Bill wrote or cowrote eight of the eleven tracks on *Has Been*, including "Together," sharing songwriting credit on the song with Elizabeth and Lemon Jelly.

Has Been was released in early October 2004 and reached a very respectable twenty-two on the *Billboard* charts; the online music magazine *Pitchfork* called Bill "the ultimate icon for Generation Irony," noting that the album's "humor and candor give it a fair amount of staying power... It's so confusing, enthralling, sincere, profound, and trite that it's nothing short of a mirror to society's own incongruities. Which, really, is quite an achievement."[37] "Has there ever been a more eminently slappable man in American pop-cultural history than Shatner?" asked one critic, referring to the "sheer chutzpah" of Shatner's rendition of Pulp's "Common People." "He's aware of his own limitations and has managed to cannily stitch them into his public façade, but he's essentially still untalented."[38]

Entertainment Weekly called the album "alternately comic and, believe it or not, touching," and in late October, Ben Folds, who was performing at the El Rey Theater in Los Angeles, beckoned Bill onstage to a raucous welcome. Reading lyrics on a music stand, Bill performed "Has Been" (with Joe Jackson singing backup vocals and Folds on drums and keyboards), "It Hasn't Happened Yet," and, removing his sports jacket, "Ideal Woman," "Common People," and "I Can't Get Behind That" (which he performed on the album with Henry Rollins). Then, raising his arm above his head, he gave the audience the finger before launching into his *The Transformed Man* rendition of "Lucy in the Sky with Diamonds." The crowd ate it up. Others weren't as charitable.

"At the El Rey on Thursday night, Shatner ended his five-song perf with "Lucy," but something felt off. He's in on the joke now," *Variety* noted. "The aud is still laughing at him, but Shatner knows it now and plays up the awfulness, turning it into camp. It's brittle and desperate (and not just a little sad) to see the Emmy-winning actor turn himself into a singing monkey. The material from his recently released *Has Been* fared somewhat better."[39]

Bill's collaboration on *Has Been* with Henry Rollins resulted in an unlikely friendship between the two men, who were thirty years apart in age but lived only blocks from each other in Los Angeles. They became "pals," and Bill would often invite Rollins over to his house to watch *Monday Night Football* along with his other celebrity (and non-celebrity) friends. "At least for me, Bill is one of the nicest people I've ever met in my life and it's one of the oddest friends I have in that I've been going to Bill Shatner's house every year since 2003," Rollins said. "Every once in a while, his assistant will contact me: 'Hey, Bill really wants to see you. Are you free for next Wednesday?' It's great to see him and his amazing wife and I truly value that friendship—I look forward to seeing him and I really enjoy hearing what he's up to . . . and it's become this thing where I really look forward to football season."[40]

Has Been took on a life of its own; in 2007, Margo Sappington, the choreographer behind the controversial 1969 off-Broadway revue *Oh! Calcutta!*, infamous for its onstage nudity, adapted *Has Been* into a vehicle for the Milwaukee Ballet. She called the show *Common People* (the album's opening track). Bill financed a filming of the Milwaukee Ballet's performance of *Common People*, which appeared two years later as the documentary *William Shatner's Gonzo Ballet*, premiering at the 2009 Nashville Film Festival.

*   *   *

Bill turned seventy-five in March 2006 and showed no signs of slowing down. *Boston Legal*, now in its second season, continued to be a popular draw for ABC in its new Tuesday-night time slot, and Bill's peers continued to laud the series. For the duration of its run and in its various iterations, John Laroquette, Taraji P. Henson, and Saffron Burrows, among others, joined *Boston Legal*. Bill earned four consecutive Emmy Award nominations as Denny Crane but no further statuettes.[41] James Spader won his second Emmy Award as Alan Shore in 2007, and *Boston Legal* won a Peabody Award in 2005. That same year its season was cut short to accommodate a new ABC medical drama called *Grey's Anatomy*.

"I consciously made the decision how I thought Denny Crane would be the great lawyer he was supposed to be and had been, and that remnants of that great lawyer were still around," Bill said of his onscreen alter ego. "What I gathered from all the words I had to learn [as Denny Crane] . . . was that his legacy really didn't matter. He wanted to live life to the fullest while he still could, and if that meant doing something illegal or unpalatable, he would do it because it would cause [his] enjoyment of life. I think the character believed that he had been a great lawyer and was filled with the torment that he no longer was."[42]

Bill kept busy in other venues. He starred in a silly reality show for Spike TV called *Invasion Iowa*, in which he (and a retinue of actors) descended on the bucolic town of Riverside, Iowa (known in *Star Trek* mythology as the birthplace, in 2233, of Captain James T. Kirk), where they snookered locals by pretending to shoot a science fiction movie on location. He was inducted into the Broadcasting & Cable Hall of Fame in New York City, accompanied by Elizabeth—"who is young, tall and slender, and wore a slinky knit dress, cut perilously low in the back."[43] He informed reporters covering the festivities that he recently passed a kidney stone, which he later auctioned off for $25,000 via Julien's Auctions to the website GoldenPalace.com—donating the proceeds to Habitat for Humanity. "This takes organ donors to a new height, to a new low, maybe," he said. "How much is a piece of me worth?"[44]

Bill's colorful, quirky public image—and his ability to laugh at himself (to a point)—translated into ratings for cable's Comedy Central network, which invited him to be the fourth celebrity "roasted" (following Denis Leary, Jeff Foxxworthy, and Pamela Anderson) on a no-holds-barred television special. *The Comedy Central Roast of William Shatner*, hosted by "Roast-master" (and huge Shatner fan) Jason Alexander, aired in late August 2006 with "roasters" including Farrah Fawcett, Nichelle Nichols, Kevin Pollak, Betty White, and George Takei. (White: "We all know Shatner's nuts, but George has actually tasted them!")

Nothing was off-limits on the roast, save for jokes about Nerine (at Bill's request). His colleagues took potshots at the predictable Shatner targets: his sketchy hair, his girth, his Halting. Acting. Style. Leonard Nimoy couldn't attend, but he and Bill pre-taped a sketch in which Bill calls Nimoy at home, inviting him to participate in the roast. Nimoy forcefully declines. "Roasts are for pigs!" he says. "Why are you doing this? Is it for the food?" Bill hangs up, thinking Nimoy is off the line (he's not): "Pointy-eared pussy!" he says. The roast opened to nearly 4 million cable viewers—big numbers for Comedy Central—and was nominated in 2007 for a Primetime Emmy Award as Outstanding Variety Special. That award went to *Tony Bennett: An American Classic*.

Bill ponied up $200,000 to be launched into space on Richard Branson's planned Virgin Galactic space ship, joining a long waiting list for a project that, nearly fifteen years later, still has not come to fruition. In 2007, during a hiatus from *Boston Legal*, he played an investigative reporter in the ABC miniseries *Everest*, which was based on the true story of the first Canadians to reach the vaunted summit of Mount Everest. Although he had a frenzied work schedule, Bill found time to complain about being left out of the eleventh *Star Trek* movie, a prequel film called, simply, *Star Trek* and directed by J. J. Abrams, with Chris Pine and Zachary Quinto playing Kirk and Spock, respectively. "How could you not put one of the founding figures into a movie that was being resurrected? That doesn't make good business sense to me," he griped. "I've become even more popular than I was playing Captain Kirk—I'm good box office and I get publicity."[45]

("I know he's upset," said Leonard Nimoy, who appeared briefly in the movie, "but his character died three movies ago, so it would have been very difficult to get him into this one."[46]) The omnipresent *Star Trek* franchise would reappear in Bill's life five years later.

In March 2006 Bill poked fun at his musical career in *Living in TV Land: William Shatner in Concert,* a surreal journey through his daily life that aired on oldies cable network TV Land and was loosely tied to the 2004 album *Has Been.* Bill was a co-producer on the special, which followed him behind the scenes on the set of *Boston Legal,* riding broncos at a rodeo, flying to a *Star Trek* convention in Las Vegas with Leonard Nimoy and Kate Mulgrew (Captain Janeway on *Star Trek: Discovery*), and accepting his Emmy Award for *Boston Legal.* It also featured his friends, family (wife Elizabeth and daughters Leslie, Lisabeth, and Melanie) and costars (including Candice Bergen) who offered up their (sometimes cheeky) takes on Bill Shatner and his music. "I found out early on that he's William Shatner, not Captain James T. Kirk," said his *Boston Legal* costar Mark Valley. "I hate to say it, but there's a certain amount of disappointment that goes with that."

Age was starting to catch up with him—but just a little.

In late January 2008, nearing his seventy-seventh birthday, Bill had hip-replacement surgery at Cedars-Sinai Medical Center in Los Angeles. The routine surgery reportedly took a short-lived alarming turn when Bill's heart started beating erratically before returning to its normal rhythm. He was both shaken and stirred and vowed to lose some weight once he returned home and began his recovery. Within days of returning from the hospital, Bill was up and walking and issued a statement denying that anything had gone awry during his operation. "I'm in absolute perfect health. I've never felt better in my life," he said. "Somebody made up an absolutely foolish story. My Best, Bill." He felt well enough to appear four weeks later as a guest on Oprah Winfrey's daytime television talk show, *Oprah,* on one of its "TV Icons" segments (and to pitch his upcoming autobiography, *Up Till Now*)—walking onstage with a cane but otherwise looking fit and healthy in a dark brown sports jacket and blue shirt.

* * *

In the spring of 2008, ABC renewed *Boston Legal* for a fifth and final season comprising thirteen episodes, including a two-hour series finale. Viewership had fallen from a high of nearly 13 million viewers in 2004, its maiden season, to around 9 million viewers a week in Season 4, and ABC didn't see the point of spending any more money on a series that was ranked fiftieth among all prime-time shows. "When you do an odd show that tonally is just distinct, I think the shelf life is a little shorter," series creator David E. Kelley said in retrospect.[47] "When it's really a series about mining the eccentricities of its characters, after a while that gets a little old. I felt our race was pretty much run. The worst thing we could all imagine is that we continued to work on it and stopped loving it. The time was right to say goodbye."[48] Bill fired a parting shot at ABC, saying, "[*Boston Legal* was] on the wrong network . . . I don't think NBC or CBS would have cancelled us."[49]

The plan in that final scene was for Denny Crane's Alzheimer's disease—always lurking just under the surface—to progress to the point where it would impact his career. "There's an interesting chord being played, in a scene I'm paying a lot of attention to, in which I say, 'I think I'm slipping,'" Bill said before the season launched. "Later on, I say, 'I'm slipping.' Then I say, 'I know I'm slipping.' I think Kelley is planning on something dire, with some disposition or some disposal." [50]

The two-hour series finale of *Boston Legal* aired on December 8, 2008, with a suitably whimsical, eccentric episode, "Last Call," in which Alan Shore and Denny Crane get married. It was Denny's call: he wanted to marry Alan, he said, for practical purposes, and since same-sex marriages were legal in Massachusetts, that would give Alan the power of attorney to make critical medical decisions for Denny as his Alzheimer's took over. "I've always wanted to remarry before I die. I just have," he said to Alan. "And like it or not, you're the man I love."

The episode ended with Denny and Alan and Carl (John Larroquette) and Shirley (Candice Bergen) marrying in a double civil ceremony in Nimmo Bay—officiated by (ultraconservative) Supreme Court Justice Antonin Scalia (played by actor Jack Shearer), who, in the episode's plotline, happened to be in the area on a fishing trip. (Shearer reprised his "Scalia" character in the 2008 HBO movie *Recount*, about the 2000 presidential election.) It was the liberal-leaning Kelley's final *Boston Legal* "fuck you" to the right. Bill had the honor of uttering the series' final line. "It's our wedding night," Denny says to Alan as they slow-dance on the balcony. Bill later wrote about the "intensity of the relationship" between Alan and Denny: "Certainly there has never been a stronger bond between two men portrayed on a series."[51]

Bill segued seamlessly from the end of *Boston Legal* to the premiere of his next television series, *Shatner's Raw Nerve*, which premiered on cable's The Biography Channel (partly owned by ABC) about a week before the two-hour *Boston Legal* series finale.

Shatner's Raw Nerve was an interview show in which Bill chatted with celebrities on a studio set as they sat inches apart from each other in chairs— and, starting with Season 2, on an S-shaped couch (designed by Bill). "I wanted to be on the edge of personal space that is shy of violating a person's privacy but close enough to suggest intimacy," he said. "I was trusting my intuition from my past [talk show] experience when I'd ask myself, 'Why is this desk in between me and the person I'm talking to?'"[52] The show's producer, Scott Sternberg, added: "He wanted to have direct eye contact [with his guests] and not be at an angle. He wanted to be able to touch them, and for them to be able to touch him . . . he is just curious about everything and I think that's what makes him really good in terms of asking questions—he's a really good listener."[53]

Each celebrity (among them Kelsey Grammer, Judith Sheindlin, a.k.a. "Judge Judy," porn star Jenna Jameson, Scott Bakula, Regis Philbin, and Bill's *Star Trek* castmates Leonard Nimoy and Walter Koenig) was asked to bring an item from their personal lives to their interview as they sat opposite Shatner on the couch. "That was Bill's idea, to bring something from home that was meaningful for them," Sternberg recalled.

> He felt he could get a really good story out of it and really open up his guest a little bit more to things that maybe would not come out in other talk shows that are limited to six-minute segments, at best. One of the things we did is that we never stopped recording the show; it usually went to an hour or an hour-and-a-half knowing we had to cut it down to a half-hour show. But you never know when the magic or gold was going to happen—and normally [on *Shatner's Raw Nerve*] it did.
>
> When we booked people on the show they were not coming to talk to a talk-show host, they were coming to talk to Bill Shatner—and that was an experience for them. They couldn't believe they were there.

"I've spent my life enjoying myself talking to friends . . . and rather than dally with the incidental stuff, I find myself going to the heart of somebody's issue — whether it's a momentary issue or a deep-seated issue," Bill said. "I sort of acted by intuition to begin with [on *Raw Nerve*] . . . it was a voyage of discovery in the first few shows and then I began to realize that . . . the character of this show would assume the character of my personal life."[54]

Bill proved to be a considerate, penetrating interviewer; at times, *Shatner's Raw Nerve* was thoughtful and provocative. A bald Walter Koenig—who surprisingly accepted an invitation to appear on *Shatner's Raw Nerve* after criticizing Bill in his 1998 autobiography, *Warped Factors*—was extremely blunt when it came time for him to sit opposite his nemesis on the S-shaped couch. Koenig told Bill that he and the other *Star Trek* costars lived in fear that Bill would fire them at any time, despite never witnessing such behavior on his part, and scolded Bill for "frequently" stealing scenes from the supporting players. "There was a self-involvement on your part. Where was the guy who was supposed to be the leader of the troupe?" Koenig said. "Where was the guy who was supposed to be the guy we could go to, our friend? And we never felt that way."

Bill didn't flinch and appeared to take Koenig's criticisms to heart. "That resonates with me," he said, cradling a coffee mug. "The man I am now is much more inclusive . . . and now that I hear you and hear the human wail of 'What about me?' coming from a young actor makes me cry inside for you and regret in all my heart that I never reached out to you guys and put my arm around you and said, 'You guys are great, this is a wonderful show, I hope we make another movie together.' I am so sorry that I wasn't capable then of doing that."

"The amazing thing is the reason that Walter was booked [on the show] was because he wanted to come on and blast Bill and really resolve the issues between them," Sternberg said. "Bill said, 'I didn't realize the dislike, or I didn't remember any of that kind of stuff' and ultimately he apologized to him, which I think helped close the circle for Walter." No circles were closed when Leonard Nimoy sat opposite Bill on *Shatner's Raw Nerve*. "These two guys were like brothers but also had issues," Sternberg recalled. "Bill would say, 'Well, Leonard, don't you remember when...' and Leonard would say, 'That's not the way it happened! What the fuck are you talking about Bill! You're making it up!'"[55]

Walter Koenig's visit to *Shatner's Raw Nerve* gave Bill the opportunity to bring up another sore subject when he implored Koenig to "Help me with George Takei." In 2008, Takei married Brad Altman in a Buddhist ceremony, with Koenig as his best man and Nichelle Nichols as his "best woman." Bill wasn't there. Was he even invited? Takei insisted he was. Bill insisted he wasn't. That fueled yet another in a long list of public spats between them over perceived slights that were initially ignited by Takei's 1995 memoir, *To the Stars*. Old grudges died hard between Mr. Sulu and Captain Kirk . . . if they died at all.

Two months after Takei's wedding, Bill was interviewed online when the subject arose. "There's such a sickness there, it's so painfully obvious that there's a psychosis there," he said of Takei by way of explaining why he wasn't invited. ". . . There must be something else inside George that is festering . . . Why would he go out of his way to denigrate me?" Takei, in turn, criticized Bill during his frequent visits to Howard Stern's radio show (Takei's "Oh my" exclamation was a favorite *Howard Stern Show* sound bite) and implied that Bill was picking another fight to drum up publicity for *Shatner's Raw Nerve*, which was about to premiere. He also slammed Bill for not attending a 1994 event honoring their *Star Trek* costar James Doohan (Scotty), who was very ill at the time. "It was shocking," he told Stern.[56] Their on-again/off-again feud would continue to erupt for another decade. "I really haven't rubbed anyone the wrong way," Bill insisted to the *New York Post* while discussing *Shatner's Raw Nerve*. "I think you're referring to some cast members from *Star Trek*. I've asked them numerous times to see if I can assuage their bitterness. I don't know what their problem is, quite frankly, so I've given up on trying to make it better. I don't like any ill-feeling, and if there was something I could do to correct it, I would. But nothing seems to work."[57]

What worked for Bill Shatner was keeping busy, and his workload only seemed to increase as he neared his eightieth birthday and shifted his slate of projects into high gear. In early 2010, fourteen months after the finale of *Boston Legal*, Bill signed on for his next network television series, a starring vehicle placing him front-and-center. He followed that, in quick succession, by releasing another album and revisiting *Star Trek* (and Captain Kirk) on the big screen.

CHAPTER 15

$#*! Happens

Bill's new TV series was a product of the digital age, apropos for the man whose face had, a decade before, launched Priceline.com into the stratosphere. The Internet was opening new avenues of communication almost daily, or so it seemed, and the series was adapted from a Twitter feed called @shitmydadsays, launched in August 2009 by writer Justin Halpern. Halpern used the feed to tweet a stream of random musings from his father, Sam—grumpy, sardonic, funny, expletive-filled rants that quickly gained an online following (including actor Robb Corddry). By November 2010, @shitmydadsays had amassed nearly 2 million followers and landed Halpern a book deal (from HarperCollins) and a television development deal from Warner Brothers. The studio announced in February 2010 that Bill would star in the pilot episode for a planned CBS sitcom called *$#*! My Dad Says*. (The title was modified for television.) @shitmydadsays was the first Twitter account in the history of the Internet to be translated into a television show.

In May, CBS let its advertisers know that it was adding *$#*! My Dad Says* to its fall schedule, with Bill in the lead role of seventy-two-year-old Dr. Edison Milford "Ed" Goodson III and Ryan Devlin playing his son, Henry. Will Sasso, Nicole Sullivan, and Tim Bagley rounded out the cast. Bill's old pal, Ben Folds, composed the show's opening theme song, called "Your Dogs."

(In a case of life imitating art, Bill's personal Twitter feed, @williamshatner, would prove to be extremely popular, accruing over 2.5 million followers—not including the author, as I was blocked by Shatner on Twitter after he learned about this book.)

"CBS was basically like, 'We'll make the pilot IF you get one of these ten actors—they sent us a list and Shatner was on the list and it just seemed like a really interesting choice," said Justin Halpern, who helped develop the show and was credited as one of its four co-creators. "John Lithgow was on the list, and also people who were never going to do it, like Gene Hackman." *$#*! My Dad Says* began shooting that summer, with Jonathan Sadowski replacing Ryan Devlin as Henry Goodson.

"The thing that was most shocking to me was that [Shatner] has an insane work ethic," Halpern said. "He was doing two other shows while he was doing ours, and he was having to perform in front of a live audience, and he was like eighty at the time. It sounds clichéd, but he was like the first one there and the last one to leave.

"He always knew his shit, and he is older, so there were times we would have to pre-shoot some stuff because it's just too rigorous to go through a whole shoot in one night in front of a live audience," he said. "But he would memorize a lot of shit in a little amount of time. He's got an ego, like any big actor, but he is also very self-aware of what makes him funny and so we never had a problem."[1]

$#! My Dad Says* premiered on September 23, 2010, to nearly 13 million viewers, a strong ratings number, but the critics were mostly harsh in their assessments of the show (and often kinder to Bill regarding his performance).

"Shatner is occasionally quite funny as a curmudgeonly retired doctor whose relationship with his son (Jonathan Sadowski) never quite developed," wrote the *Philadelphia Daily News*. "The problem is that neither has the show, which at its best plays like a series of one-liners—essentially what those who followed Justin Halpern's more graphically titled Twitter feed got, but in Shatner's voice—and at its worst, tries, maybe a little too hard, to make us feel something for the guy delivering them."[2] Bill's Ed Goodson was, said the *Boston Globe*, "Archie Bunker without the satirical spin, and without the overt prejudices that made Archie so edgy."[3] The *San Francisco Chronicle*: "Face it, *$#*! My Dad Says* was a bad idea from inception to pilot."[4] Other critics called it "dismal" (*Slant* magazine),[5] "hopelessly old school" (*San Jose Mercury News*),[6] and "irrelevant, a wholly generic sitcom so divorced from its source material that you have to pinch yourself to remember it had anything to do with the Internet, or with the world after 1985" (*New York Times*).[7]

Despite the criticism, the show's viewership never drastically fell off, but CBS announced in May 2011 that it was cancelling the series after one season and eighteen episodes. "For as crappy as that show was, and it really wasn't Bill's fault at all, I think Bill did exactly what we were hoping he would do," Halpern said. "The experience was amazing. I think it was the tone of [the series]. I don't think that was the best. I don't think a multi-camera sitcom was the best format for that character . . . because he's a guy who's not trying to be funny . . . and it was very much a punch line setup. It doesn't capture what that character is. And also, you can't go as dark as you need to go." Halpern said that even his father, Sam, upon whom Shatner's Ed was based, wasn't a fan: "My dad could not have given less of a shit. He did not love that show. He didn't really care."[8]

Bill didn't appear to be too broken up over the show's cancellation, though he did chide CBS for dropping the axe. "It was too popular. And we were getting it right," he said. "I don't know what happened in CBS's mind. I'm told that it's in the top ten in Canada, and here it was in the top twenty most of the time. So, I don't understand that. I went into the series with tremendous trepidation, and I would look at it the same way now, even more so. I can create the things I am creating without having that onus on me."[9]

He took some solace following the show's cancellation in being honored with an honorary degree by McGill University, regaling the assembled crowd at his alma mater's graduation ceremonies with tales of growing up in Montreal, directing McGill's *Red and White Revue* ("I made better use of the sofa than the desk") and his long Hollywood career. "Don't be afraid to make an ass of yourself," he proclaimed. "I do it all the time and look what I got."

Earlier that year, Bill was back in the recording studio working on his fourth album, called *Seeking Major Tom*. It was released on October 11, 2011, and featured Bill covering twenty space-themed songs—including David Bowie's "Space Oddity," Roger McGuinn's "Mr. Spaceman," and Sting's "Walking on the Moon"—in his by-now-familiar spoken-voice shtick.

(The album's title was a takeoff on "Major Tom," the character in Bowie's anthemic "Space Oddity" who would reappear in other Bowie songs. Its cover illustration featured Bill, in a spacesuit, floating in orbit above the Earth with a rocket and a satellite whizzing by on either side of him.)

Bill was backed on *Seeking Major Tom* by a bevy of A-list musicians, including Sheryl Crow, Steve Howe, Johnny Winter, Ritchie Blackmore, Peter Frampton, Dave Davies, pal Brad Paisley, and drummer Carmine Appice.

For good measure, he threw in a spoken-word cover of Queen's "Bohemian Rhapsody," though he'd never heard the song before recording it, and shot a strange video to accompany the tune.

"A lot of people loved it and some people didn't like it," Bill said of the album. Reviews ranged from the enthusiastic to the snarky. "Although the variety of supporters helps, *Seeking* is at least eight songs too long; the concept and Shatner's style often wear out their welcome," sniped one critic. "Shatner's desire to be taken seriously as an artist seems to be at odds with his penchant for self-parody."[10]

"*Seeking Major Tom* is one of the most epic musical moments of 2011, and it works because — like the original *Star Trek* series or Shatner's recent masterful acting performance on *Boston Legal*—it has replayability," wrote TheTune.net. "There's no one in the world at all like William Shatner, and I'd hazard that there never will be—therefore, there will never be a cover album at all like this one."[11] *Popmatters* was more succinct: "*Seeking Major Tom* is a sleek dog that's fallen in the swimming pool and doesn't deal well with the extra weight. It stumbles awkwardly around the kitchen knocking over chairs, stopping every once in a while to shake its paws miserably."[12]

Bill had better luck that year with his new documentary, *The Captains*, a big-screen feature that eventually aired on cable's Epix network in the United States. The film had a novel concept, as Bill travelled around the world to interview five other actors who'd played starship captains in the *Star Trek* franchise (both on television and in the movies): Patrick Stewart (*Star Trek: The Next Generation*), Avery Brooks (*Star Trek: Deep Space Nine*), Kate Mulgrew (*Star Trek: Voyager*), Scott Bakula (*Star Trek: Enterprise*), and Chris Pine (the alternate-universe version of Captain Kirk in 2009's *Star Trek*).

"It's just an idea that occurred, and it seemed like a good thought, it seemed like a commercial thought," he said, admitting that he didn't know the other actors save for "a respectful nod in their direction when I would see them," although he did have dinner with Patrick Stewart a few times.[13] The ninety-six-minute movie, which featured a bevy of co-producers—notably several Canadian production companies—also featured smaller interviews with other actors associated with *Star Trek*, including Rene Auberjonois (Bill's *Boston Legal* costar who played Odo in *Deep Space Nine*), Christopher Plummer (*Star Trek VI: The Undiscovered Country*), Walter Koenig, Grace Lee Whitney (Yeoman Rand from the original series), and Garrett Wang (Harry Kim in *Star Trek: Voyager*).

The Captains premiered in July 2011 to mixed reviews, with the *New York Times* calling it "largely about William Shatner" but "pretty tolerable as vanity projects go," while TrekMovie.com claimed: "[It's] overly long, a big self-indulgent, and possibly over ambitious. The direction and editing are trying a bit too hard with Shatner not really letting the core content of his interviews stand out." It did note, however, that it "is still a must-watch for any Trekkie."[14] [15]

*   *   *

Bill donned his author hat again that fall with the release of *Shatner Rules: Your Guide to Understanding the Shatnerverse and the World at Large*, a tongue-in-cheek take on self-help books cowritten by Emmy-winning comedy scribe Chris Regan (Comedy Central's *The Daily Show with Jon Stewart*). The 272-page book, published by Dutton, featured Bill spouting faux Zen philosophy ("There are many lives in a lifetime"; "The journey must be taken in individual moments. Enjoy the ride for the ride") and ruminating on his life and career. He even took a few jabs at his favorite celebrity target, *Star Trek* costar George Takei, writing that "he's been saying mean things about me for nearly 40 years now" and claiming that Takei's 2008 marriage to Brad Altman was a publicity stunt. Nonetheless, the book was generally well-received. "Lurking beneath the *Star Trek* cracks and self-deprecating hairpiece jokes, this is a portrait of a man nearing the end of his days, taking stock of his life and wrestling with his two distinct personalities," wrote the critic for the *National Post*. "But through it all, the reader gets a keen sense that William Shatner knows exactly who the character of William Shatner really is, and that he's the one having the last laugh."[16]

The cancellation of *$#*! My Dad Says* failed to put a dent into Bill's television career; if anything, he now had the time and freedom to pick and choose projects that appealed to him without the onus of a weekly series and its grueling production schedule. For the next few years, his television appearances were, for the most part, guest-starring roles for one or two episodes. He played Frank O'Hara, the estranged father of Det. Juliet O'Hara (Maggie Lawson), on two episodes on the popular USA Network cable series *Psych* and guest-starred on the third-season premiere of ABC's cop drama *Rookie Blue* (a Canadian import) as a belligerent drunk driver with a built-in antagonism toward the police. "For a guy his age he is such a badass," said series star Missy

Peregrym. "He's really tough. He was getting his ass kicked and kicking other people's asses. It was awesome."[17]

In January 2012 Bill announced his return to the Broadway stage in a one-man show, *Shatner's World: We Just Live In It*, which was slated to premiere in February at the Music Box Theater on West Forty-Fifth Street for a limited run (through March 4) to be followed by a fifteen-city national tour. It was his first appearance on The Great White Way in nearly fifty years, since ending his run as Paul Sevigne in *A Shot in the Dark* at the Booth Theatre.

Shatner's World began its journey to Broadway the previous year, in February 2011, when Bill was flown to Australia by a Sydney production company, Spiritworks, to appear onstage in an interview show called *Kirk, Crane and Beyond*, a testament to his international popularity. He toured with the show throughout Australia and New Zealand, sitting onstage with a moderator who prompted him with questions about his life and career—and, of course, about *Star Trek* and *Boston Legal*. It was a successful venture that eventually took Bill to Canada with the show retitled to *How Time Flies: An Evening with William Shatner*.

"We finished the six cities, got good reviews, and people clapped and I sang some songs," Bill said. "And I thought, 'Well, that's over. I've done that. And then Canada said, would I tour Canada? Same kind of show, and they offered me an interlocutor who was a nationally known character. I worked the show out a little bit better and got to Toronto—which is the high point in Canada—and they usually tear you apart. And they didn't tear me apart. It was very well attended."[18] When he was asked to bring the show to Broadway, he decided to ditch the interviewer—"that's not a one-man show"—and rewrite the show in order to let his anecdotes flow more smoothly. "The New York people came to Los Angeles and we started to put the visuals together. And I thought, 'This isn't good enough, I'm fucking going to be laughed at, I'm going to be laughed off the stage. This is terrible . . . But the more I did it, the faster I got, the more rhythm I got, it started to take shape."[19] *How Time Flies* took Bill to six Canadian cities, including Vancouver, Winnipeg, and Montreal, with a press release promising "a wild ride through his life and career" and Bill "singing songs as only he can." The show ran for nearly three hours and the reviews were mostly positive. "The end is coming, and William Shatner knows it," noted one critic. "He's so preoccupied with it that he's begun a pilgrimage across Canada to ensure his legacy is secure . . . Ranging from funny to morbid, Shatner talked a lot about his own mortality . . . Unfortunately, the show's moniker wasn't its mantra. Shatner might look great for 80, but like some octogenarians, he can be a windbag when he gets talking about the past."[20]

No matter; when word broke that Bill was returning to Broadway following his run in Canada, he threw caution to the wind, issuing a typically blustery press release announcing his return to the boards with *Shatner's World:* "I've been pretty busy since I last played the Music Box," he said mistakenly. (He never starred in a Broadway production in that theater.) "I've been refurbished; I hope the theater has been too. My plan has always been to return to Broadway every 50 years. I can't ask my fans to wait for me longer than Halley's Comet, so I'm coming back." *Shatner's World* would, the press release promised, feature "this internationally known icon and raconteur, known as much for his unique persona as for his expansive body of work" reminiscing on his sixty-year career.

Scott Faris, a veteran of several Broadway productions, was hired to direct the show. Faris worked as a stage manager on *Cabaret, Grease*, and *Chicago* before he got the call for *Shatner's World*. "He didn't know me from Adam, and I called him, he's got the stentorious voice, he said, 'Hello, Scott, this is Bill Shatner,'" Faris recalled. "At first I thought, 'Bill Shatner? He's not on my radar at all.' I watched *Star Trek* as a kid and I knew he had a hit with *Boston Legal*, and once I was hired, I started watching everything he did and read his autobiography."

Bill sent Faris some DVDs from the Australian production of *Kirk, Crane and Beyond* for context and research purposes; Faris, who was in Berlin, Germany, at the time, took copious notes. "I watched them all and said to him, 'Some of it is too much and needs to be cut, what do you think that is?' and he said to me, 'You tell me,' which I loved as a challenge." Faris was due to fly from Berlin to Los Angeles to meet Bill, where they would be followed by a documentary camera crew filming it all for posterity. "I was going to meet him for breakfast the next morning and I got to the place early and was listening to music from his album with Ben Folds with headphones on," Faris said. "A car pulls up directly in front of me and it's Bill Shatner. He stepped out and was looking at me, sort of with his brow down and I point at myself and I point at him. He says, 'You're Scott Faris. Well, this is very fortuitous that we met in the parking lot.'"[21]

The meeting went smoothly. "I told him, 'This is a play, therefore no stories that don't support the journey can be included' and he said, 'I completely agree with you' and we hit it off," Faris said. "We had some breakfast and went to a brief rehearsal which was nothing but fun. He was delightful, witty, funny, and demanding, but I was used to that, having been around stars, so that didn't bother me at all." They rehearsed the show for a week at a dance studio on La Brea Avenue, and Bill, who was hosting his annual Super Bowl party at his house, invited Faris, who accepted the invitation. "It was a huge party with his kids, his grandkids, his friends, and TV and film guys from various parts of his career," he said. Faris mentioned to one of Bill's costars from *Boston Legal* that he was directing him in a one-man show. "He just laughed at me and said, 'Good luck directing Bill.' I told him we'd been working for a week and he'd been nothing but agreeable."

They flew back to New York and began rehearsing for *Shatner's World* in a studio on East Thirty-First Street in Manhattan to prepare for the show's opening night. "It's me giving you some varied aspects of my life that I think are interesting and entertaining, and dramatizing who I am and what I am and why I am," Bill told a reporter. "I don't have the answers to those questions, but in the dramatizations of these stories, I hope that you may have an answer that will satisfy you." He called the idea of doing a one-man show on Broadway "daunting" and said he'd been asked to return to the Broadway stage "several times" but never had the time to commit to this sort of project. So, what changed? "But this was like a dream come true, because I could come to New York, be part of the Broadway stage one more time and not have to have an extensive commitment that would take me away from my family."[22]

The hard work paid off. *Shatner's World* opened on February 14, 2012, to mostly positive reviews, though eyewitnesses reported that Bill was heckled by audience members every now and then. The project got off to an inauspicious start when Bill came down with food poisoning or the flu (he wasn't sure which) the night before the show's preview performance after dining at the Four Seasons with Elizabeth. "At this point now, what are you going to do? Laugh me off the stage? I'm not going to die . . . so I go into my Broadway opening frightened to death that I'm going to fail," he said. "And I have the stomach flu—which means you can go from here to there, to the toilet, because you have no command of your bowels whatsoever. And

I'll tell you the life lesson I learned . . . You never know what you can accomplish until you try."[23]

In the show, Bill spent over ninety minutes on stage—seated in a rolling armchair, with a large projection screen behind him—regaling theatergoers with stories from every phase of his life: his childhood in Montreal, his four years at McGill, the mid-1950s Stratford Festival years, working in live television in New York, *Star Trek*, *Boston Legal*, Priceline.com, Ben Folds . . . and on and on. He told stories about his love of horses and, naturally, got in a few zingers at George Takei, though he largely avoided mentions of Leonard Nimoy or his other *Star Trek* castmates.

"We kind of fluffed it up, adding a projection screen; we wanted a bit of a space-age thing," Faris said. "The producers always wanted Bill to hit on *Star Trek* . . . I came up with this idea that we would play the start of the *Star Trek* music, like he was going to do, 'Space: the final frontier'—he interrupts from offstage and says, 'Oh no, I'm not gonna do *Star Trek*!' and crashes that idea, yelling at the stage manager. It got a big laugh. He certainly didn't suffer fools gladly. When the producer made the suggestion about *Star Trek*, he said, 'I'm not doing that. That's the worst idea I've ever heard.' He was just like, flat-out 'No!' He didn't mince words."[24]

The *New York Times* called the show a "chatty, digressive and often amusing tour of his unusual acting career . . . Mr. Shatner shows a welcome tendency to poke fun at himself that anyone who has seen his commercials for the travel Web site Priceline.com will probably recognize," while the Associated Press noted the preoccupation with death in Bill's observations: "He lingers on the supposed final words of Timothy Leary ("Of course") and Steve Jobs ("Oh, wow"), wondering what it all means. 'What happens at the other end? I don't know!' he demands, almost screaming . . . It is very much like Shatner himself, a little out of date, a little bizarre, but endearing nonetheless."[25] [26]

"People loved it," Faris said. "They were saying, 'This is absolutely delightful. He's funny. He's fun.' I lived uptown at that time and would walk to the theatre in the weeks of the run. He'd go, 'Scotty, glad you're here, I'm having trouble with this joke, let's work on it.' He was calling me Scotty, which just cracked me up. He brought Brad Paisley in to perform a song as a guest artist in the closing show. I staged that."

Shatner's World exceeded expectations and garnered Bill glowing reviews as it moved from Broadway to a touring production in major cities throughout the United States. He sat for a round of interviews to promote the show, and in September, the producer of *Shatner's World*, Innovation Arts & Entertainment, announced that it was adding another twenty cities to the tour, taking its run through 2013. "His new solo stage act might be pulled together from anecdotal scraps," *Variety* noted, "but it gets by with humor and good-natured charm."[27] Bill would continue to tour with a pared-down version of the show in subsequent years—"a suitcase show with less production values," said Faris, now an associate professor of theatre practice in stage management at the USC School of Dramatic Arts.

Shatner's World, or at least a reasonable facsimile thereof, was staged even without its star, or his cooperation. In January 2014, Phil Soltanoff and Joe Diebes launched *An Evening with William Shatner Asterisk*, an off-Broadway show staged at the New Ohio Theater on Christopher Street in the West Village. Directed by Soltanoff and written by Diebes, it cobbled together snippets of audio and video of Captain Kirk from the original *Star Trek* series and projected this onto a large screen abutted on either side by video screens with titles. "The juxtaposition of Kirk's strenuously virile utterances with Joe Diebes's highfalutin text may sound like a one-joke concept," one critic wrote, "but Mr. Soltanoff continually, deliciously alters the temps, cadences and presentation."[28]

It was obvious that Bill would never escape the clutches of Captain James T. Kirk, and while he grew to embrace his role in the *Star Trek* mythology, the franchise continued to mushroom into other areas. In April 2014, NASA honored Bill with its Distinguished Public Service medal, the highest award bestowed by NASA to nongovernment personnel. It presented the award to Bill (wearing a leather jacket and cowboy hat) in Los Angeles during his annual Hollywood Charity Horse Show. He was receiving the medal "for outstanding generosity and dedication to inspiring new generations of explorers around the world, and for unwavering support for NASA and its missions of discovery." Bill's association with NASA included his recent narration of a NASA documentary celebrating the thirtieth anniversary of the space shuttle missions and, in 2013, hosting a video presentation about Curiosity, the rover sent to Mars to explore that planet.

*   *   *

Bill released his fourth spoken-word album, *Ponder the Mystery*, in October 2013 on Cleopatra Records. The fifteen-track album was produced by Billy

Sherwood, who played most of the instruments and who recruited keyboard-ists Rick Wakeman and Tony Kaye, both of whom played with Sherwood in the progressive rock group Yes. The album also included contributions from notable musicians, including ex-Doors guitarist Robbie Krieger, Al Di Meola, Vince Gill, and Foreigner founding member/guitarist Mick Jones.

Bill, who wrote all lyrics, described the album's theme as "a guy in de-spair who is living on a beach, and it takes him through the last hour of the day at sunset through twilight, into darkness and the sounds of the night in which he regains his fervor, his love of life based on the beauty of what he's seeing around him."[29] He shot a kaleidoscopic video to promote the album, and in late October, following its release, he performed *Ponder the Mystery* live at small venues in Southern California (Hermosa Beach, Agoura Hills, and San Juan Capistrano) accompanied by Kaye and Circa, Sherwood's pro-gressive rock band that included several former members of Yes.

"Shatner's reflections are somewhat scatterbrained throughout *Ponder the Mystery*, but that's what makes the compilation so intriguing," wrote *Music Times*. "The eighty-two-year-old performer initially ponders one word or phrase, and eventually blossoms that concept into a lyrical conun-drum of insightful thoughts and ideas. Some may find Shatner's creative talent genius, others probably think it's laughably crazy, but overall the experience is amusingly enjoyable."[30]

That was the vibe that Bill hoped for when he signed a deal to host his first web series, *William Shatner's Brown Bag Wine Tasting*, which premiered on Ora.TV in June 2014 and found him collaborating, once again, with *Shatner's Raw Nerve* producer Scott Sternberg. (Ora.TV is also the Internet home to former CNN stalwart Larry King, whose *Larry King Live* morphed into *Larry King Now* on the streaming network in 2012.) "It was his idea," Sternberg said of *Brown Bag Wine Tasting*. "He called me up and said, 'I have an idea. I'm gonna knock on doors and take bottles of wine and share wine with people and I'm gonna ask them what they think about it.'"[31]

Bill said that he was inspired to do the series—parts of which were shot in his house in Studio City—by a friend of his, Mike Horn, a broadcaster who was also a sommelier, and by the success of his Bio Channel talk show, *Raw Nerve*. "I'd been casually drinking wine for years before that, but now came specific and distinct knowledge of this estate and that varietal," he said, "and so it occurred to me in one of those conversations that since I liked wine, but knew nothing about it, and I'd had an interview show that had done well . . . we would combine the wine and conversation, so that the wine became an introduction to the conversation."

William Shatner's Brown Bag Wine Tasting ran for two seasons; over the course of the series, Bill sat down with, among others, Wil Wheaton and LeVar Burton from *Star Trek: The Next Generation*, comedian Adam Carolla, television personality Nigel Lythgoe (*So You Think You Can Dance*), and actor Misha Collins (best known for The CW television series *Supernatural*). "The hook was, we'll put [the wine] in a brown paper bag so no one knows the wine, not even Bill," said Sternberg. "Then, at the end, after the interview, the other hook [for the series] was to describe the wine as if it was something in your business or occupation, using terms you use on a daily basis like, 'This tastes like a bad tax return.' That also helped with Bill's sense of humor, which is outstanding."

William Shatner's Brown Bag Wine Tasting won a TasteTV Award from the Academy of Media Tastemakers, a "diverse and respected association of food & wine editors, writers and bloggers, chefs, fashion journalists, television producers and stations, online video platforms, mobile device providers, retail and technology enterprise experts." He received his TasteTV Award in January 2015 at a red-carpet reception held at the Egyptian Theatre in Hollywood.

CHAPTER 16

"He's Just This Life Force"

Facing his own mortality was becoming a central theme in Bill's philosophical outlook on life. He would eventually translate those feelings onto the written page in the form of a 2018 book, but in the meantime he was confronted with the death of one of his dearest friends—and resounding public backlash about how Bill handled this delicate situation.

In February 2014, one month before he turned eighty-four, Leonard Nimoy announced that he was suffering from chronic obstructive pulmonary disease (COPD), a progressive lung disease that made breathing difficult. Nimoy attributed his illness to his smoking habit, although he'd given up cigarettes thirty years before. Within a year's time his COPD progressed rapidly, and on February 19, 2015, he was taken to UCLA Medical Center, suffering from chest pains. He lapsed into a coma soon thereafter and died, at home in Bel Air, on February 27.

Bill and Leonard made their final on-camera appearance together the previous year, filming a German-language television commercial for Volkswagen to introduce its new Golf electric car. The forty-five-second ad, underscored by the familiar *Star Trek* opening theme, ended with Nimoy, driving a futuristic car, pulling up to Shatner (driving the new electric Volkswagen with a *Star Trek*-obsessed young boy in the passenger seat). Nimoy stops and glances over at the Volkswagen. *Faszinierend* ("Fascinating"), he says, raising his eyebrows a la Mr. Spock. The commercial shoot marked the last time Bill and Leonard would see each other.

Nimoy's death made headlines around the world and was followed by a public outpouring of grief from fans and colleagues alike, including President

Barack Obama, officials from NASA, and Nimoy's original *Star Trek* costars Nichelle Nichols and George Takei. "Today, the world lost a great man, and I lost a great friend," Takei wrote on Facebook. "We return you now to the stars, Leonard. You taught us to 'Live Long And Prosper,' and you indeed did, friend. I shall miss you in so many, many ways."

Bill released a statement. "I loved him like a brother," he said. "We will all miss his humor, his talent, and his capacity to love." Nimoy's traditional Jewish funeral was held in Los Angeles on March 1, 2015. Over three hundred people attended the private ceremony. Bill, who always referred to Leonard as his "brother," was not one of them—and he used his Twitter account to explain his notable absence. "I chose to honor a commitment I made months ago to appear at a charitable fundraiser," he wrote. "A lot of money was raised. So here I am; tell me off. So, my daughters Melanie and Lisabeth are attending Leonard's services. I feel really awful. Here I am doing charity work and one of my dearest friends is being buried."

Bill was in Palm Beach, Florida, attending a Red Cross fundraiser at Donald Trump's Mar-a-Lago Club, when he heard the news about Leonard's death. "He had a good, long life," Bill told a local television station. "He did a lot of things. He inspired a lot of people. He was loved by a lot of people and he loved a lot of people."

The fact that Bill missed Nimoy's funeral, for whatever reason, did not sit well with some people. Actor Burt Reynolds, one of Nimoy's close friends, took a swipe at Bill shortly thereafter while he was being honored at Lynn University in Boca Raton, Florida. The seventy-nine-year-old Reynolds was, by this time, visibly frail; he needed assistance and walked with a cane. (He died from a heart attack in September 2018 at the age of eighty-two.) Reynolds turned emotional in recounting how he'd spoken to Nimoy just before he died. "We were . . . two hours on the phone, talking about everything," he said, his voice cracking. "He was a wonderful, wonderful guy and I loved him very much. We are going to miss him a hell-of-a-lot more than the other guy."

Burt Reynolds's biting words were a bit surprising; if there was any bad blood between him and Bill, it was not public knowledge. Throughout their wildly divergent careers, Bill and Reynolds were linked, in the public consciousness, by their obvious toupees (the good, the bad, and the ugly). They were friendly enough that Reynolds asked Bill for advice when he needed help with his sparse pate. "You know, if I had it to do over again, I would do it natural," Reynolds said. "Not wear a toupee. But I ended up seeing this guy William Shatner sent me to. Edward Katz. He's a genius at what he does. Best guy in the business."[1] (Katz's other celebrity clients included actor Tony Curtis, ABC News anchor Peter Jennings, and director Mike Nichols.)

In April 2015, a month after Nimoy's funeral, word broke in the media that Bill was writing a book about his relationship with Leonard. It was called *Leonard: My Fifty-Year Friendship with a Remarkable Man* and was published by Thomas Dunne Books in February 2016, one year after Nimoy's death. Bill wrote the bestselling book with his longtime collaborator David Fisher and dedicated it to "my dear friend Leonard Nimoy and his loving family." The book's biggest revelation was that Bill and Leonard were not speaking for five years leading up to Nimoy's death, save for their brief interaction shooting the Volkswagen commercial in 2014. Bill said he didn't really know what caused Nimoy's animosity. "No one could give me an answer," he wrote. "It remains a mystery to me."

He thought that Nimoy's iciness might have been related to Bill's 2011 documentary, *The Captains*. Nimoy did not want to appear in *The Captains* and was angry when a cameraman filmed him at a convention without his permission. At least that's what Bill surmised. "Essentially, he stopped speaking to me," he wrote. "It made no sense, and I reached out to him several times to try to heal this problem, but I never got a response."[2] Bill told television talk show host Meredith Vieira that "it wasn't a feud"—and that he'd written Nimoy a note when he heard about his grave condition: "I heard that he was dying and I never got any response to it, so this dear, dear friend of mine went to his death and I don't know why I couldn't comfort him in his last moments."[3] Bill included his "last note" to Nimoy in *Leonard*. In the three-paragraph missive, he laid bare his feelings for his "brother," remembering their laughter together, how Nimoy regaled him with stories of his father and grandfather, and how Bill had "a deep love for you Leonard—for your character, your morality, your sense of justice, your artistic bent whether it's painting pictures or as an actor . . . You're the friend that I have known the longest and the deepest. I have missed you terribly and have longed for those dinners we used to have."

Bill added another layer of intrigue to his estrangement from Nimoy in his 2018 memoir, *Live Long and . . . What I Learned Along the Way.* "My closest friend was Leonard Nimoy. We were born four days apart and raised in Orthodox Jewish homes," he wrote. "We shared so much throughout our careers. I loved Leonard, and he used to refer to me as his brother. Yet at the end of his life and for reasons I still don't know, he was not my friend. I would call him, and he wouldn't answer the phone or return any messages. He died and I didn't feel welcome at his funeral."[4]

Bill was, though, still a welcome presence on television, and in early 2015, he signed on for *Better Late Than Never*, an NBC road trip reality series that was adapted from a South Korean television hit called *Grandpas Over Flowers*. The NBC version was executive-produced by Emmy-winning actor Henry Winkler, who was also a member of the cast. Bill joined Winkler and fellow men-of-a-certain-age travelers George Foreman, the former heavyweight boxing champ turned entrepreneur (the George Foreman Grill) and ordained minister; and Terry Bradshaw, the legendary NFL quarterback who led the Pittsburgh Steelers to four Super Bowl titles in the 1970s and segued to a successful analyst/cohosting career on *Fox NFL Sunday*. The men visited Japan, Hong Kong, Thailand, and South Korea with comedian Jeff Dye as their "guide," immersing themselves in the local culture and needling each other in the goofy, feel-good series, which was filmed over thirty-five days in the summer and fall of 2015.

"Bill is prickly, funny, informed, energetic . . . he's just this life force," Winkler said. "I ride with him in the van whenever we go anywhere, whatever city we're in. He's got like five or six books going at one time on his phone—he's reading or he's memorizing for his one-man show or he's explaining the fin shape of a dolphin. Or he's looking out the window and is completely fascinated by the color of the sand in Marrakesh."

"You know, he's very opinionated. He's very idiosyncratic," Winkler said. "If you engage him in a conversation, make sure you have at least forty-five minutes, because he knows a lot about any question you ask him."[5] *Better Late Than Never* premiered in August 2016 and, boosted by NBC's coverage of the Summer Olympic Games in Brazil, averaged 8 million viewers a week. It was renewed for a second season, which aired from December 2017 through February 2018, and featured Bill and company trekking to Sweden, Lithuania, Germany, Spain, and Morocco.

"The best thing about the trip [is that] I don't think I would be able to endure it at all without those occasional talks that William Shatner and I had," said Foreman. "He came with his intelligence and objectivity to the fullest. You're not going to sway him with words, but he would listen, and he was always curious. When things were getting a little shaky for me, I'd lean over to him, and I'm telling you, the guy was gifted with more wisdom than anyone I had run into with the Hollywood scene. He's no different from anyone else—don't get me wrong—but he's full of wisdom and with an ear to hear."

Foreman recalled an intense moment in the second season of *Better Late Than Never*, when the group traveled to Lithuania. The visit resonated not only for Bill—whose paternal roots were planted in the region—but also for Foreman.

> We were in Lithuania and we had a kind of reenactment of those people being caught in those camps. I had a blindfold on, and I actually felt what those people had gone through—being asked questions. They didn't really want an answer, just a reason to kill them. I felt it, and when I took my blindfold off, I just broke down crying uncontrollably. Shatner caught me crying and he said, "That's all that fierce competition and meanness you had in boxing coming completely out there to the sensitive man you've become." The glue [for the show] would not have been there without William Shatner and his wisdom. He was the most understanding fella, as far as I'm concerned . . . everybody keeps their feelings to themselves. I know that, I'm a minister by profession, but occasionally we'd sit and he'd blurt out an actual, honest-to-goodness opinion about something. Those were the best moments. If I had to tell you I miss the show, I'd be lying—I miss William Shatner.

Bill turned eighty-five on March 22, 2016, content that all his skeletons in his closet—romances, marriages, divorces, palimony suits—were happily buried in the graveyard of his past. That was about to change.

In early April of that year, Bill was hit with a $170 million paternity suit by a sixty-year-old Florida insurance broker named Peter Sloan, who also called himself Peter Shatner. Sloan's birth mother was a Canadian actress named Katherine Burt (later Kathy McNeil), who gave Peter up for adoption when he was five days old. In 1983, Sloan went in search of his biological parents and eventually found Burt—who told him that she had a brief romantic liaison with Bill in 1956. (Peter was born in December 1956). She also told Peter that his father was either Bill Shatner or a Montreal law student she called "Chick," though she was "more certain" it was Bill—who, she said, had known about the baby's birth since 1962. "She revealed my father was William Shatner," Sloan said. "My jaw dropped to the floor, basically." (Burt and Shatner appeared together in "Forever Galatea," an episode of the CBC's *General Motors Theatre* that aired on December 4, 1956.)

In 1984, E. Arthur Kean, a Hollywood producer and a Sloan family friend, arranged a meeting between Peter Sloan and Bill on the set of *T. J. Hooker.* "I said, 'Mr. Shatner, I'm Peter Sloan' and he said, 'You're the one,'" Sloan said later, describing how he spent two hours talking with Bill in a production trailer on the *T. J. Hooker* set. Bill told Sloan that he did not remember Katherine Burt. "He said, 'What do you want Peter? What can I do for you? Do you want me to introduce you to the casting directors?'" Sloan recounted. "'No,' I said. 'I just wanted to hold my father in my arms,' and I literally started to cry. And he cried. And then he lifted me up and held me in his arms."[6]

Sloan claimed that, during their meeting, Bill admitted that he was his father and "was willing to talk further at another time" but then called Sloan back shortly thereafter to say he could not publicly admit to anything. They met again in 2011 at an Orlando comic book convention, where Sloan paid to have his picture taken with Bill and spoke to him briefly. (Two years earlier, Sloan registered the website Petershatner.com.) "Mr. Shatner has three lovely daughters, but no sons," Bill's publicist told the *New York Post* after the paternity suit was made public. "Mr. Shatner is aware of the lawsuit, but there's nothing there because he isn't his father."

In 2016, Sloan, using the name Peter Shatner, published a book, *The Search*, in which he documented the trail he claimed led him to Bill as his biological father. There was no proof, other than Katherine Burt's recollections, and Bill refused to take a DNA test to prove or disprove Peter Sloan's claim. The paternity suit was permanently dismissed in June 2018 by Judge James Whittemore of United States District Court, Middle District of Florida, Tampa Division. Whittemore ruled that Sloan sought "to establish paternity, but under the guise of tort action sounding like defamation" and that, because Bill is a Canadian citizen living in Los Angeles—without business ties to that part of Florida—the court had no personal jurisdiction over him. "The alleged defamatory statements . . . could not have been as a matter of law, false when made," Whittemore wrote.[7]

But the story wasn't over. On January 14, 2019, Sloan, now sixty-two and living in Clearwater, Florida, filed papers in the Pinellas County Court seeking to legally change his name to "Peter Shatner"—claiming the Shatner surname as his "birthright." One week later, he received a cease-and-desist letter from Bill's attorney in Miami. How Bill's camp learned of Sloan's legal filing remains a mystery; Sloane theorized that Bill was alerted to the court papers after Sloan posted information about it on social media. Sloan describes himself as "Son of William Shatner" on his Twitter biography.

Bill's attorney, John B. Atkinson, requested the cease-and-desist since Sloan's legal petition to change his name was signed under oath—constituting perjury, Atkinson said. "These falsities and failures clearly indicate that the Petition has an ulterior motive or illegal purpose that may invade the property rights of Mr. Shatner and others," Atkinson wrote. A news story on Sloan's attempts to change his name ran in the *Tampa Bay Times*, which pointed out that Atkinson's request "notes that Sloan has publicly stated the adoption agency described his biological father as an unnamed 'law student.' What's more, the request says, Sloan's defamation suit was dismissed by the US District Court in Tampa on the grounds that 'it has never been established' that Shatner is the biological father."[8]

"They are trying to scare me," Sloan told the newspaper. "It won't work... I am Peter Shatner. No one can prove otherwise. If they want to, let's get that DNA test."

* * *

Star Trek turned fifty years old on September 8, 2016. Its golden anniversary not only spurred headlines around the world—and ruminations in print and online regarding its indelible and enduring impact on pop culture—but tributes from a galaxy of *Star Trek* actors past and present, including George Takei, Nichelle Nichols, John Cho, Patrick Stewart, Brent Spiner, and LeVar Burton. Bill noted the anniversary but kept it short and sweet on his preferred social media platform, Twitter: "HB2U! #StarTrek50. My best, Bill." He had over 2.5 million followers on Twitter and wasn't shy about "blocking" fellow Twitter users from seeing his account, or directing messages to him, if he felt slighted or insulted or for reasons known only to him.

The *Star Trek* franchise continued to flourish on the big screen and on television, but it would venture forth without Bill at the helm as Captain James T. Kirk. Moviegoers flocked to *Star Trek Into Darkness* and *Star Trek Beyond* in 2013 and 2016, respectively, and in the spring of 2018, Paramount announced that the studio had two more *Star Trek* movies in development.

The advent of streaming television helped to recharge the franchise on the small screen. CBS's digital subscription platform, CBS All Access, launched new *Star Trek* shows and announced additional upcoming entries in the genre. The fifteen-episode prequel series *Star Trek: Discovery* premiered in September 2017 on CBS All Access and proved to be a critical and popular success. It was renewed for a second season, which kicked off in January 2019. Bill wasn't a part of the show but still managed to inject himself into the *Discovery* universe when, in the middle of its maiden season, he blocked *Star Trek: Discovery* star Jason Isaacs (Captain Gabriel Lorca) on Twitter, apparently over comments Isaacs made in an online interview when he was asked about the possibility of recruiting Captain Kirk for a visit to *Star Trek: Discovery*. "Kirk doesn't come along for ten years and when we meet him, he's 26, so it would be a weird timeline if they met," Isaacs said. "If you have stunt celebrity cameo casting, it completely pulls [viewers] out of it. They feel like they're watching a *Saturday Night Live* sketch."[9] Bill's Twitter ban on Isaacs lasted two days before he unblocked Captain Lorca. "He who must not be named's bff is now unblocked," Bill tweeted, with Isaacs responding in kind on his Twitter feed: "Undoubtedly. Here's what people miss with @WilliamShatner: the unbroken continuity and cross-pollination between the sublime, disruptive, iconic performances—as Kirk & Denny amongst others—and the provocative, take-no-prisoners tweeter. I'm all in."

CBS All Access also announced plans for a new animated series, *Star Trek: Lower Deck*, and in August 2018, it was seventy-eight-year-old Patrick Stewart's turn to return to the *Star Trek* fold. Stewart surprised everyone by announcing he would reprise his iconic television role as Captain Jean-Luc Picard from *Star Trek: The Next Generation* in a new, as-yet-untitled CBS All Access series that would, he tweeted, "endeavour to bring a fresh, unexpected and pertinent story to life once more." Bill congratulated Stewart but said he was through with *Star Trek*. "I'm wishing Patrick all the best," he told the *Toronto Sun*. "I hope he does really well going back to *Star Trek*, but that isn't for me."[10] He amended that statement shortly thereafter, telling the website Trekmovie.com that he "would jump at the chance" to return as Kirk "if they can find a way of writing a fifty years older captain and it was meaningful and had something to do with the plot."[11]

Still, Bill kept busy and showed no signs of slowing down, continuing to appear on television, writing another book, and returning to the recording studio.

He narrated and cowrote the sixteen-episode digital graphic novel series *William Shatner War Chronicles*, which was part and parcel of Shatner Singularity, a comic book imprint he cofounded with LNL Partners. He guest-starred as Mark Twain in an episode of the CBC television series *Murdoch Mysteries* and materialized in a story arc of the Syfy series *Haven* as Croatoan, a creature (in human form) able to erase people's memories. He promoted his *Haven* role on Twitter and even found time in his manic work schedule to provide the voice of the pony Applejack's maternal grandfather, Grand Pear, in the animated children's series *My Little Pony: Friendship Is Magic*, set in the magical land of Equestria. He flew to Italy to shoot his role as Lord Ogmha in *Creators: The Past*, an Italian-language sci-fi/fantasy movie starring Gerard Depardieu. (The movie's logline: "*Creators: The Past* brings us back to the year 2012, to the prophecies of the Maya and how our planet escaped a total catastrophe and extraterrestrial invasion.") He also began working on his next book, *Spirit of the Horse*.

Published in 2017 and cowritten by Jeff Rovin, with whom Bill collaborated on the 2016 book *Zero-G: A Novel*, the three-hundred-page *Spirit of the Horse* covered Bill's love of his maned companions—combining anecdotes from his personal and professional lives with historical ruminations on all things equestrian with chapter titles such as "My First Time," "The Winged Horse," "Wild Horses," and "Horsing Around on the Set." Bill dedicated the book to the many horses he worked with over the years (a very long list, including "Da Vinci," "Sparkle," "Tucker Belle," and "Boston Legal"). There were no photographs in the book, but Bill was pictured on its front and back covers posing lovingly with one of his horses. "This book was inspired by my desire not only to give my perspective on the excitement of the race and my love of horses," he wrote in his introduction, "but to share the thoughts and experiences of others."[12]

In November 2018, Bill was honored with the Dale Wilkinson Lifetime Achievement Award from the National Reining Horse Association for being "a dedicated horseman," with the organization's spokesperson saying, "[Bill has been] a high-level promoter and fundraiser for the sport of reining. He has won numerous world championships in several equine events."

The honors continued. In December 2017, he joined 120 others in receiving the Order of Canada, the country's second-highest honor for merit, from Canadian Governor General Julie Payette. Bill was inducted as an "Officer" for "his contributions to popular culture spanning theater, television, and film, and for his philanthropic support of causes related to health care, the environment, and the well-being of children." Though Bill lived in Los Angeles and had not resided in Canada for over sixty years, he was an enthusiastic supporter of his native country, earning its eternal gratitude and other honors, including his star on Canada's Walk of Fame in 2000 and his inclusion in the closing ceremonies of the 2010 Winter Olympics in Vancouver. In 2011, while he was starring in *$#*! My Dad Says* on CBS, Bill was honored for his "Lifetime Artistic Achievement" with a Governor General's Performing Arts Award in Canada as "actor, director, producer, writer, spokesman and philanthropist." He accepted the honor with his typical, strangely worded panache set off with a dash of self-deprecation. "One lives many lifetimes in a lifetime. This is just one lifetime award—I expect to be back to get another in a few years," he told the *Toronto Globe and Mail*. "[Lifetime achievement] does suggest that you accept the award and then drop dead. But I don't want to be a bother—carting me off stage and all that."[13] He was, he said, a Canadian "in my heart."

Bill was heavier now, with a puffy face and a hairline that improved with age. In early 2018, as he closed in on his eighty-seventh birthday, he was back in the recording studio to work on his next album, and his first foray into country music. This time around he teamed with Jeff Cook, the lead guitarist of popular country/Southern rock band Alabama. "I had known Bill for a while, and I didn't know he could sing," Cook said. "We have a mutual friend in Heartland Records, and not knowing that Bill and I were acquainted, [Heartland president] Brian Curl got this idea and thought we could make it work." Bill and Cook recorded the album, called *Why Not Me?*, at Cook's studio in Fort Payne, Alabama, with Cash Creek, Home Free, and Neal McCoy making guest appearances. "Country music is the epitome of reaching out in pure terms from a musical and a lyrical standpoint," Bill said with his usual bombast. "It's that purity that I love. When Brad Paisley sings a song, not only are you humming the melody, but you are understanding the words."

"He got in there, did what we went in to do," Cook said. "He was really great to work with. We had to find something that really lent itself to what we were trying to do. I think we got a good recording out of it."[14]

The tracks on *Why Not Me?* included "Friends Don't Let Friends Drink Alone," "Beam Me Up," and "Too Old to Be Vegan," a humorous track Cook called "a novelty . . . a type of song that people haven't heard before."

In conjunction with the album's debut in August, Bill announced the upcoming release of *Shatner Claus: A Christmas Album*, which he recorded in his inimitable spoken-word style.

That album was released on December 7, 2018, on the Cleopatra Records label and featured Bill's usual eclectic group of musical collaborators, including ZZ Top guitarist/lead singer Billy Gibbons, Rick Wakeman, Brad Paisley, Judy Collins, Ian Anderson, and Henry Rollins—with chestnuts including "Winter Wonderland," "Run Rudolph Run," "Jingle Bells" (with Rollins), "Silent Night" (a duet with Iggy Pop), and "Little Drummer Boy." A close-up photo of Bill graced the album's cover; he wore a Santa hat and hip dark sunglasses and posed beside a Christmas tree.

"I picked songs by lyric or by familiarity," he said about the album.

> There are two major pieces in the album. One is a poem by a veteran [Blades Anthony] who came back [from Afghanistan] bruised by battle. He had written a large number of poems. When he had written a large number of songs about the torture of battle, I said, "This could make a one-man show. Can you write me something about before you went into the Marines and now that you're out of the Marines?" He couldn't. And then I said, "Could you write a Christmas song?" and he wrote a Christmas song about what it's like to be overseas and wondering how it is back home. It's a beautiful poem. We set it to music, and it's one of the major pieces in the album; the other is the Christmas story, which we set to music.[15]

Brad Paisley said the album came together earlier that year, when Bill came to see one of his concerts and told him he had a Christmas project in mind. "Bill is one of the biggest inspirations to me on how to live your life that I've ever met, or ever will," Paisley said. "He is constantly moving. Sharks never sleep —they're always in motion. He is that. With him, it's one thing after another . . . He exhausts me. It's an amazing thing to watch."[16]

The fall of 2018 also saw the publication of yet another Shatner tome, *Live Long and . . . What I Learned Along the Way*. Cowritten by frequent collaborator David Fisher, it featured Bill ruminating on growing older and sharing his philosophy on life yet offered little else beyond what he had previously shared in his other books and in the thousands of William Shatner interviews over his long career. Bill admitted this with tongue planted firmly in cheek. "I am not a font of wisdom," he wrote in *Live Long and* .

. . "I'm the guy who saved the Starship *Enterprise* for seventy-nine weeks and ended up kissing James Spader on a patio."

Bill did reveal, though, that he was diagnosed with prostate cancer in 2016, which was, unfortunately, not unusual for a man his age (eighty-five at the time he was diagnosed). But it turned out to be a false alarm; he was told by his doctor to cut back on the testosterone supplements he'd been taking, and once he did so, he was sent for more blood work, which came back normal. "Three months later I took another PSA test. It had gone down to one. One," he wrote. "The doctor guessed that the testosterone had resulted in the elevated PSA level."[17]

He was coming to grips with his age . . . but just barely.

In mid-April 2017, Bill began a monthlong shoot for his next movie, an independent romantic comedy called *Senior Moment*, in which he played Victor Martin, a retired Navy pilot and NASA aircraft tester with a penchant for younger women. Victor tools around town in his vintage 1955 Porsche convertible with his best friend (played by Christopher Lloyd), but he has an accident and loses his driver's license, throwing his world into a tailspin—until a visit to the Department of Motor Vehicles changes his life.

The movie was shot in Palm Springs, California, and was partly funded by producer Gina Goff, who was surprised to hear that Bill was interested in the project after she sent him the script. "I was fortunate enough to find an investor who was a huge William Shatner fan and he agreed to back his offer, which was a start but wasn't enough," she said. Goff raised the rest of the capital and was able to complete the movie, which included costars Esai Morales, Katrina Bowden, and Jean Smart.

It didn't seem to matter to Bill how big or small the parts were now, as long as he was working and keeping busy. He played Harvey Dent, a.k.a. Two-Face, in the straight-to-video animated movie *Batman vs. Two-Face*, costarring original *Batman* television stars Adam West, Burt Ward, and Julie Newmar. (West died at the age of eighty-eight in June 2017, four months before the movie premiered at New York Comic Con.)

Bill attended the launch of *Batman vs. Two-Face* and, ever the showman, managed to come up with a "motivation" for his animated character: "What I challenged myself with was to try and do the voice organically. This is a good word. So, it all was one thing. Rather than playing the straight voice and then using technology to do the bad guy. So, I allowed the bad guy to emerge out of the good guy, much like a Jekyll and Hyde thing." He took it a step further (without being asked), likening Harvey Dent to Stephen Paddock, who earlier that month shot and killed fifty-eight people and wounded nearly nine hundred others attending a Las Vegas music festival in the worst mass shooting in US history.

"What was going on in what's-his-name's head in Las Vegas when he shot that window out and began to spray bullets? Here he was. A mild-mannered guy—very much a Harvey Dent character—and all of a sudden he is doing one of the most incredibly—I hate to use the word 'evil' because I don't know whether I believe that there is good and evil—but this man who sought to terrorize and kill and maim as many people as possible, knowing that he was going to die in the end . . . What vicious, monstrous thing was going on in his head? And how you might relate that, in reality, to a Harvey Dent character."[18]

A return to television as a series regular didn't appear to be on the horizon for Bill at this stage of the game. *Better Late Than Never*, which took him around the world with Henry Winkler, George Foreman, Terry Bradshaw, and Jeff Dye, was cancelled by NBC after its second season aired in early 2018. But later that year the Hollywood trade press reported that plans were in the works to revive Bill's old series, *Rescue 911*, which aired its last episode on CBS in 1996. The reboot would, once again, be hosted by Bill, but unlike the original version, this iteration would air live each week, with each two-hour episode following first responders (firefighters, EMTs, police) with a live panel of first responders commenting on the action. The format hewed closely to *Live PD*, which premiered on cable network A&E in October 2016 and was renewed for nearly three hundred episodes airing through 2019.

He wrote the original story for and starred in *Devil's Revenge* (originally called *The Relic*), a big-screen psychological thriller costarring Robert Scott Wilson and Jeri Ryan (Seven of Nine from *Star Trek: Voyager*), and when he wasn't shooting movies, riding his horses, or writing books, he kept busy picking fights on Twitter. The size of the target didn't seem to matter much to Bill, who weighed in with his unsolicited opinions and/or often "blocked" whomever he decided to feud with.

In July 2018, he launched a Twitter war against the Association for Library Service to Children—on behalf of the long-dead author Laura Ingalls Wilder (1867–1957) and her popular *Little House on the Prairie* book series, based on her pioneer childhood in Wisconsin, Missouri, and Kansas. The Association decided to change the name of its Laura Ingalls Wilder Award ("for significant contributions to youth literature") to the Children's Literature Legacy Award after concerns were raised about Wilder's portrayal of African Americans and Native Americans. (Example: "The only good Indian is a dead Indian," one of the books' white characters says.) The decision was based on "the fact that Wilder's legacy, as represented by the body of work, includes expressions of stereotypical attitudes inconsistent" with its "core values of inclusiveness, integrity and respect and responsiveness."

Some critics thought the name change was an example of censorship and bowing to political correctness, an opinion Bill shared on Twitter. "Did you hear about the Laura Ingalls Wilder Award being renamed over negative lines on the indigenous people of America?" he tweeted. "I find it disturbing that some take modern opinion & obliterate the past. Isn't progress @ learning from our mistakes?" He was applauded by some but criticized by others, most notably two academics: Ebony Elizabeth Thomas, an associate professor at the University of Pennsylvania, and Brigitte Fielder, an assistant professor of comparative literature at the University of Wisconsin at Madison.

Fielder took her Twitter account private when Bill blasted her as a "troll," while Thomas continued to needle him and even questioned the gender politics of *Star Trek*. Bill, she said, "seriously needs to stay in his lane"; he fired back by tweeting to the Twitter accounts of both professors' institutions to "look at the content of their faculty online," while suggesting the University of Pennsylvania "should also check out their professor who cannot seem to stay in her lane & uses 2018 sentiments on 50 yo TV shows." Bill continued to tweet about Thomas and poke the bear—she had just earned tenure, he wrote, while he was a published author a dozen times over. The kerfuffle eventually died down. "Go ahead & block me like everyone else you disagree with," Thomas tweeted at Bill. "I'll still be a #StarTrek fan."[19]

He engaged in a much more bizarre Twitter feud with Sebastian Bach, the former lead singer for the heavy metal band Skid Row, who is thirty-seven years younger than Bill. Their digital fight started when Bill disliked a Tweet that Bach liked and sent him an emoji of a purple devil face, to which Bach responded by calling Bill "a dickhead" and threatening to stop by Bill's house in his Studio City neighborhood in LA: "I'll see you at your home. I will run past your fucking house every day until the day I die," Bach tweeted to Bill. "Deal with me with your phaser cell phone bullshit." He also referred to Bill as "emoji man." "Maybe you need to unfollow me if you cannot stand interacting," Bill tweeted back. "Troll? He liked a tweet. I replied to him.

I do that. He follows me. If he doesn't like what I say he can unfollow. It sounds like he's not having a good night so it's better to stop interacting with him." He did.

Maybe Bill was just bored or was trying to remain relevant in pop culture via social media. Whatever the case, he continued to pick fights on Twitter. In July 2016, he clashed with the website The Mary Sue (its goal: "highlighting women in the geek world and providing a prominent place for the voices of geek women"). It ran a story, headlined "William Shatner Says, 'A Woman's Place in the Fridge,' Remains the Worst," which quoted Bill during his appearance at the Montreal Comic-Con.

He was there to celebrate the fiftieth anniversary of *Star Trek* with Kate Mulgrew (*Star Trek: Voyager*)—the first female captain as a series regular in the franchise's history—and with *Star Trek* veteran Brent Spiner (Lt. Commander Data). Bill joked onstage that he'd never seen Mulgrew in *Voyager*, eliciting a cry from the audience that "a woman's place is on the bridge!" Mulgrew glanced sideways at Bill. "Or in the kitchen, as the case may be," she responded. Bill countered with "a woman's place is in the fridge"—and then repeated the phrase several more times. The Mary Sue took him to task. "It's hard to think of a way that Shatner's comments could have possibly been respectful to women," it reported. Bill fired back, saying that he was just sharing an inside joke with Mulgrew. "Apparently killing women & stuffing them in refrigerators is some kind of trope in comics," he tweeted. "Who knew?"

Then, in March 2017, Bill launched a tweetstorm against Nick Viall, a former star of ABC's *The Bachelor* who was now competing on the network's other reality show, *Dancing with the Stars*. Bill fired the first online salvo—"My goal for #DWTS is to knock Bachelor Nick out ASAP. Who is with me?"—and followed that with several more negative anti-Viall tweets ("#Dontvote4Nick #DWTS," "Anyone but the vile one"). When Viall refused to take the bait, Bill called a truce: "As a Dad w/daughters I'm not happy w/what you've done in the past. Maybe you've matured now?"

Four months later, for reasons known only to Bill, he picked another online fight, this time with fans of the television series *Outlander*, a time-traveling sci-fi epic airing on the Starz cable network. Bill liked the series and had clashed the year before on Twitter with *Outlander* fans who wanted to see stars Sam Heughan and Caitriona Balfe—lovers on the small screen—embark on a real-life relationship, known in the parlance of fandom as "shipping."

Bill took it upon himself to scold the shippers: "You and your group terrorize the fandom," he tweeted. "And they are not dating so stop shaming them for being good friends in real life."

A year later he reignited his Twitter feud with *Outlander* fans, tweeting a photo of Heughan with his girlfriend, MacKenzie Mauzy, and adding a smiley-face emoji and writing "Adorbs!" followed by three heart-shaped emojis. He then took it one step further, referring to *Outlander* shippers as "snowflakes" and "SJWs"—terms often used by the political right to criticize those on the left. ("Snowflakes" referring to overly emotional, easily offended, entitled people unable to deal with opposing opinions and "SJWs" referring to "social justice warriors.") One Twitter user asked Bill if he was the target of "an entire army of trolls?" "No," Bill tweeted back, "just certain snowflakes in fandoms who don't like to hear truths or differing opinions." The short-lived controversy ended within a day as Bill lost interest.

Bill kept the Twitter ball rolling into 2018, finding new targets at random or injecting himself—and his opinions—into the national discussion. In July, he took on autograph-seekers in a three-day Twitter tirade with this opening salvo: "How about you just don't ask me? Most who follow me know I don't give autographs in public." In December, he argued with his fans when several radio stations in the United States and Canada pulled the song "Baby, It's Cold Outside" from their Christmas lineup, feeling that the tune, written in 1944 by Frank Loesser—and featured in the 1949 movie *Neptune's Daughter*—was sexist and promoted "rape culture" in the wake of the growing #MeToo movement against sexual harassment and sexual assault. "Call in to CBC radio all day and get them to play 'Baby It's Cold Outside' over and over until midnight!" Bill tweeted. "I would think that censorship of classics because certain 'types' need to judge things through their own 2018 myopic glasses and demand they be stricken from history is important. Or is this 1984 only 34 years too late?"

He characteristically took it one step further in a television interview. "In 2018 we have the MeToo movement, which I think is great, that these hidden forces are exposed and not to be allowed and women have equal rights," he said. "I've got three daughters and am all for that. But if you look back at things that were written and said 20, 30 years ago, it's a different context. And you've got to judge it by that context. Rape and pillage, absolutely not, those are crimes against humanity. But saying 'would you make love with me?' and the opposing party says yes or no, I can't fathom what's wrong with that . . . I've tweeted about it just to get it out there and have some fun with the people who think differently. On my part there's no animosity, just a difference of opinion."[20]

Bill's social media voice was often cheeky and humorous. "Get your Icosahedron die ready for I'm out to win this game!" he announced on Twitter—his roundabout way to announce that he would finally appear on CBS's science-nerd sitcom *The Big Bang Theory*, which had been trying to lure him as a guest star for several years. (He'd passed on previous offers, reportedly because he didn't like the way he was written into the show.) The show's cocreator, Bill Prady, was a big *Star Trek* fan; he'd written "Bliss," a 1999 episode of *Star Trek: Voyager*. *The Big Bang Theory*, which morphed into a huge hit several seasons after its premiere in 2007, spawned an equally successful spinoff, *Young Sheldon*, and was in its twelfth and final season when Bill broke the news in January 2019 regarding his upcoming visit.

He would not be the first celebrity—nor the first *Star Trek* alumnus— to drop in on *The Big Bang Theory* and its core cast of characters: brilliant Sheldon Cooper (Jim Parsons); his equally brilliant wife (as of Season 11), Amy Farrah Fowler (Mayim Bialik); across-the-hall neighbor Penny (Kaley Cuoco); and their geeky pals Leonard Hofstadter (Johnny Galecki), Howard Wolowitz (Simon Helberg), and Rajesh Koothrappali (Kunal Nyar). Past episodes included appearances from cast members of *Star Trek* iterations, including George Takei, Leonard Nimoy (voice only as Sheldon's Mego Mr. Spock action figure), LeVar Burton, Wil Wheaton, and Brent Spiner. The big-screen *Star Wars* franchise wasn't ignored, either, with James Earl Jones, Carrie Fisher, and Mark Hamill visiting *The Big Bang Theory*. "Get ready for the ultimate Dungeons and Dragons battle coming soon," the show's Twitter feed announced, mentioning Bill and other "special guests" in the episode, including Joe Manganiello, Kevin Smith, Kareem Abdul-Jabbar, and Wheaton.

"I think we reached out to him a couple of times over the years and for one reason or another it didn't quite work out, whether it was scheduling or whatever," *The Big Bang Theory* showrunner/executive producer Steve Holland said about the episode, which aired February 21. "Coming to our final season, we knew we had a wish list of people we still wanted to be part of the show, and [Shatner] was at the top of that wish list. So, we reached out to him again—I got on the phone and chatted with him about what we were thinking about. At that point we didn't have a script, but I think he felt like he wanted to be part of this before it came to an end."

Holland said Bill was also willing to appear on the episode since he'd done several Priceline.com commercials with series costar Kaley Cuoco. "They're friendly, so I think he was excited. When I got on the phone with him, one of the things he asked was, 'Will I get to play a scene with Kaley?'" (He did.) Bill spent one day on the set of *The Big Bang Theory*—"watching Shatner and Kareem Abdul-Jabbar chat between takes was really fun," Holland said—and Bill enjoyed playing a heightened version of his public persona.

"That shouldn't be surprising that he's so good. He's been doing this a long time, especially playing himself and it was really interesting to watch him work," Holland said. "He would play [the scene] for a couple of takes until he found a delivery he liked and then really locked into it. He was certainly willing to poke fun at himself." *Star Trek*, Holland said, resonated strongly with the show's writers—which made Bill's appearance in its final season so special. "This show is so rooted in pop culture; our writers are fans and therefore our characters are fans. And I think, in a weird way, the original *Star Trek* was almost ground zero for pop culture fandom. I don't think you have Comic Con or the Marvel movies [without it], and I think it really goes back to this weird little sci-fi show that only ran for three seasons in the '60s."[21]

*   *   *

Bill continued to roll along as he inched closer to his eighty-eighth birthday. He continued touring with his one-man show, *William Shatner Live*, and proved to be as unpredictable as ever during one four-hour event. Sitting through a screening of *Star Trek II: The Wrath of Khan* at De Anza College in Cupertino, California, he took questions from audience members and had trouble remembering a few words ("ultrasound," "cotton gin," and some people's names) and needed to be prompted by members of the audience. Prowling around the big stage, he started coughing and joked that the audience would be there "when William Shatner finally died." He flashed moments of humor ("I realized the universe didn't give a shit"; "I'm too old to be a vegan") and turned maudlin in explaining why he didn't attend "brother" Leonard Nimoy's funeral in 2015 ("Fame and fortune [are] dust in the wind. What does matter and what lasts till the end of human experience are good deeds"). [22]

He made his onstage debut at the Grand Ole Opry in Nashville, Tennessee, in February, where he was joined by Alabama cofounder/guitarist Jeff Cook, Bill's collaborator on his country album *Why Not Me?* The television and movie roles were few and far between now. There was still the hoped-for reboot of *Rescue 911* that Bill would host, and in March 2019, the cable network History announced that Bill would host and executive-produce *The UnXPlained*, an upcoming series that would "explore the facts behind the world's most fascinating, strange, and inexplicable mysteries." In the same announcement, History said it was renewing another series, *In Search Of*, for a second season. That series had a "six degrees of separation"-kind of connection to Bill. *In Search Of* was hosted by Zachary Quinto—who played Spock in the big-screen movies *Star Trek*, *Star Trek Into Darkness*, and *Star Trek Beyond*—and was a revival of the late-1970s syndicated television series hosted by the original Spock, Leonard Nimoy. Nimoy, in turn, replaced intended host and *The Twilight Zone* creator Rod Serling, who died before production began.

In the meantime, Bill discovered the joys of electric bicycles, and with his days as the Priceline.com pitchman long behind him, he turned his gaze to Pedego Electric Bikes, starring in a series of advertisements for the company and appearing as the keynote speaker at its annual dealer conference. He also talked up Pedego in various interviews. "I live in the hills of the San Fernando Valley, so going up a hill on a bike is meaningful and emotional—giving you a good day or a bad day," he told the *Los Angeles Times*. "Well, with the electric assist, every day is a good day! The e-bike got me outside and got me fitter. Going up the hills is not a problem. I've got an arthritic back from all the horseback riding, my muscles are tender, yet I go back to my car when the bike ride's over and I feel perfect."[23]

Bill appeared in three Pedego ads airing on various media platforms (Facebook, Google)—including one spot, "The Doctor," set in a proctologist's office—and he shot a minute-long online promotional spot for Pedego featuring video of the extended Shatner clan, including Elizabeth, riding their Pedego bicycles along the beachfront in California: "We take many trips together and it's unifying, it's joyful, and it really is something we all look forward to."

He reveled in his family life. The extended Shatner clan numbered thirteen now, including five grandchildren (three boys, two girls), and Bill, the family patriarch, relished his role as a grandfather. "I have the time now to grab a grandchild and talk and hug and kiss them and make sure that I'm taking time to be with them and to give them some aspect of the things I've learned," he said. "Family is totally encompassing. I see my daughters every weekend. And we go off on holidays together—everything from skiing to snorkeling.

"The acting is great, and I've had a wonderful career, but the people in my family mean the most to me. The thing you have to remember is that life is for the living. You only have this minute, this little particle that goes *kachung!*—and then is gone.

"You have such a short time to live and you've got to help other people, be kind, and just love."[24]

Notes

CHAPTER 1

1. Biography, A&E, 2006
2. Coolopolis.blogspot.com, April 16, 2018
3. Geni.com
4. Shatner and Fisher, Up Till Now, 8
5. Shatner and Fisher, Up Till Now, 8
6. Shatner and Fisher, Up Till Now, 8
7. Shatner interview, Archive of American Television, 1999
8. "Captain on the Bridge," The Biography Channel, 1999
9. Shatner, Marshak, and Culbreth, Shatner: Where No Man, 28
10. "Captain on the Bridge," The Biography Channel, 1999
11. "Captain on the Bridge," The Biography Channel, 1999
12. Shatner interview, Archive of American Television, 1999
13. Author interview
14. Lafond, Peach Cobbler Stories, 20
15. Nestruck, "How Shatner Became Shatner," The Globe and Mail, October 25, 2013
16. Yarnell, "The Children's Theatre Turns 75," The Metropolitan, January 15, 2009
17. "Captain on the Bridge," The Biography Channel, 1999
18. Childrens-theatre.ca/william-shatner-talks-about-his-experience-childrens-theatre
19. Shatner, Marshak, and Culbreth, Shatner: Where No Man, 31
20. Ralph, "Shatner Brought Audience to Tears," Summercampculture.com
21. Weisblott, "William Shatner," Lifestyles Magazine, 2012
22. Shatner, Marshak, and Culbreth, Shatner: Where No Man, 32
23. Shatner and Fisher, Up Till Now, 16

24. Author interview
25. "Biography: William Shatner," A&E, 1999
26. Shatner, Marshak, and Culbreth, Shatner: Where No Man, 32
27. Shatner interview, Archive of American Television
28. Author interview
29. Author interview
30. Author interview
31. Shatner, Marshak, and Culbreth, Shatner: Where No Man, 32
32. Shatner and Fisher, Up Till Now, 18
33. Shatner, Marshak, and Culbreth, Shatner: Where No Man, 62
34. Shatner and Fisher, Up Till Now, 18
35. Shatner interview, Archive of American Television
36. McGill University Alumni Magazine, 2010
37. Fields, "New Star on Movie Horizon," New York Post, December 23, 1957
38. Shatner and Fisher, Up Till Now, 19
39. Shatner interview, Archive of American Television
40. "That's Show Business," Yuma Sun, April 12, 1961
41. "Coward's Comedy in Ottawa," New York Times, November 17, 1953

CHAPTER 2

1. Stratfordfestival.ca/aboutus/ourhistory/timeline
2. Fields, "New Star on Movie Horizon," *New York Post*, December 23, 1957
3. Shatner and Fisher, *Up Till Now*, 23
4. Author interview
5. Author interview
6. Author interview
7. Shatner and Fisher, *Up Till Now*, 37
8. Shatner and Fisher, *Up Till Now*, 39
9. Shatner interview, Archive of American Television
10. Shatner and Fisher, *Up Till Now*, 23
11. Shatner, Marshak, and Culbreth, *Shatner: Where No Man*, 55
12. Shatner interview, Archive of American Television
13. Archive of American Television
14. Radio, TV Highlights, *Winnipeg Free Press*, April 28, 1956
15. Shatner interview, Archive of American Television
16. Shatner and Fisher, *Up Till Now*, 39
17. Hall, *Life Before Stratford*, 240
18. Atkinson, "New Shylock: Stratford (Ont.) Shakespearean Festival Opens," *New York Times*, July 1, 1955
19. Author interview
20. Plummer, *In Spite of Myself*, 209

21. Author interview

22. Nestruck, "Shatner and Plummer Reunite," *The Globe and Mail*, August 23, 2010

23. Shatner, Archive of American Television

24. "Stricken at Stratford," *Montreal Gazette*, August 11, 1956

25. Johnson, *Montreal Star*, August 11, 1956

26. "Understudy Wins Curtain Calls," *Medicine Hat News*, August 11, 1956

27. "Crowther, "Staging at Canadian Festival Is Filmed," New York Times, January 8, 1957

28. Moran, "TV Talk," *Oil City Blizzard*, March 4, 1955

29. Shatner and Fisher, *Up Till Now*, 36

30. Fields, "New Star on Movie Horizon," *New York Post*, December 23, 1957

31. "U.S. Actor's Ban Hit," *New York Times*, March 10, 1956

32. Gould, "Before Going West," *New York Times*, December 17, 1957

33. Shatner and Fisher, *Up Till Now*, 43

34. Shatner, Marshak, and Culbreth, *Shatner: Where No Man*, 64

35. Falconer, "He Is Legend," *Cinema Spy*, December 11, 2007

36. Shatner and Fisher, *Up Till Now*, 51

CHAPTER 3

1. Moon, "Shatner's Adventures in Hollywood," *Maclean's*, October 26, 1957

2. *Variety* Staff, "The Brothers Karamazov," *Variety*, December 31, 1957

3. Brooks, "Bringing the Karamazovs," *New York Times*, September 29, 1957

4. Gould, "Prejudice Dissected," *New York Times*, June 20, 1958

5. Shapard, "Shatner Talks About TV," *New York Times*, August 10, 1958

6. "Shatner a Regular," United Press International, May 19, 1958

7. Shatner, Marshak, and Culbreth, *Shatner: Where No Man*, 67

8. Zolotow, *New York Times*, June 13, 1958

9. Sabbath, "Young Canadian Actor," *Montreal Gazette*, October 28, 1958

10. Haydon, "The World of Suzie Wong," *South China Morning Post*, July 11, 2017

11. Shatner, Marshak, and Culbreth, *Shatner: Where No Man*, 68

12. Atkinson, "Theatre: Suzie Wong," *New York Times*, October 11, 1958

13. *Montreal Star*, October 18, 1956

14. Shannon, *Washington Times*, April 18, 1959

15. Shatner and Fisher, *Up Till Now*, 61

16. Shatner and Fisher, *Up Till Now*, 65

17. Shatner and Fisher, *Up Till Now*, 62

18. Haydon, "The World of Suzie Wong," *South China Morning Post*, July 11, 2017

19. Danzig, "Why Canadians Succeed," United Press International, April 7, 1959

20. Haydon, "The World of Suzie Wong," *South China Morning Post*, July 11, 2017

21. Heimer, "TV Cameos: William Shatner," King Features Syndicate, 1967

22. Shatner and Nuyen would reunite on several future projects, including an episode of *Star Trek*, the 1973 television movie *Horror at 37,000 Feet*, and a 1974 episode of *Kung Fu*.

23. Danzig, "Why Canadians Succeed," United Press International, April 7, 1959

24. "Hollywood Actor," *Red Bank Register*, July 14, 1961

25. Shatner and Fisher, *Up Till Now*, 95

26. Shatner and Fisher, *Up Till Now*, 50

CHAPTER 4

1. "Actor Shaken Up," *Van Nuys Valley News and Green Sheet*, April 21, 1961

2. Author interview

3. Author interview

4. "The Intruder" DVD extras

5. "New Film Dramatizes School Integration Fight," *Ebony*, July 1962

6. Shatner and Fisher, *Up Till Now*, 69

7. "New Film Dramatizes School Integration Fight," *Ebony*, July 1962

8. "The Intruder" DVD extras

9. Shatner and Fisher, *Up Till Now*, 74

10. Shatner and Fisher, *Up Till Now*, 75

11. Shatner and Fisher, *Up Till Now*, 76

12. Shatner and Fisher, *Up Till Now*, 76

13. Shatner interview with the Paley Center

14. Shatner and Fisher, *Up Till Now*, 80

15. Edelman and Kupferberg, *Matthau: A Life*, 133

16. Savery, "Trio of Broadway Shows," *Montreal Star*, October 28, 1961

17. Humphrey, Mirror Syndicate, July 14, 1961

18. Savery, "Trio of Broadway Shows," *Montreal Star*, October 28, 1961

19. Siskind, "Stage Career Still Uncertain," *Montreal Star*, December 12, 1964

20. *Variety* Staff, *Variety*, December 31, 1961

21. Author interview

22. Crowther, "'The Intruder,'" *New York Times*, May 15, 1962

23. Author interview

24. *Montreal Star*, January 19, 1963

25. "Biography," A&E, 1999

26. Shatner and Fisher, *Up Till Now*, 99

27. Shatner and Fisher, *Up Till Now*, 98

28. Boucher, "Before They Were Heroes," *Los Angeles Times*, August 3, 2011

29. Shatner and Fisher, *Up Till Now*, 93

30. Archive of American Television

31. Author interview

CHAPTER 5

1. Shatner, Marshak, and Culbreth, *Shatner: Where No Man*, 51

2. Shatner and Fisher, *Up Till Now*, 98

3. Shatner and Fisher, *Up Till Now*, 112

4. Archive of American Television

5. Author interview

6. Hammond, "CBS Prosecutor Won't Win 'Em All," *New York Post*, January 3, 1965

7. Harrison, "The Chance of a Lifetime in the Twist of a TV Dial," *Washington Star*, January 31, 1965

8. Shatner and Fisher, *Up Till Now*, 97

9. Gould, "TV: An Assistant D.A.," *New York Times*, February 1, 1965

10. Williams, "On the Air," *New York Post*, February 1, 1965

11. CBC radio interview, CBC archives, March 1, 1965

12. Shatner narrated the 1963 movie *Operation Bikini* starring Tab Hunter and Frankie Avalon but was not listed in the movie's credits.

13. Shatner and Fisher, *Up Till Now*, 88

14. Liebenson, "Eerie Cult Classic ," *Los Angeles Times*, July 11, 2001

15. The twice-divorced Stevens, who was forty-one at the time, married Ames, twenty-eight, in the fall of 1965. They divorced in 1966.

16. Weaver, *I Was a Monster Movie Maker*, 220

17. Shatner's involvement with *Incubus* wasn't finished. Several nude scenes were added into the movie in 1968, and Shatner provided the voiceover narration (in English) while he was filming *Star Trek*. The movie's infamy lived on due to the unfortunate fates of its costars. Eloise Hardt, who played Amael, was kidnapped and murdered in the Hollywood Hills in 1968; Ann Atmar (Arndis) killed herself in October 1966 just weeks before the movie opened. In January 1966, Milos, the Incubus himself, shot and killed his girlfriend, Barbara Ann Thomason—who was married to Mickey Rooney at the time—before turning the gun on himself.

18. Lloyd Bridges was Roddenberry's first choice to play Captain Pike, but he turned the role down because he didn't want to be associated with a science fiction television series.

19. Archive of American Television
20. Solow and Justman, *Inside Star Trek*, 63
21. Shatner and Kreski, *Star Trek Memories,* 70

CHAPTER 6

1. Archive of American Television
2. Shatner, Marshak, and Culbreth, *Shatner: Where No Man*, 56
3. Shatner and Fisher, *Up Till Now*, 97–98
4. Archive of American Television
5. Gross and Altman, *The Fifty-Year Mission*, 93
6. Shatner and Kreski, *Star Trek Memories*, 77
7. Shatner and Kreski, *Star Trek Memories*, 79
8. "Biography," A&E, 1999
9. Shatner and Kreski, *Star Trek Memories*, 80
10. Takei, *To the Stars*, 233
11. Halliday, "'Hyphen' Profound, Delightful Comedy," *Salt Lake Tribune*, March 25, 1966
12. Archive of American Television
13. Gardella, "Shatner Takes Weighty Approach," *New York Daily News*, August 23, 1966
14. Archive of American Television
15. Gardella, "Shatner Takes Weighty Approach,"*New York Daily News*, August 23, 1966
16. Archive of American Television
17. Archive of American Television
18. "Biography," A&E, 1999
19. *TV Guide*, November 26, 1966
20. Solow and Justman, *Inside Star Trek*, 306
21. Biography, A&E, 2006
22. Shatner and Kreski, *Star Trek Memories*, 195
23. Archive of American Television
24. Hauck, *Captain Quirk*, 103
25. Solow and Justman, *Inside Star Trek*, 236
26. Solow and Justman, *Inside Star Trek*, 236
27. Shatner was likely referring to his hairpiece. He's never admitted to wearing a hairpiece; in a 1967 *New York Times* article headlined "Modern Men Discover Fountain of Youth," Shatner is mentioned—along with John Wayne, Rex Harrison, Sean Connery, Mel Ferrer, Henry Fonda, and others—as "an estimated 10 to 20 percent of male performers" wearing "rugs or doilies, as they are sometimes called."
28. Shatner and Fisher, *Up Till Now*, 123–124

29. *People* Staff, "*Star Trek*'s Stars Trek," *People*, July 20, 1992

30. Solow and Justman, *Inside Star Trek*, 238

31. Solow and Justman, *Inside Star Trek*, 239

32. Whitfield and Roddenberry, *The Making of Star Trek*

33. Hauck, *Captain Quirk*, 105

34. Biography, A&E, 2006

35. Solow and Justman, *Inside Star Trek*, 305

36. Archive of American Television

37. Hauck, *Captain Quirk*, 127

38. Shatner and Fisher, *Up Till Now*, 135

39. Shatner and Fisher, *Up Till Now*, 135

40. Author interview

41. Rand was let go from *Star Trek* in the first half of its inaugural season for budgetary reasons.

42. Whitney, *The Longest Trek*, 81

43. Trenkews.net, Nov. 7, 2011

44. Author interview

45. Doohan and David, *Beam Me Up, Scotty*, 149

46. Archive of American Television

47. Michaelson, "William Shatner by Starlight," *Los Angeles Times*, May 4, 1968

48. Archive of American Television

49. Prelutsky, "Five Seconds to Live," *Los Angeles Magazine*, October 15, 1967

50. Shatner's hairpiece was not often mentioned in the press. In the 1996 book *Inside Star Trek: The Real Story*, Robert Justman writes that Shatner "wore lifts to help him attain his advertised height of 5'11'"" and that Shatner began the first season of Star Trek with "two new toupees," which he rotated, wearing one while the other was cleaned by the makeup department. They cost $200 apiece. One of the toupees vanished between Seasons 1 and 2.

51. Alan Baker, NBC's director of program publicity during that time, estimates that NBC received a total of 12,000 letters re: *Star Trek* in January and February 1968, according to *Star Trek: The Real Story*.

52. The *New York Times* noted Star Trek's renewal on February 21, 1968, a week before NBC's on-air announcement. "In an effort to attract a larger audience, the series will be shifted from Fridays at 8:30 p.m. to Mondays at 7:30 p.m."

53. Page, "Capt. Kirk Gets the VIP Treatment," *Los Angeles Times*, August 17, 1968

54. Gross, "Science Fiction and Reality," *New York Daily* News, December 1, 1968

55. Page, "Capt. Kirk Gets the VIP Treatment," *Los Angeles Times*, August 17, 1968

56. Cowboys and Indians: The Premiere Magazine of the West via horsenation. com.

57. Shatner, "Horse of One's Own," *Los Angeles Times*, November 3, 1985

58. Gross, "Science Fiction and Reality," *New York Daily News*, December 1, 1968

59. Shatner and Rovin, *Spirit of the Horse*, 96

60. Horsenation.com, June 12, 2014

61. Solow and Justman, *Inside Star Trek*, 395

62. Solow and Justman, *Inside Star Trek*, 398

63. Shatner and Fisher, *Up Till Now*, 135

64. "Shatner's Wife Wins Divorce," *Tucson Daily Citizen*, March 10, 1969

65. Shatner and Fisher, *Up Till Now*, 136

66. Model, "Full Speed Ahead," *Cigar Aficionado*, September/October 2006

67. Nimoy, *I Am Spock*, 115

68. "Missing Links in the TV chains," *Broadcasting*, 48–52

69. "Turnabout Intruder" warranted its own honorary "Close Up" segment in *TV Guide*, accompanied by a photo of Shatner as Captain Kirk and an in-depth description of the episode's plotline.

70. Takei, *To the Stars*, 277

CHAPTER 7

1. Michaelson, "William Shatner by Starlight," *Los Angeles Times*, May 4, 1968

2. Shatner and Fisher, *Up Till Now*, 136, 145

3. Sagaftra.org

4. Shatner, Marshak, and Culbreth, *Shatner: Where No Man*, 76

5. Delatiner, "Space Captain Moves into Comedy," *Newsday*, July 24, 1969

6. Shatner and Kreski, *Get a Life!*, 224

7. Adler, "'Asylum' Doesn't Beat 'The Band,'" *New York Times*, December 13, 1970

8. Wagner, *Anne Francis: The Life and Career*, 100

9. Campbell, "Shatner Shines in 'Itch,'" *Daily Herald*, April 26, 1972

10. Author interview

11. Shatner, Marshak, and Culbreth, *Shatner: Where No Man*, 76

12. Shatner, Marshak, and Culbreth, *Shatner: Where No Man*, 77

13. Fitzgerald, "William Shatner Masters Destiny," *Montreal Gazette*, October 3, 1980

14. Biography, A&E, 2006

15. Hardy, "Variations on a Theme," *Montreal Gazette*, July 3, 1971

16. Gardella, "Shatner on Stage," *New York Daily News*, May 25, 1969

17. Gent, "TV: Tearing Off Masks," *New York Times*, May 7, 1969

18. Gould, "'Andersonville Trial' Is Revived," *New York Times*, May 18, 1970

19. Peabodyawards.com

20. Shatner and Fisher, *Up Till Now*, 163

21. Buchalter, "Star Trek's Straight Arrow," *People*, July 5, 1982

22. Gould, "N.B.C. Presents Lawrence Ferlinghetti," *New York Times*, February 26, 1967

23. Shatner, Marshak, and Culbreth, *Shatner: Where No Man*, 250

24. Shatner, Marshak, and Culbreth, *Shatner: Where No Man*, 254

25. Shatner and Fisher, Up Till Now, 164

26. Shatner and Fisher, *Up Till Now*, 165

27. Martin, "Shatner back down to Earth," *The Globe and Mail*, January 6, 1973

28. Author interview

29. Author interview

30. Author interview

31. Author interview

32. Author interview

33. Shatner wrote in his memoir, *Up Till Now*, that he wasn't overly concerned about being naked with Dickinson and that it was she who was apprehensive about their nude scene. "My only worry is that I'm going to get an erection," Shatner told Corman. He did not mention the gaffer's tape in his recollection of shooting the scene.

34. Author interview

35. Author interview

36. Shatner, Marshak, and Culbreth, *Shatner: Where No Man*, 251

37. Gross and Altman, *The Fifty-Year Mission*, 233

38. Buck, "Star Trek Canceled," Associated Press, April 5, 1972

39. "Biography," A&E

40. Pierce, "Alexander of 'Seinfeld,'" *Deseret News*, August 12, 1992

41. Buck, "Star Trek Canceled," Associated Press, April 5, 1972

42. Buck, "Star Trek Canceled," Associated Press, April 5, 1972

43. Montgomery, "'Star Trek' Sparks Future Nostalgia," *New York Times*, February 19, 1973

44. "Shatner, McClure Are Un-Alike," *Hamilton Spectator*, October 25, 1975

45. Archive of American Television

46. Shatner and Fisher, *Up Till Now*, 170

47. Hauck, *Captain Quirk*, 147

48. Bawden, "Shatner Hooked on Stardom," *Montreal Gazette*, October 23, 1975

49. Ebert, *Chicago Sun-Times*, August 15, 1975; Eder, "Film: 'The Devil's Rain,'" *New York Times*, August 8, 1975

50. "Doug McClure Happy," *Times-Reporter*, October 31, 1975

51. Williams, "Shatner Back in the Saddle," *New York Post*, August 20, 1975

52. Author interview

53. Archive of American Television

54. Gross and Altman, *The Fifty-Year Mission*, 295

CHAPTER 8

1. Shatner and Fisher, *Up Till Now*, 141

2. Joan Winston, "Captain Kirk's Long Trek," *New York Post*, December 10, 1977

3. Hodenfield, "Star Trek's Shatner," *New York Post*, September 3, 1977

4. "Shatner to Star Again," *Montreal Gazette*, July 20, 1977

5. Hodenfield, "Star Trek's Shatner," *New York Post*, September 3, 1977

6. Archive of American Television

7. UPI, "'Star Trek' Will Rise Again," *Montreal Gazette*, June 20, 1977

8. "Mr. Spock's Spot Uncertain," *New Times*, November 8, 1977

9. Hodenfield, "Star Trek's Shatner," *New York Post*, September 3, 1977

10. Lanken, "Shatner Expects 'Trek' Post," *Montreal Gazette*, July 20, 1977

11. Dillion, "Shatner Sticks to Tarantulas," *Montreal Gazette*, August 31, 1977

12. "Mr. Spock's Spot Uncertain," *New Times*, November 8, 1977

13. "Mr. Spock's Spot Uncertain," *New Times*, November 8, 1977

14. Dillion, "Shatner Sticks to Tarantulas," *Montreal Gazette*, August 31, 1977

15. "Shatner to Command Enterprise Again," *Canadian Press*, October 20, 1977

16. Horrorpedia.com

17. Author interview

18. Bleecker wrote several books about Lee: *The Life and Death of Bruce Lee*, *The Bruce Lee Story*, and *Unsettled Matters*, which he coauthored with Lee's widow, Linda Lee.

19. "Mr. Spock's Spot Uncertain," *New Times*, November 8, 1977

20. "Mr. Spock's Spot Uncertain," *New Times*, November 8, 1977

21. Hofsess, "McLuhan's 'The Third Walker,'" *Cinema Canada*, June 1978

CHAPTER 9

1. Gross and Altman, *The Fifty-Year Mission*, 370

2. Shatner and Fisher, *Up Till Now*, 200

3. Marilyn Beck, "Hollywood Gossip," *Pacific Stars and Stripes*, Nov. 12, 1979

4. Takei, *To the Stars*, 324

5. Shatner and Fisher, *Up Till Now*, 201

6. Gross and Altman, *The Fifty-Year Mission*, 350

7. Shatner and Fisher, *Up Till Now*, 201–202

8. Gross and Altman, *The Fifty-Year Mission*, 364

9. Gross and Altman, *The Fifty-Year Mission*, 364

10. Takei, *To the Stars*, 326

11. Canby, "'Star Trek,' Based on TV," *New York Times*, December 8, 1979

12. Schickel, "Warp Speed to Nowhere," *Time* magazine, December 17, 1979

13. Denby, "Voyage to the Bottom," *New York* magazine, December 24, 1979

14. Ellison, "Ellison Reviews TREK," *Starlog*, April 1980

15. Shatner, Marshak, and Culbreth, *Shatner: Where No Man*, 241

16. Fitzgerald, "William Shatner Masters Destiny," *Montreal Gazette*, October 3, 1980

17. Fitzgerald, "William Shatner Masters Destiny,"*Montreal Gazette*, October 3, 1980

18. Paramount rejected Roddenberry's script for the second *Star Trek* movie. Submitted in May 1980, it was a time-traveling tale which took the USS *Enterprise* back to 1963 in a world where President John F. Kennedy is not assassinated—and, in fact, meets with Captain Kirk in the Oval Office.

19. Archive of American Television

20. Gross and Altman, *The Fifty-Year Mission*, 395

21. Gross and Altman, *The Fifty-Year Mission*, 414

22. Gross and Altman, *The Fifty-Year Mission*, 418

23. Archive of American Television

24. Archive of American Television

25. Takei, *To the Stars*, 340

26. Archive of American Television

27. Rogerebert.com

28. *Variety* Staff, "Star Trek II: The Wrath of Khan," *Variety*, December 31, 1981

29. Gross and Altman, *The Next Fifty Years*, 430

CHAPTER 10

1. Author interview

2. Author interview

3. Author interview

4. *TV Guide*, August 14, 1982

5. *TV Guide*, August 14, 1982

6. Christian and Grant, *Babylon Confidential*, 47

7. Pagesix.com, September 1, 2007

8. O'Connor, "Tough Cop, Broadway Extravaganza," *New York Times*, March 12, 1982

9. Winfrey, Knight Ridder Newspapers, March 12, 1982

10. *This Is Your Life*, December 27, 1989

11. Bierly, "Adrian Amed: PopWatch 'Teen Idol,'" *Entertainment Weekly*, December 30, 2008

12. Krupnick, "Lean Years Are Over," Newhouse News Service, June 23, 1982

13. *Variety* Staff, "Airplane II the Sequel," *Variety*, December 31, 1981

14. Beck, Marilyn, September 16, 1982

15. Smith, *Bill & I*, 157

16. Smith, *Bill & I*, 17

17. Shatner and Rovin, *Spirit of the Horse*, 130

18. Smith, *Bill & I*, 31

19. Smith, *Bill & I*, 161

20. Smith, *Bill & I*, 17

21. Buchalter, "Star Trek's Straight Arrow," *People*, July 5, 1982

22. Shatner and Fisher, *Up Till Now*, 262

23. Hauck, *Captain Quirk*, 242

24. One of the dialogue exchanges between Hooker and McGuire is an inside reference to the *Star Trek* episode "The Apple." "I owe you one, Hooker," McGuire says. To which Hooker replies: "I remember saying the same thing to you seventeen years ago."

25. Lachman, "Stars Ripped Over Laos Raid," *New York Post*, February 1, 1983

26. Lachman, "Stars Ripped Over Laos Raid,"*New York Post*, February 1, 1983

27. Kalech and Schermerhorn, "Paramount Sets Gutted," *New York Post*, August 26, 1983

28. The blaze, which caused $3 million in damage, destroyed about 350,000 square feet of outdoor sets and damaged four sound stages. The cause was later determined to be arson.

29. Gross and Altman, *The Fifty-Year Mission*, 469

30. Stark, "Leonard Nimoy Directs," *People*, June 11, 1984

31. Gross and Altman, *The Fifty-Year Mission*, 449

32. O'Connor, "From Explicit Sex to Gratuitous Passions," *New York Times*, September 16, 1984

33. Maslin, "Latest in the 'Star Trek' Series," *New York Times*, June 1, 1984

34. Ebert, "Star Trek III: The Search for Spock," *Chicago Sun-Times*, June 1, 1984

35. Mackay, "Search for Schlock," *Toronto Globe and Mail*, June 2, 1984

36. Peterson, "More Missions for Shatner," Knight Ridder Newspapers, June 1, 1984

37. *New York Post*, September 24, 1984

38. Author interview

39. Closerweekly.com, March 21, 2019

40. Archive of American Television

41. Gross and Altman, *The Fifty-Year Mission*, 479

42. Gross and Altman, *The Fifty-Year Mission*, 479

43. Gross and Altman, *The Fifty-Year Mission*, 483

44. Burden, "Voyage Is Not Over," *New York Post*, November 26, 1986

45. Leerhsen et al., "Star Trek's Nine Lives," *Newsweek*, December 22, 1986

46. Shatner and Fisher, *Up Till Now*, 144

47. Burden, "Voyage Is Not Over," *New York Post*, November 26, 1986
48. "Did Shatner Jump the Gun," *Los Angeles Times*, December 17, 1986

CHAPTER 11

1. Associated Press, *Chicago Sun-Times*, March 29, 1990
2. Finn, "Spaceship to Show Ring," *New York Times*, November 8, 1986
3. "Actress Does Time-Traveling," United Press International, March 11, 1987
4. "Shatner Tussles with Rookie," *New York Post*, July 25, 1987
5. Jarvis, "Review: Broken Angel," *People*, March 14, 1988
6. Shirley, "White Rich Kids," *Los Angeles Times*, March 14, 1988
7. "Gorilla Trek for Shatner," Associated Press, April 4, 1988
8. "Biography," A&E, 2006
9. Seniorvoicealaska.com, June 1, 2015
10. Gross and Altman, *The Fifty-Year Mission*, 505
11. Gross and Altman, *The Fifty-Year Mission*, 496
12. Archive of American Television
13. Gross and Altman, *The Fifty-Year Mission*, 501
14. Gross and Altman, *The Fifty-Year Mission*, 498
15. O'Connor, "New Star Trek Series," *New York Times*, October 5, 1987
16. Laurence, *San Diego Tribune*, September 29, 1987
17. Doohan and David, *Beam Me Up, Scotty*, 198
18. *Daily Gleaner*, August 30, 1979
19. Gross and Altman, *The Fifty-Year Mission*, 499
20. Haun, "Sequel's Skipper," *New York Daily News*, June 4, 1989
21. *Daily Gleaner*, August 30, 1989
22. Gross and Altman, *The Fifty-Year Mission*, 509
23. Archive of American Television
24. Kempley, "Star Trek V: The Final Frontier," *Washington Post*, June 9, 1989
25. Ebert, "Star Trek V: The Final Frontier," *Chicago Sun-Times*, June 9, 1989
26. Thomas, "Star Trek V: The Final Frontier," *Los Angeles Times*; Clark, "Star Trek V," *USA Today*; Carr, "Star Trek V: The Final Frontier," *Boston Globe*, June 9, 1989
27. "Actor Shatner Turns Writer," United Press International, October 30, 1989
28. *People* Staff, "Review: 'Trek War,'" *People*, Nov. 27, 1989
29. Robertson, "Shatner Shucks Phaser for a Pen," American Library Association, October 1, 1989
30. *Publisher's Weekly*, Aug. 1, 1990
31. Hauck, *Captain Quirk*, 270
32. Author interview

33. Brooke, "Shatner Captains Real Life Drama," *New York Post*, April 18, 1989

34. Author interview

35. Author interview

36. Buck, "'Rescue 911' Gives Networks a Rare Hit," Associated Press, June 25, 1990

37. "Shatner Denies Palimony Claim," *Los Angeles Times*, January 26, 1990

38. "Capt. Kirk Encounters an Old Nemesis," *New York Post*, January 26, 1990

39. *Star Magazine*, May 5, 1987

40. Barr, "Model Hits Married Star," *National Enquirer*, January 1, 1990

41. Glynn, *Tabloid Culture*, 47

42. Gross and Altman, *The Fifty-Year Mission*, 524

43. Gross and Altman, *The Fifty-Year Mission*, 527

44. There was talk of incorporating *Star Trek: The Next Generation* stars Patrick Stewart and Brent Spiner into the movie to meet their alter egos, Kirk and Spock, but the idea was quashed by Paramount's TV department. *The Next Generation* was still going strong in syndication and there were fears of diluting its brand—and of clashing egos.

45. Takei, *To the Stars*, 400

46. "Biography," A&E, 1999

47. Takei, *To the Stars*, 406

48. Shatner and Kreski, *Star Trek Memories*, 303

49. Maslin, "Aging Trekkers to the Rescue," *New York Times*, December 6, 1991

50. Wloszczyna, "'Trek VI' Sails Jauntily," *USA Today*, December 6, 1991

51. *Variety* Staff, "Star Tek VI: The Undiscovered Country," *Variety*, December 6, 1991

52. Sheehan, *Hollywood Reporter*, December 6, 1991

CHAPTER 12

1. "Biography," A&E, 1999

2. Shatner and Kreski, *Star Trek Memories*, 300–301

3. "Biography," A&E, 1999

4. Shatner and Kreski, *Star Trek Memories*, 303

5. Doohan and David, *Beam Me Up, Scotty*, 159

6. "Star Trek Memories," *Publisher's Weekly*, November 1, 1993; Bray, "In Short: Nonfiction," *New York Times*, December 26, 1993

7. "Shatner, Wife Ending 20-Year Marriage," Associated Press, February 4, 1994

8. Shatner and Fisher, *Up Till Now*, 164

9. Ahrens, "Real Face of William Shatner," *Washington Post*, April 10, 2001

10. Nichols, *Beyond Uhura*

11. Takei, *To the Stars*, 327

12. Takei, *To the Stars*, 356

13. Koenig, *Warped Factors*, 233

14. Gross, "William Shatner and His Coworkers," Closerweekly.com, March 21, 2019

15. Koenig, *Warped Factors*, 277

16. In the original script, Soran killed Kirk by shooting him in the back. This was changed because it was felt that Kirk deserved a more "heroic" death, according to the special DVD/Blu-ray edition of *Star Trek Generations*.

17. Biography, A&E, 2006

18. Comicbook.com, September 6, 2018

19. Maslin, "Major Star Date," *New York Times*, November 18, 1994

20. Kempley, "Star Trek Generations," *Washington Post*, November 18, 1994

21. Schwarzbaum, "Star Trek Generations," *Entertainment Weekly*, November 25, 1994

22. The never-ending fascination with Shatner's hair reared its head again in November 1994, when Shatner was promoting *Star Trek Generations*. According to *Captain Quirk* author Dennis William Hauck, Shatner was wrapping up a phone interview with Tampa radio station WFLA when DJ M. J. Kelley brought up the sensitive subject. "I hope this is not a sensitive question—the hairpiece. It's the best I've ever seen." "I don't wear a hairpiece," Shatner replied. "That's the stupidest question I've ever heard. 'M. J.' must stand for 'Most Jerk.' That's a stupid question by a stupid person." Shatner hung up.

23. Turan, "Star Trek Generations" *Los Angeles Times*, November 17, 1994

24. Martin, "Getting College Credit," *New York Times*, January 8, 1995

25. "William Shatner Sued," *Allentown Morning Call*, September 20, 1994

26. Hoogenboom, "Everyday Heroes Key to Success," *Xenia Daily Gazette*, June 6, 1992

27. Author interview

28. Author interview

29. "TekWar," *Variety*, January 17, 1994

30. William, "'Tek War' Surrenders," *Los Angeles Times*, January 19, 1994; Tucker, "TekWar," *Entertainment Weekly*, Jan. 28, 1994

31. Benson, "Action Packs Wallop," *Variety*, January 19, 1994

CHAPTER 13

1. Shatner and Fisher, *Up Till Now*, 263

2. Vasquez and Weiss, "Shatner's Wife Glamorous, Generous," *Boston Globe*, August 20, 1999

3. "Cute little nose," *Boston Globe*, August 20, 1999; "She was a typical girl," *Los Angeles Times*, October 13, 1999

4. "She was like a windup doll," *Boston Globe*, August 20, 1999
5. Shatner and Fisher, *Up Till Now*, =264
6. Shatner, "Sound of Silence," *People*, May 19, 1997
7. Hiassen, "Alien Sound Hits Shatner," *Baltimore Sun*, February 8, 1997
8. Shatner, "Sound of Silence," *People*, May 19, 1997
9. Howsyourhearing.org, 2011
10. Shatner, "Sound of Silence," *People*, May 19, 1997
11. Shatner and Fisher, *Up Till Now*, 265
12. Shatner and Fisher, *Up Till Now*, 266
13. "Biography," A&E, 1999
14. "Weddings of the Year," *People*, June 22, 1998
15. Shatner and Fisher, *Up Till Now*, 267
16. Shatner and Fisher, *Leonard*, 199
17. Shatner and Fisher, *Up Till Now*, 267–268
18. Gettelman and Haynes, "Shatner's Wife Found Dead," *Los Angeles Times*, August 11, 1999
19. Thompson, *Keeping the Dream Alive*
20. Bloomberg Television, December 15, 2015
21. Fortune.com, September 6, 1999
22. Bloomberg Television, December 15, 2015
23. Schaal, "A Supermodel," Skift.com, June 13, 2016
24. Schaal, "Legendary Pitchman," Skift.com, June 13, 2016
25. CNN, December 20, 2002
26. Krugman, "To Boldly Go," *New York Times*, October 8, 2000
27. Tharp, "Priceline Flatline," *New York Post*, September 28, 2000
28. Holson, "What Shatner Hath Wrought," *New York Times*, June 6, 2000
29. Shatner and Fisher, *Up Till Now*, 272–273
30. Gliatto, "A Sad Discovery," *People*, August 23, 1999
31. Shatner and Fisher, *Up Till Now*, 275
32. Gettleman and Haynes, "Shatner's Wife Found Dead," *Los Angeles Times*, August 11, 1999
33. Gliatto, "A Sad Discovery," *People*, August 23, 1999
34. Vasquez, "Shatner's Wife Glamorous, Generous," *Boston Globe*, August 20, 1999
35. Gettelman, "Alcohol, Pills Are Blamed," *Los Angeles Times*, October 13, 1999
36. Gliatto, "A Sad Discovery," *People*, August 23, 1999
37. Gettleman and Haynes, "Shatner's Wife Found Dead," *Los Angeles Times*, August 11, 1999
38. Gliatto, "A Sad Discovery," *People*, August 23, 1999
39. Gettleman, "Alcohol, Pills Are Blamed," *Los Angeles Times*, October 13, 1999
40. Shatner and Fisher, *Leonard*, 199

CHAPTER 14

1. Hewitt, "Miss Congeniality," Knight Ridder/Tribune News Service, December 20, 2000

2. Carr, "Miss Congeniality," *Boston Globe*, December 22, 2000

3. Horsesinthesouth.com, Sept. 14, 2011

4. Shatner and Fisher, *Up Till Now*, 310

5. Lipworth, "Shatner Boldly Goes Philosophical," *The Mirror*, March 27, 2005

6. Shatner and Fisher, *Up Till Now*, 312

7. Biography, A&E, 2006

8. Lipworth, "Shatner Boldly Goes Philosophical," *The Mirror*, March 27, 2005

9. Shatner and Fisher, *Up Till Now*, 239

10. Shatner and Fisher, *Up Till Now*, 240

11. Campaignlive.com, May 13, 2002

12. Luxebeatmag.com

13. Lifestylesmagazine.com, 2006

14. Archive of American Television

15. Stone had guest-starred in a Season 4 episode of *T. J. Hooker*, "Hollywood Starr," as vice cop Dani Starr, which was intended to launch a *T. J. Hooker* spinoff series built around her character. The episode's cast included Jonathan Goldsmith, later to star in ads for Dos Equis beer as "The Most Interesting Man in the World." ABC passed on the pilot.

16. Archive of American Television

17. Archive of American Television

18. Archive of American Television

19. Archive of American Television

20. Archive of American Television

21. Archive of American Television

22. Archive of American Television

23. Author interview

24. Archive of American Television

25. Biography, A&E, 2006

26. Author interview

27. Lowry, "Boston Legal," *Variety*, September 30, 2004

28. Stanley, "Sexism Suffuses New Season," *New York Times*, October 1, 2004

29. Flynn, "Boston Legal," *Entertainment Weekly*, November 12, 2004

30. Lloyd, "Glossy, Quirky Kelley Special," *Los Angeles Times*, October 1, 2004

31. Archive of American Television

32. Therumpus.net, August 14, 2012

33. StarFest Denver, 2017

34. Biography, A&E, 2006

35. Bemis, "William Shatner's New Enterprise," *New York Times*, October 10, 2004

36. Bemis, "William Shatner's New Enterprise," *New York Times*, October 10, 2004

37. Pitchfork.com, October 17, 2004

38. Slantmagazine.com, September 30, 2004

39. Mirkin, "William Shatner/Ben Folds," *Variety*, October 24, 2004

40. *The Joe Rogan Experience* podcast, August 9, 2018

41. Shatner was beaten those years (2006–2009) by Alan Alda (*The West Wing*), Terry O'Quinn (*Lost*), Zeljko Ivanek (*Damages*), and Michael Emerson (*Lost*).

42. Archive of American Television

43. Robertson, "Oh, Captain! My Captain!" *New York Times*, October 26, 2005

44. *The Today Show*, January 20, 2006

45. *Extra*, November 23, 2007

46. *New York Times*, November 15, 2007

47. He initially wasn't so understanding when ABC decided to cancel *Boston Legal*. "ABC didn't want us back," he told one reporter. "It's as simple as that. They didn't even want us back for this year at all. We had to fight to get back on with thirteen [episodes]. It's not a product they care to market."

48. Archive of American Television

49. EW.com, December 9, 2008

50. Steinberg, "Boston Lawyers," *New York Times*, September 19, 2008

51. Shatner and Fisher, *Up Till Now*, 327

52. Author interview

53. Author interview

54. Starr, "He's All Ears," *New York Post*, November 30, 2009

55. Author interview

56. Tucker, "Shatner and George Takei Still Feuding," *New York Post*, July 21, 2014

57. Starr, "He's All Ears," *New York Post*, November 30, 2009

CHAPTER 15

1. Author interview

2. Gray, "Shows Making Their Debut," *Philadelphia Daily News*, September 23, 2010

3. Gilbert, "Only the Title Is Fresh," *Boston Globe*, September 23, 2010

4. Goodman, "'My Dad Says,' 'Outsourced,'" *San Francisco Chronicle*, September 23, 2010

5. King, "Review: 'S#*! My Dad Says,'" *Slant Magazine*, September 20, 2010

6. Barney, "Trick or Tweet?" *San Jose Mercury News*, October 19, 2010

7. Hale, "Twitter-Size Gimmick," *New York Times*, September 22, 2010

8. Author interview

9. Keller, "Getting Canceled," *New York* magazine, August 1, 2011

10. Consequenceofsound.net, October 31, 2011

11. Thetune.net, October 14, 2011

12. Finley, "Shatner: Seeking Major Tom," *Popmatters*, January 19, 2012

13. Keller, "Getting Canceled," *New York* magazine, August 1, 2011

14. Hale, "To Boldly Go," *New York Times*, July 21, 2011

15. Trekmovie.com, July 22, 2011

16. Hartley, "Book Review: Shatner's Rules," *National Post*, December 9, 2011

17. Bourdeau, "Missy Peregrym on 'Rookie Blue,'" *Huffington Post*, May 23, 2012

18. Therumpus.net, August 2012

19. Therumpus.net, August 2010

20. Dedekker, "Review: 'An Evening with William Shatner,'" *Regina Leader-Post*, October 22, 2011

21. Author interview

22. Itzkoff, "Set Phasers to Stunned," *New York Times*, January 11, 2012

23. Therumpus.net, August 2012

24. Author interview

25. Isherwood, "Shakespearean Who Soared," *New York Times*, February 16, 2012

26. Kennedy, "Shatner Boldly Tackles Death," Associated Press, February 16, 2012

27. Suskin, "Shatner's World," *Variety*, February 21, 2012

28. Grode, "It's Bitesize Captain Kirk," *New York Times*, January 10, 2014

29. Lewis, "Shatner Again Explores New Worlds," *Los Angeles Times*, October 10, 2013

30. Musictimes.com, October 10, 2013

31. Author interview

CHAPTER 16

1. Gq.com, December 1, 2015

2. Shatner and Fisher, *Leonard*, 268–69

3. *The Meredith Vieira Show*, February 23, 2016

4. Shatner and Fisher, *Live Long and . . .*, 16

5. Author interview

6. Nbc4i.com, January 23, 2019

7. Guzzo, "Court Dismisses Suit," *Tampa Bay Times*, June 25, 2018

8. Guzzo, "Shatner Tries to Stop," *Tampa Bay Times*, January 22, 2019

9. Metro.co.uk, November 14, 2017

10. Daniell, "Shatner Says He's Done," *Toronto Sun*, August 30, 2018

11. Trekmovie.com, September 7, 2018

12. Shatner and Rovin, *Spirit of the Horse*, 3

13. Trekmovie.com, March 3, 2011

14. *Billboard*, August 7, 2018

15. Scott, "Shatner on His Christmas Album," *Parade* magazine, December 7, 2018

16. Lewis, "William Shatner Boldly Explores," *Los Angeles Times*, November 23, 2018

17. Shatner and Fisher, *Live Long and . . .*, 4

18. Butler, "Shatner Likens His 'Batman' Villian," United Press International, October 8, 2017

19. Insidehighered.com, July 6, 2018

20. Parry and Boswell, "MeToo Has Become Hysterical," *Daily Mail*, December 18, 2018

21. Starr, "How 'Big Bang Theory' Snared 'Star Trek' Legend," *New York Post*, February 13, 2019

22. De Paul, "Shatner of 'Star Trek,'" *Daily Californian*, January 15, 2019

23. Wallack, "Horses and E-Bikes," *Los Angeles Times*, November 3, 2018

24. Lipworth, "Shatner: My Family Values," Theguardian.com, March 14, 2014

Selected Bibliography

Altman, Mark A., and Edward Gross. *The Fifty-Year Mission: The First 25 Years*. New York: Thomas Dunne Books, 2016.

Doohan, James, and Peter David. *Beam Me Up, Scotty*. New York: Simon & Schuster, 1996.

Hauck, Dennis William. *Captain Quirk: The Unauthorized Biography of William Shatner*. New York: Kensington Books, 1995.

Koenig, Walter. *Warped Factors*. Dallas: Taylor Publishing, 1997.

Justman, Robert H., and Herbert F. Solow. *Inside Star Trek: The Real Story*. New York: Pocket Books, 1996.

Lafond, Suzanne. *Peach Cobbler Stories: A Gift of Memories from Mamie/Grand-Mere*. Batavia, NY: KingAuthor Productions, in association with Anthem Publishing, 2013.

Nichols, Nichelle. *Beyond Uhura: Star Trek and Other Memories*. New York: G. P. Putnam's Sons, 1994.

Shatner, Lisabeth. *Captain's Log: William Shatner's Personal Account of the Making of Star Trek V: The Final Frontier*. New York: Pocket Books, 1989.

Shatner, William, Sondra Marshak, and Myrna Culbreath. *Shatner: Where No Man . . . The Authorized Biography of William Shatner*. New York: Grosset & Dunlap, 1979.

Shatner, William, and Chris Kreski. *Get a Life!* New York: Simon & Schuster, 1999.

———. *Star Trek Memories*. New York: HarperCollins, 1993.

Shatner, William, and David Fisher. *Leonard: My Fifty-Year Friendship with a Remarkable Man*. New York: Thomas Dunne Books, 2016.

———. *Up Till Now: The Autobiography*. New York: Thomas Dunne Books, 2008

Shatner, William, and Jeff Rovin. *Spirit of the Horse*. New York: St. Martin's Press, 2017.

Smith, Dalan E. *Bill & I: Building William Shatner's Belle Reve Ranch*. Self-published, CreateSpace, 2012.

Takei, George. *To the Stars*. New York: Simon & Schuster, 1994.

Index